For the College Library
in appreciation for your
hospitality.

April 1973

UP FROM NEVER

Prentice-Hall, Inc., *Englewood Cliffs, N.J.*

UP FROM NEVER

by
Joseph N. Sorrentino

Up from Never by Joseph N. Sorrentino
Copyright © 1971 by Joseph N. Sorrentino
All rights reserved. No part of this book may be
reproduced in any form or by any means, except for
the inclusion of brief quotations in a review, without
permission in writing from the publisher.
ISBN 0-13-938977-6
Library of Congress Catalog Card Number: 79-153951
Printed in the United States of America T
Prentice-Hall International, Inc., London
Prentice-Hall of Australia, Pty. Ltd., Sydney
Prentice-Hall of Canada, Ltd., Toronto
Prentice-Hall of India Private Ltd., New Delhi
Prentice-Hall of Japan, Inc., Tokyo

Second printing . . . . October 1971

To my mother and father;
to Tommy Quinn, "The Thousandth Man";
and to Miss Lawsen, who helped me discover another me

Contents

PROLOGUE: SONNY MEOW

*Coney Island in the winter is a ghost town. Huge waves lumber to-
ward the land, stumble and roll when they hit, and then acquire
grace gliding up the beach. Moonbeams illuminating the sand reveal miles of miniature craters trampled out by human feet, but
not a single walker is about. Under the boardwalk the juke joints
that blared with rock 'n 'roll last summer are boarded up and their
chairs stacked. Wharf rats deserting the beach skulk up the splintered stairs to the boardwalk, where shimmering signs displayed
over a hive of small shops advertise a bevy of sugary specialties:*
THE WORLD'S GREATEST SALTWATER TAFFY / THE COLDEST MELON
IN CONEY / SEE OUR JUMBO COTTON CANDY MADE. *Beneath
the signs, wooden hatches reinforced by iron gates seal in the shops'
novelties until next season. Along the dark back streets where
barkers' shouts once lured strollers, salt air quietly eats into vacant
ticket booths. The rides stand motionless. Bumping-cars remain in
the same jam they were in at the last bell. The roller coaster lies
dormant, a wheeled caterpillar in a steel cocoon, and under an as-
bestos canopy the party-colored ponies of the carousel hibernate.
The spook house witch, her hyena laugh silent, stares vacantly as
five youths pass.*

▼▼▼

*It was Bib's idea to steal the guns. He remembered a shooting gal-
lery in one of the little alleys off the midway.*

*"Where is this fuckin' place?" Tony asked, getting angry out of
apprehension.*

"It's right by the Wonduh Wheel," Bib answered.

*"I hope those guns ain't bolted ta the counter or else it's gonna
be some job ta get 'em off," Petey broke in.*

*"They're not. It's just a thin metal chain about that thick." Jerry
held up his thumb and forefinger almost pinching as a measure.*

*Whitey lingered in front of the wax museum, held by its gallery
of morbid figures. After reading an account of one recently head-
lined tragedy, he raced to catch up with the others who were fast
approaching the Wonder Wheel.*

Below the wheel's silver arc the sign of an arcade announced:
SHOOT LIVE AMMUNITION. *Spying his goal, Tony quickened his
strides to take the lead. From a distance his runty height made it
seem ludicrous for him to be the leader—he was only 5'6" com-*

pared to Bib's 5'9" and Jerry's towering 6'2"—but up close his appearance was intimidating. His black hair combed straight back accented dark eyes. For fourteen his face seemed hard. His firm jaw was sculpted of heavy bone, and when he talked his Adam's apple bobbed beneath the skin of his thickset taut neck. Tight chino pants exposed his powerful squat legs, and even through his winter jacket tense chunks of arm muscle could be seen. Tony's nickname was Sonny Meow because he once smashed a cat against a brick wall, crushing its skull, and then whirled it around by the tail to splatter everyone with blood. The name was not used to his face.

The shooting gallery was doubly barricaded. A wire mesh screen with a tumbler lock shielded two padlocked purple doors.

"Gimme the cutters," Tony grunted up at Jerry.

Jerry removed a long pair from under his mackinaw and handed them to him. The strong jaws of the cutters snapped the two locks in quick succession and Jerry guided open the unwieldy doors. Eight repeating rifles glinted on the counter, flanked on each end by a submachine gun. Instinctively, Tony moved to one of the automatic weapons. "Grab these mothers. They'll really do the job on her."

"Nill, Tone," Jerry said. "Those don't fire live rounds."

Each cradled in his arm a stack of rifles and several of the straw-like tubes of .22 ammunition.

▚▚

The next night Bib hopped into his father's battered, box-shaped Hudson and drove to Papa Joe's Candy Store. The other four were waiting there. All climbed in with Bib except Tony, who went back into the candy store. As Whitey got in he checked the back seat to see if the lower cushion was snug in its grooves. He wasn't sure he had pushed it all the way back when they loaded the car earlier that morning. Satisfied, he patted the seat and said to the others, "I wouldn't want that ta be spotted in case we got stopped."

"Why should we get stopped?" Bib asked.

"Wid five guys in the car the bulls might pull us over."

"Yeah, jus' ta break chops." Jerry illustrated by cupping his crotch in his hands.

"Ya think she'll be there now?" Petey asked.

"Shit, I'd take book on it. We'll soon find out. Here comes Tony."

Tony jumped into the back. "The kid's got her on the phone now. Let's burn rubbuh."

The Hudson snorted out in low gear, struggling up the slope on 66th Street. Then, with Bib's foot flooring the accelerator, the vehicle snaked around downhill traffic.

Tony grumbled. "You drive like a twat."

The car turned left onto Fourth Avenue, heading toward the higher numbers.

"I wonduh if she believed what the kid was puttin' ta her on the phone?" Whitey looked at Jerry.

"We ain't gonna know till we get there, that's fa sure."

Tony leaned forward in his seat to avoid the prickles of the shredding upholstery. "When the fuck are ya gonna make ya old man get some seat covers in this bomb?"

"Next score, Tone, I'm gonna make him junk this shebang an' get a sharp lookin' Chevy I seen fa sale."

"Would he go fa that action?" Petey asked.

"Ya don' know my ol' man. He can hardly talk English."

"So what?"

"So like he's deaf. He can't understand what nobody says in this country. No, he's woise, he's blind. He can't read a line. He has ta come ta me fa everythin'. Whatever I say he listens. Tony's ol' man is the same. All they know how ta do is break up the streets wid a pickaxe."

"If the bulls ever chase us in this thing they could walk an' still head us off," Petey said, ending the car talk.

"Hey, there's her school!" Whitey said, pointing to the tower of Fort Hamilton High School in the distance.

"Pull over when we pass it," Tony said as he cuffed Bib behind the neck. "About two blocks from the house."

As the car cruised past the school its passengers tensed. Two blocks later the car halted in front of an apartment house. Tony snapped orders: "Petey, get off ya ass so we can move outta the seat. Jerry, jump out and grab the lights."

"Wait," Whitey said as he grabbed Jerry's arm. "Tony, I still think it's gonna look more suspicious to cover the lights," he argued.

"They won't shine this way."

"Tony, ya wrong."

"Shut the fuck up, scumbag, before I jack ya head in right

here." Tony's lip quivered and they all knew that meant he was about to explode.

Whitey shut up. Jerry climbed out of the car and draped handkerchiefs over the headlights. No one thought of turning off the lights.

Jerry got back in and Bib eased the car forward. A man who passed while walking a dog never looked up. The car turned the corner. The back window slid down and the barrel of a pump rifle nosed out and angled up.

The episode's ending was reported in the New York Daily News the next day:

SHOT UP HOME
OF TEACHER, 5
BOYS CONFESS
By Nat Kanter and David Quirk

Equipped with a man-sized arsenal, five Brooklyn youths—the ringleader a tough and cocky 14-year-old—were rounded up last night and promptly confessed that they were the gang that sprayed the home of blond and pretty . . . , Fort Hamilton High School teacher, with a shower of .22-caliber slugs Wednesday night.

1
THREE POOL-
ROOMS IN FOUR BLOCKS

Home was a 3½-room apartment in Brooklyn, on the top floor of a two-story brick building. I shared the living room with my three brothers. My sister Madeline slept in the half room, and Ma, Dad, and the baby had the bedroom. My aunts and uncles were tenants on the first floor. Grandma, our landlady, lived in the cellar.

▪▪

The alarm clock set for school sputtered on the windowsill. An alerted mouse scooted under the overstuffed chair. Pale, grayish light penetrated the frosted window and splashed rumpled clothes hung across the back of the opened Castro sofa bed. I lazily untangled myself from my brothers' arms and legs twisted about me. If I got up before them there was a fair chance I would get a pair of matching socks. Dipping one leg out from under the blanket to test the air, I quickly withdrew it. The morning chill filled the room. Grabbing my pants and shirt, I got dressed under the covers.

The radiator started to spit and clank. "Granma must be shoveling in coal," I thought. I got up, stretched, and groggily looked around the room. A round mirror on the wall was missing a hunk of glass. The carpet was now a faded straw color with only a corona of its original brown. The venetian blinds drooped lopsidedly to the right or left depending on which ribbon was ripped. My sister Madeline's rubber doll, which I used for a punching bag, swung from a necktie noose in the doorway. Near the radiator was a small bookcase with the beginning issues of a set of A&P encyclopedias. My three brothers cuddling in the Castro reminded me of our puppies in their basement box.

"Youse better be up before I come in there wid the broom," Ma hollered from the kitchen.

"We're up, we're up," I yelled back.

My older brother Anthony opened his eyes. "What time is it?"

"It's okay, you can sleep," I said. "It's still early."

I dragged the bookcase to the windowsill to improvise parallel bars. Straddling the two surfaces, I slowly went down and up, counting to myself.

"Better hurry up before Ma catches ya," my sister Madeline said, passing the open door.

"Hey, where ya going?" I yelled, chasing her.

"Ta the bathroom, and you're after me."

"Wait a minute before ya go in. Whadda ya gotta do, number one or number two?"

"Number two."

"Listen, I only gotta do number one. Let me go in foist. I'll be right out."

"Awright, but you better not comb ya hair."

Opening the bathroom door I turned back to her. "Ya know, I shouldn't even have ta ask ya ta go foist. Ya should step aside just out of respect fa ya elders."

A diaper clogged the toilet bowl. "Oh, no," I moaned, getting down on my knees. Tweezing a tiny corner between my fingers, I flushed the diaper in and out to get rid of its load. Then I flung it on the top of the washboard in the tub. With the splendor of a newly christened ship, the diaper eased down on the board's incline to join the flotilla of diapers waiting to be scrubbed.

Dad's razor had been left out on the sink, so I lathered for a quick shave. I had no whiskers but I wanted to get my stroke down for when that cool day came. After my face I shaved my chest to speed the growth of hair on it.

"Hurry up in there," Madeline ordered, knocking on the door.

"Hurry up in there," I mimicked in a high voice as I came out.

As I passed the kitchen Ma yelled, "Don't walk around barefoot. You'll get yourself a cold."

Shoes were heaped under the Castro. Ransacking among them, I weeded out a pair and carefully examined the size of the holes—if a hole was too large, a cardboard patch placed inside would soon squeeze out. After putting on the best pair, I went to the closet to get my jacket. There was only one closet in the apartment for the eight of us. "Ya need a friggin crowbar," I muttered, pushing aside clothes and mothball canisters to reach my jacket. "Better get a tie, too, for assembly."

I didn't know what assembly was going to be like in junior high. In the sixth grade we listened to records. My friends hated the longhair music they played, but I loved it. When "Fingal's Cave" was on I closed my eyes and pictured a cliff as high as the clouds, with the ocean doing somersaults against its side. My favorite was "Dance Macabre" by Saint-Saëns. It was so eerie it made me feel like I had no skin. Once, during a Tschaikovsky suite, the music teacher asked for a volunteer to interpret it. I went up to the stage and made motions with my arms and jumped around. All the kids

laughed, which is why I did it, but the teacher thought I was a tal.
ent and selected me to star in the graduation play. I played the
part of a witch who held ten lovely maidens captive. The only
scene I can remember clearly was one where I whipped them,
shouting, "Dance, maidens, dance." My classmates thought it took
special nerve to get up on the stage in front of everyone, but I enjoyed the vibrations of a reacting audience.

"Can I get in the closet now?" Madeline said, ending my day-
dream.

"Whadda ya doin', shadowing me?"

"I gotta get my coat."

"Well, let me get a tie foist, damn it." Quarrying deep inside I
found a fat brown tie with crossbars that made it look like a boa
constrictor. The knot I made bulged as if the thing had swallowed a
native. When I walked into the kitchen, Dad was sitting at the
table in his Department of Sanitation khakis, sipping coffee and
squinting at the racing entries in the *Daily Mirror.* He glanced up
and then resumed his study. Ma sat across from him with her
blouse open, breast-feeding baby Camille and stroking Madeline's
hair.

"Hey, Ma," I said as I pulled a card out, "would ya fill out this
vaccination thing. I gotta bring it to school by tomorruh."

"Can't youse see I ain't got no time fa youse big ones. Ask ya father. I got a little baby to feed."

"Dad, Ma told me to make ya fill this out. I need it signed."

"What is it? I got no time ta read nuttin' now. I'm late as it is."

"Could ya do it tanight?"

"I'm not gonna be home tonight. Got a music job wid the com-
bo."

"Oh, youse never have time fa my things."

The path to P.S. 259 from my corner took the shape of an "L" over
eleven city blocks. The lower stem was a narrow, tar-paved side-
street streaked with chalk markings for games of patsy, stoop ball,
triangle, and the scribbled valentines of small girls. Worn apartment buildings—two, three, and four stories high, with fire escapes
on kitchen windows—lined the street. Hard-working *manuáles,*
mainly immigrants from Italy and first-generation Americans, clustered here with their families. Small, one-man stores occupied the

sidewalk level of some structures. A glazier's fresh putty bordered the clear new pane set in the bookmaking parlor, replacing the window shattered by Tom Dewey's racket squad in a recent raid.

The long stretch to school was along Fort Hamilton Parkway. Apartments seemed to alternate with gas stations on this busy thoroughfare. The noise of automobile traffic was swelled by staticky radios on windowsills and BMT trains rumbling into the Fort Hamilton station. Newsstands outside candy stores carried seven newspapers, whose front pages ranted violent headlines and played up gory pictures. The usual scenes were of firemen carrying someone in a stretcher out of a charred building, or a kid lying near the wheel of a truck, his body covered by a blanket, his mother crying and the driver putting his hands over his eyes. At 65th Street you could see the cross on top of St. Rosalie's Church; my brother Anthony's homing pigeons used it as a landmark flying back from Staten Island. Police cars from two precincts kept watch on three poolhalls within four blocks but ignored the many local gambling establishments, including the $20-million-a-year operation of bookmaker Harry Gros. Women sitting on the stoops wagged their tongues and rocked their baby carriages. Here and there in the neighborhood were dilapidated wooden buildings, holdovers from the days of the horse and wagon. Once they tore down one of these relics and hundreds of rats panicked out into an ambush of men who bashed them with hammers while kids had a field day with their Red Ryder BB guns. On Sunday the busy spots were the Fortway Theater and the Greek's luncheonette a short stroll away. No trees grew here; the only greenery along the way were the painted leaves on Bryer's ice cream signs.

Junior High School 259 was located on the edge of everyone's neighborhood. The Irish came from the streets in the high numbers, the Norwegians from Little Norway on Eighth Avenue, the Italians from the south side, the Jews from Thirteenth Avenue, and the Polish from pockets all around. The buttermilk brick building was clean but stained with stinky urine on the bottom. Students jabbered outside the gate waiting for the bell. The Ungraded Class began to line up at the entrance and kept breaking into goony laughter. Across the street a meeting was being held by a gang of seniors who wore black satinette jackets with DEVILS S.A.C.

blocked out in red on back.

I walked up to two boys who were talking, hands jabbing back and forth. One of them was Joey Mappito, who everyone considered the best dresser around. He was wearing creamsicle pants with black saddle stitching and chartreuse pistol pockets. After your eyes adjusted to the colors, you noticed that Mappy was a short, dark teenager with a nose that would have helped in a photo finish and a brawny build which came from working out with a home-made barbell constructed from a pipe and cement-filled flower pots.

The overgrown, sandy-haired, good-looking boy with him was Bobby Stroloski, a Pole, part-Italian on his mother's side.

"Sarry, babe," Bobby greeted me by my nickname.

Mappy's head swiveled around and he said, "Hi, Sarry."

"Whadda ya say, Bob, Mappy."

"Me and Bobby's jus' been arguin' about what's a natural. He says there ain't no such thing." Mappy's hand juggled air as he talked. "Ain't it when a guy's good at somethin' wid no practice or nuttin'. Like take Danny Charms, he could never before have played stickball but still put one over two sewers his foist time up."

"That's what I thought."

"I tol' ya, ya don't know shit." Mappy pounded Bobby's chest. "Ya dumb Polack."

"Here comes Richie." I said, craning over Bobby's shoulder.

"Yeah, look at the cheap Kraut finishing off his crumb buns before he gets to us," Bobby mocked.

Richie Berder shuffled in on us. "Hey, youse guys hear what happened yesterday? Tony Bavimo and the guys from Papa Joe's shot at a teacher at Fort Hamilton."

"Where'd ya hear that?" I asked in awe.

"I just passed Silverrod's and saw it in the papers. They got pichers on the front page of her windows wid alla bullet holes in them."

"Ya mean they killed her?" Bobby asked.

"Naw. They were just tryin' ta scare her, the papers say."

"What they wanna scare her fa?"

"Ya know Jimmy Rosone, Benny Masinella's cousin who lives upstairs from him on 74th Street? Remember—the one who had trench mouth last summer wid alla dark stuff on his teeth."

"Yeah, what about 'im?"

"He was afraid she was gonna fail 'im in somethin' and his fodder would break his ass if he did, so he went and told da Papa Joe boys about it."

"Does it say which one did the shootin'?" Mappy asked.

"It don' tell."

"It had ta be Bavimo" I said. "Ya don't think he's gonna make the other guys do it while he stands there takin' pichers."

"Yeah, who else would have the balls," Richie agreed.

▰▰

The seventh-graders filed noisily into the auditorium. The boys sat on the side facing the Abraham Lincoln portrait. The girls made their way to the section facing George Washington. Off to the side of the stage, the principal spread the notes for his speech on the piano. The music teacher at the keyboard chomped down on a fawning smile for him. When the students were seated and the chatter hushed, the principal began speaking.

My eyes and mind separated as I thought about what Richie had said. None of us who were talking about Tony Bavimo had ever met him. But he was my idol because of stories I heard from the older boys on my block. Huddled in a hallway with them, I learned about the time he dropped Blubberhead, the toughest guy on Thirteenth Avenue, and the time he starched three Nishskies—as we called Norwegians—when they bothered his steady, and how he could lift hundred-pound potato sacks over his head, one in each hand. I thought: "Opening up wid guns. On the front page and everythin'. That Bavimo's somethin'."

▰▰

2 "Gimme a clean towel, Ange," Dad called, in his morning voice from the bathroom.

"There's one under my smock hanging on the door," Ma answered, shutting off the kitchen faucet.

"There's nuttin' here."

"Use a sheet then."

"Well, you get it."

Dad came into the kitchen and Ma began to scold. "Don't come in here drippin' water, and put on an undershirt. Have some modesty."

"I gotta dry off first."

"Well, put somethin' around yourself. Don't walk around here barechested."

"Whadda ya makin' such a big stink about?"

"Because it's vulguh ta show that ugly chest hair."

"I go ta the beach like this and nobody squawks."

"I don't care. It's still vulguh ta walk around the house like that. Ya never see Paul next door walk around his apartment widout a shirt."

"Plenty of the boys on the job eat widout a shirt when it's hot, and their wives don' bellyache."

"Oh, ya're just a garbage man. You greaseball Sorrentinos don't know nuthin' about refinement."

"Your family does, eh, wid ya mother who runs after tenants wid a hatchet."

"At least my family turned out a lawyuh."

"Ya mean ya cousin Dom? He's no lawyuh *cetrul* [jerk]. He's only a clerk at the court."

"Well, he's still an educated man, not like you who went up ta the thoid grade."

"Sixth grade, dumbie."

"Don't call me dumb and stop raisin' ya voice, monster. Here's a sheet, go dry yaself an' get dressed. I got enough aggravation around here."

I grabbed my books and walked into the kitchen. "Fa cryin' out loud, Ma, ya have conniptions over nuttin'."

"Shut up, you." She brushed by me to open the oven. Charred toast was layered upon the racks. I took out two slices and scraped them over the sink.

Dad came back in combing his hair, which was parted perfectly straight. He was a good-looking man—dark, lean, and tall for an Italian. His wavy black hair shaded into a rim of premature gray above the ears. I saw his chin as pointy, his nose sharp but well-formed, his Latin eyes, volatile brown. Below his mouth grew a jot of beard, sign of a horn man, which he claimed strengthened his lip. When Dad walked down the block, women on the stoops stopped rocking their carriages. Mappy's mother called him a ladies' man.

Dad worked at the main garage of the Sanitation Department. Years before he worked out of the 62nd Street branch. That was only a block away from our house so I often saw him on the job when I was playing in the street. They had him doing different things depending on the season. In the warm months he pushed a long porcupine broom or followed a garbage truck around, dumping cans in the back. The kids next door used to put me down when he passed. Their father was a factory foreman. I wanted to tell them our dog was bigger than theirs, but I felt too much like crying. In the winter, though, Dad drove a snowtruck, a big orange tractor with a huge plow in front. I thought he was pretty hot stuff driving that snowtruck. Then I got back at the kids next door, reminding them that a factory foreman can't compare with a snowtruck driver.

Finishing my toast and a glass of milk, I left for school. Outside, I passed Dad's friend, Freddy, who was waiting in his car. Every morning he and Dad drove to work together.

I had been at Junior High School 259 only a week, but my direction seemed set. I was becoming the same problem student I had been at P.S. 187. My third-grade teacher at 187 once got so angry when I couldn't answer a simple arithmetic question that she rammed my head against the blackboard 2 + 3 times. In another grade, the teacher got so fed up with my troublemaking that she banged my face between both her hands as if she were playing cymbals.

My official teacher at 259, Mr. Goldfar (that name took a lot of gas outside of his ear-reach), assigned homework every day the first week, but I didn't bother to do any. Already I was known by the assistant principal, the shop teacher having reported me for sawing his model ashtray in half.

Five members of my neighborhood "*click*" were in the class, and we all sat near each other in the back of the homeroom.

"Hey, look. " I put my foot in the aisle. "I got a fourteen peg in my pants now."

"Big deal, that's like a sailor's bell bottoms," Mappy answered. "Check mine out. I got a twelve." The pants squeezed his ankle tight like a bicycle brace.

"I got a twelve, too." Richie shot his leg out.

"Whadda you got, Bobby?" I asked.

"I got only a eighteen cause my foot is too big."

"What size shoe ya take?" Mappy twitted, laughing loudly.

"Hey, Goldfart is lookin'"

"Shit on Goldfart," Mappy shrugged. "C'mon, what size, *jooche* [oaf]?"

"Fourteen triple E."

My attention was on Bobby's shoes when the side door opened and a monitor went up to Mr. Goldfar with a folder. Reading a note clipped to the folder, the teacher looked my way. "Joseph Sorrentino.'

"Yeah."

"Would you come up to the desk. There's been some kind of clerical error. Your records show you're supposed to be in 7-5 not 7-10."

"Oh, shit," I mumbled.

"Take these records down to Miss Lawsen in Room 242. Do it tomorrow morning—her class is on a trip today. She'll be your new teacher."

<hr>

On the way home from school, I stopped off at Weinstein's Italian-American grocery. A bell rang when I entered the store, but there was no one behind the counter. While I waited to be served, I glanced around the store. Yicchy loaves of bread sprouting furry green fungus rested on a bakery tray. I turned away from them and toyed with the long pole topped by metal jaws for taking items from high shelves. In a minute a stooping man about fifty years old came through a soiled curtain at the rear.

"Vell, hello beeg fellow. So how it goes mit you?"

"Fine, thanks, Murray. My mudder ga' me a list."

"Mine boy Nathan is in the back having supper. Vhy don't you go by him and say hi vhile I make out Mama's order."

I pushed the curtain aside and stepped into the apartment in the rear of the store. Scraggy Natie was leaning over the kitchen sink munching on a Yankee Doodle and making a bottle of Pepsi fizz by shaking it with his thumb over the top.

"Whadda ya doin', practicin' fa a soda fight or somethin'?"

"Hi, Joey." He turned around. "Naw, jus' gettin' out the gas. Wanna swig?"

"No, thanks."

"Whadda ya *skeeve* [think I'm unsanitary]?"

"No, I'll take a bite a ya Yankee Doodle if ya offer."

"Okay." He held out the cupcake for me, but his thumb covered the cream-filled center.

"Boy, you're lucky. You can eat anythin' ya want in the store."

Coming out of the bedroom, Mrs. Weinstein interrupted us, "So how's your sweet mama?"

"She's awright, thanks, Gertie," I answered.

"That poor voman, God bless her, I remember vhen she used to come in Mr. Weinstein's store mit two in the carriage, two on the side, and one on the vay."

"Ca . . . choo," Natie sneezed.

"Here, Nathan, blow." His mother raised an end of her apron and Natie blew.

"We're gettin' up a game of canball tanight," I said. "Ya want me ta tell ' em to choose ya in?"

"No, not tonight." He got pale. "I'm gonna study my baseball record book. Dixie Walker once hit in seventeen straight. Maybe he'll break Joe D's streak next season."

"He's got a long way ta go ta 56."

"Dija hear that Snuffy Stirnweiss ain't wid the Yanks no more? Him and Don Johnson's been traded ta the Browns."

"Yeah, I hoid about it. Ya sure ya don' wanna get in tanight?"

"Yeah, thanks anyway," he said.

"Okay, see ya."

"See ya."

Natie was the only Jewish kid in the neighborhood. Everybody had fun calling him "mockey bastard" and other names, watching his face redden, and seeing him cry until he ran home. Now he didn't come out anymore.

I walked back into the store. "Got my mudder's order ready, Murray?"

"Did Mama vant vhite or yellow American cheese?"

"Yellow, and she wanted Ronzoni fa the macaroni. She saves the coopons on the box."

"That's vhat I thought." He penciled the prices on the side of the bag and added them up. "Two thirty-six. Cash or trust?"

"Put it on the bill."

"Here, hold eet from the bottom."

Climbing up the stairs with the groceries, I could hear my seven-year-old brother Nicky whine, "Oh, no, ya not gonna put iodine on it."

"Be still and stop bein' a baby," Ma chided.

"I don' wan' no iodine. Get that outa here. Get some Mercurochrome."

"It'll only burn fa a second. Be a man."

I didn't have to see to know what came next. She dipped the thin glass spreader in the bottle with a skull on the label. I shivered, anticipating Nicky's pain.

"Ouwh, ooh, ooh. No more! No more!" He screamed.

I thought: "At least it's better than peroxide." I dreaded that medicine, which looks like harmless water but foams like a tired horse's mouth when poured over torn skin.

I walked into the apartment and passed Ma and Nicky in the bathroom. I put the bag down in the kitchen. "The groceries are on the table, Ma. Dija make the chocolate puddin' I asked ya ta?"

"I haven't got time to breathe around here and he asks me 'bout puddin'."

"Just asked."

"Put the buttuh in the icebox before it melts."

"Oh, I forgot ta tell ya, Ma. They put me in another class taday. I start in it tomorruh. There was some kind of mistake."

"As long as I don' have ta come up ta school."

Sticking my head in the bathroom I saw the brownish-red blotch on Nicky's knee. "What happened to you?"

"I got it caught on the pickets climbin' the schoolyard fence."

"Why dija climb the fence?"

"They closed it. They don't want nobody in the yard after t'ree. Youse guys are lucky. Ya got Canball Stadium to play in now."

It really was hard to find a place to play ball where you wouldn't be chased. Schoolyard signs warned: STICKBALL PROHIBITED, N.Y.P.D. It seemed a waste to lock up schoolyards after three o'clock. Very few kids used them, and then briefly, during the school day. When school was out locks on the gates or police signs forced them to play in the streets. On weekends the restrictions were even more strictly enforced against older boys. I suppose those in charge were not so much worried about the kids as the windows in the building. Maybe the rules didn't affect the school officials personally but injuries to my brothers and me while playing in the streets caused Ma three near heart attacks. When Ernie, my youngest brother, was four years old, he was sitting on the curb and almost got crushed when a car pulled out. Nicky was once smashed into a coma by a speeding car.

My own accident happened just before my ninth birthday. I had been indoors and didn't even want to go out that day. I was content punching my sister's rubber doll hanging in the kitchen doorway, but Aunt Marie was up and she and Ma were trying to gab.

"We wanna have some peace and quiet. Do you mind?" Ma said. "Why doncha go outside?"

"Yeah, why doncha go call your friend Tommy?" Aunt Marie said.

"Awright."

I gave the doll one last hard sock and then went for my jacket. I took the shortcut through the alleys to Tommy's. His father's barber shop had closed for the day and the family was still eating when I walked in. They were having tuna fish heroes and devil-dogs.

"Can't I fix ya a sandwich?" Tommy's mother asked.

"No, thanks, Viola."

"Ask him if he wants a drink, Vee." His father laughed.

"Yeah, sure, Benny." Viola puckered her lips, annoyed.

The night before Benny had talked the bartender at Andy's Tavern into serving nine-year-old Tommy and me whisky. The good thing about Benny's drinking, it always put him in a fun mood. Once he dressed up in a black SS uniform with the puffy pants, leather boots, and red swastika armband and went around knocking on doors. Back in 1945 there were some people who got shook up when they opened the door.

When Tommy finished eating we went out to pitch pennies. His older brother Paulie got in too. Before long we were looking for something new to do. Then, down the street we saw one truck slowly towing another by a chain. The truck being towed was stripped to its frame—the motor and cab were intact but in back there was no freight box, just a rectangular surface of four steel bars supported by four flat tires. Both trucks stopped at the red light.

"Come on, let's hitch a ride," I said. I climbed up onto a beam

of the skeleton truck and sat sidesaddle between the front and back
wheels on one side. The light changed and the trucks rolled out.
Tommy and his brother tagged along, walking briskly. After riding
a block, I jumped off and fell into the path of the rear wheels. A
woman in a window shrieked. Stretched out, face down, with my
feet caught by the back wheel, I was pushed forward like a cardboard box. Although I was wearing a jacket, the friction rubbed
skin off my chest. The Meerto brothers could have run up to the
driver but, numb with shock, they just watched. The truck began
to ride over me. I felt its weight but no pain. I made no outcry, but
a frightened voice in the pit of my gut murmured, "Oh, Momma, I'm
gonna die." Starting with my feet, the tire pressed my ankles
and knees almost flat. Then it sank into my back, rolled over my
shoulders and, finally, my head. I got up and walked home, to
Grandma's.

"*O poura figlio* [Oh, poor son]," Grandma cried out at the door.
Then, whack! she unleashed a backhand, yelling *"Pasa whya!"* Although she branded me "troublemaker," Grandma took me downstairs to her cellar apartment to treat my wounds. She didn't
bother calling a doctor. Unless it was also time to send for a priest,
she considered a doctor an extravagance. Her own treatment was
to scrub my wounds with hot water and Octagon soap, which was
like salting them. Grandma disregarded my yelps as she went about
patching me up. She scissored off the hanging flesh in the same un-
ruffled manner she axed a turkey's head. Nothing panicked Grandma. That was the reason I went to her first. When I finally got
upstairs Ma got upset, but not as much as she would have if I had
come straight to our apartment.

〰️〰️〰️〰️〰️〰️〰️〰️〰️〰️〰️〰️〰️

3   A morning sunburst lightened the room.
    "There she blows, " Anthony hollered. "Moby Dick."
Diving into a corner, spouting dust in the air, a giant silverfish,
whitish in color and as big as a breakfast sausage, streaked for the
closet on a jillion legs. Anthony got the name from reading classic
comics. Usually when we saw a cockroach we simply got out of bed
and crushed it. But no one dared do that to Moby Dick; he was too
big and slimy. We tried to harpoon him with shoes, thrown from
the bed, but he submerged in the deep of clothing.

I walked into the kitchen tugging the fly of my shorts to the side to make sure I was covered. Ma was standing over the stove holding Camille in one arm and stirring something in a saucepan with the other.

"Don't parade around here in ya shorts, ya got sisters."

"Aw, Ma, my pants're in the bathroom. Whadda ya cookin'?"

"Pablum."

"Bah!'

"Let me see those." She dropped the spoon and latched onto my ear.

"Whadda ya doin'? Get outta there."

"Ya call those clean?"

"Will ya stop?"

"Stand still. You always do things half-ass."

She took a napkin and burrowed it into the crevice of my ear. "Look at that. Look at all the mucky wax you missed."

"Holy Max, I coulda gone deaf."

"Is ya brother Nicky up yet?"

"The last time I seen him he said he felt sick, as usual."

"Go get that faker up before I go in there wid the broom. That sleepyhead, he'll be late fa school again."

After waking Nicky, I licked the cream out of sandwich cookies for breakfast and grabbed my books. I would be reporting to my new class today.

▰▰▰

Miss Lawsen, my new teacher, looked young, about the age to be getting married. Her face was pretty. She had a nice little nose that pointed up. Her cheeks were smooth and the flushed color a person's face becomes when turned upside down. She was taller than my mother or any of my aunts. Maybe it was the high heels she wore. Her legs had good muscles, the kind I liked to see at the beach. I could picture Miss Lawsen in a bathing suit. With calves like that it's sure her thighs filled out nicely and her behind would be bulging and round, hard to keep all inside the suit. She was there upstairs too; you could see "them" moving around, not like falsies which stay stiff. I've saved her light blue eyes and wheat blonde hair for last. They caused a very different feeling in me than the sight of her legs. None of the girls on my block were fair. They all had olive skin with dark hair and brown eyes. One lady on our street tried bleaching her hair, but it only made her look cheap. Strawberry blonde clashed with her oily dark skin and the bushes of black hair that stuck out from her armpits. With Miss Lawsen everything blended.

I sat next to a pimply-faced girl named Rose. Rose was Ping-Ponging a jawbreaker from cheek to cheek, and Miss Lawsen noticed and came over. "Get rid of it," she gently told her. Then instead of returning to the blackboard, Miss Lawsen moved toward me.

"Do you mind if I sit on your desk, Joe."

"G'head," I answered, blushing as I slid over to make room.

She settled herself on the desk, smiled down at me, and then addressed the class. "Take out your storybooks and turn to page 235."

While reaching for my book in the desk, I glanced at her legs dangling in the aisle. One foot fidgeted in the shoe in a seesaw motion. As her heel moved down, her calf flattened out; as her heel came up, her calf balled up. I was reminded of a ballerina I'd seen in the movies holding onto a rail. I had an urge to peek up her dress by dropping a pencil, but chickened out.

"Let's skip down to question number six," she said. "Neils Thorsen, would you please read it to the class."

"I forgot my book."

"Look on with Robert Mayer. Would you please let him sit with you, Robert?"

"Sure. Come on, Neils."

"Would you read it now please, Neils?"

"Why-doesn't-Jack-Arden-explain-his-mistake-to-Bess-about-the-lamp."

"No, you have the wrong place. We're skipping down to number six."

"Oh, okay. What-do-you-think-of-O-Henry's-idea-that-people-are-either-amachoors–""

"Amateurs," she corrected.

"–are-either-amateurs-or-professionals?"

"What do you think, Neils?"

Miss Lawsen's thigh swung against mine making my leg warm. When she leaned forward my hair nuzzled her loose breasts. Up close her body seemed so big to me. Neils' answer brought me back to the lesson. "Maybe it's because some do things good and others do 'em bad."

"That's one way to look at it," she said. "Did you write out an answer to that question, Knute Knudsen?"

I thought: "All Nishskies from Little Norway. There ain't nobody from my neighborhood in the whole class. Ming! I'm glad they ain't now wid her sitting on my desk."

"Joe, would you read question eight, please."

"Eight?" I looked up.

She nodded.

"Uh-why-do-you-think-Mack-the-park-bench-hobo-couldn't-win-a-fight-in-the-ring,-even-though-he-knocked-out-the-middleweight-champeen-of-the-woild?"

"Do you have a reason for it, Joe?"

"I been at the P.A.L. matches and I know a lotta guys freeze in the ring because they get butterflies. And I know one guy who lost on pernts to a guy he used to mobilize in the gym every time they sparred. Maybe that's what happened ta Mack."

When the bell rang, Miss Lawsen closed her book and slipped off my desk. I went to the wardrobe in the back to get my jacket. As I was going out the door Miss Lawsen called, "Oh, Joe, may I see you for a second, please."

"Sure, whadda ya want?"

"You did very well this afternoon. How would you like to be president of the class?"

"Me? Uh, okay." I said, surprised but pleased.

▚▚

"You're dead and you know it."

"Get outta here, you couldn't even see me."

"Ya head was stuck out. Hey, everybody, Michael's dead. I got 'im."

Kids were playing cops-and-robbers in front of the apartment when I got home from school. Inside the hall I heard jazz coming from upstairs. Dad was blowing his sax. I thought that horn was a beaut, golden-colored and shiny as anything. Dad was rehearsing for his weekend gig at Murphy's Bar and Grill. I loved to listen to Dad, but at the bar nobody noticed his playing. They all seemed to be waiting for twelve o'clock when the stripper came on. There was no stage so she danced right up close to the bar. The men could reach out and goose her—and sometimes did.

Dad considered himself a good musician and was proud that he could read music. Once when the Department of Sanitation band played on the radio, they gave him a few solo bars. "Could have gone wid the big bands," he would tell us, "but I had all you kids to think of." Then he would withdraw into himself, as though reconsidering his decision.

Everyone on the block seemed to be going into civil service. There was security in that—a regular salary, hospitalization, a pension, no more bread lines. But Dad hated getting up early in the morning to go to his job shoveling snow or hauling garbage. He wished the people wouldn't fill the cans to the brim; the strain of handling the heavy ash cans was curving his back. If only he could catch the number or a round-robin at the track he would have enough money to leave his job. He could open a little luncheonette, put the kids in there to help out. And with Peepa (Grandma's "companion" who had been a chef in Italy) making sauces, the place would have to do well.

I tiptoed into the bedroom and waited until he finished wailing on "Harlem Nocturn." "Guess what, Dad?"

Keeping the reed in his mouth, Dad turned around and creased his forehead.

"I was made president of the class by my teacher today."

He nodded, swung back around, and tootled into "Perdido."

I changed my clothes and went over to Steve's Supermarket, where I worked as a delivery boy. My hours were from four to seven or later, depending on who was running the store. If Steve's wife was in, her sweet voice hounded me until dark to scrub the cellar and the potato bins and anything else she could think of to wring her two dollars' worth out of me. It was the second time I had worked for a man whose wife was a petite tyrant.

Today I got off at seven. After supper I trotted down to play canball. The game was played with nine men and baseball rules, except that a beer can and broomstick substituted for the ball and bat. Canball Stadium attracted crowds of two and three people walking their dogs through the weedy infield. At first glance it was a billboard lot, but foot powder sprinkled in diagonal lines to an undershirt homeplate converted it to a canball park. It was a hundred and fifty feet down the right foul line, a long distance to drive a beer can.

Hulking Bobby was up so I moved back. Chanting under the lights in front of the Robert Hall Clothes billboard, I was Carl Furillo patrolling the outer garden at Ebbets Field in a night game. "No hitter, Mappy babe, put it by him. He stinks on ice." Whack! A bronze Ballantine can, caving in from a vicious swing, soared into left center. Timmy Kelly bounded over the rubbly lot tracking the tin object with the corner of his eye all the way to the base of the Levy's Rye sign, where he leaped up and made a spectacular, bloody, one-finger snag. A one-finger catch was possible because of the can-opener holes, but was a fluke.

"Told ya ya stink." I passed Bobby coming in to bat.

"Up your Aunt Tilly's."

"Batter up!" the ump barked.

I stepped up to the plate, and the outfield shifted to shallow right. I was strictly an opposite-field hitter because of a bad hitch in my swing. I always wound up with the bat to murder the can, but never got around in time. Yearning to be a homerun slugger, I had practiced swinging a barbell. My forearms grew bulky but I still couldn't reach the billboard. No matter how hard I swung, the outfielders dashed in shallow for me. Popping up again, I flung the bat against a wall.

Miss Lawsen stationed herself on my desk regularly for the remainder of the term. She treated everyone nicely, but I was her favorite. I guess it was because I was the only swarthy, black-haired boy in the class. She selected me for all the honors. If I had ever pinned on all the service ribbons and merit badges she gave me, I would have looked like a dictator. She designated me Moderator of the class on current events, and appointed me Representative to the G.O. Council. As Official Air Raid Warden, I was outfitted with a white belt, searchlight, and crash helmet in case of atomic attack. She even got me appointed Flag Bearer in Assembly. When the guys in the neighborhood saw me marching up the stage with the American flag, they had their first hint that I was a traitor.

Miss Lawsen made me feel special. Her praise inspired me to study. I wanted to excel for her. At night instead of playing ring-aleavio, canball, and the other games, I stayed home to read. Since there was no private place in the apartment, I sat in a corner with the couch pulled behind me. Until then I had dreaded books, and thinking about it now I can understand why. My uncles distrusted book learning and said that too much reading makes a person go crazy. Ma and Dad seldom read anything except *True Confessions* and the *Daily Mirror,* respectively. All my friends considered books a gruesome drag. Then I began paying attention to what books said, and started enjoying them. History became as exciting to me as a war movie, and I could remember it as vividly. At the end of the term I was on the honor roll. Worried that my friends might see my name, I asked the principal's secretary to take it down. In the space for "teacher's remarks" on my report card, Miss Lawsen wrote a long paragraph on what an ideal student I was. Dad didn't even look at the report card and Ma was hardly impressed. She told me to sign the card for her.

Miss Lawsen didn't last long as a teacher. At the end of the year she married a handsome college graduate and became a housewife. After her marriage she invited the class to her home for a party. I didn't go.

4 "I hate you," Madeline screamed as Ma rinsed her head under the hot water. "Ya blinding me. I got shampoo in my eyes. My eyes!" She started to cry.

"What're ya crying about?" Ma scolded. "Be quiet or I'll give ya somethin' to cry about."

"I think ya should use scalding water to wash her hair wid all the nits she's got," I said.

"I'll kill him." Madeline shouted, lunging at me.

"Get ya head under there and shut up," Ma ordered, pulling her back by the forelock and shoving her head under the faucet. "And ya stop being pesky," Ma said to me.

The doorbell buzzed. Ma dashed out of the bathroom.

"See who's at the door, Joey," she said, going into the closet. "If it's the seltzer man or any of the bill collectors, tell 'em I'm not home."

I walked out on the landing, weaving my head to try to make out the blurred figure in the vestibule downstairs.

"Got any old junk?" a voice yelled up.

"Hold on." I went back inside. "It's only the junk man, Ma. We got anythin' for him?"

"Tell him he can take those rags near the garbage cans down there." She came out of the closet. I stepped back into the hall. "You can have the rags down there by the cans."

"Thanks."

KILROY EATS IT, I etched into the wall with a bobby pin.

"Ya slow as molasses. Whadda ya still doin' out there?" Ma yelled.

"Just killin' time."

"Go see if your uncle has left yet. Your father wanted me ta give him a slip."

"Which uncle?"

"Your Uncle Tony. But wait a minute before ya go." She came out on the landing and handed me a strip torn from a brown paper bag. It had a list of names and was wrapped around two crinkled dollars held tight by a rubber band. "If he's still there tell him ta put this in fa your Father."

I jumped down the wooden staircase three steps a leap.

"*Animale, disgraciato, fidend,*" Grandma roared from the basement. "I come upa there wid a hatcha and cuta your head off you keepa jumpa downa mya stairs."

My uncle's apartment was in the rear of the first floor. I hurried in. "Hey, Unc, my old man wants ya ta put this in fa him." I handed him the packet.

"What, he give ya twen'y horses wid two bucks again? That stiff."

"I think they're 'if' bets."

"Yeah, him and his 'if' bets. I got nuttin' better ta do than figure his lists wid all the arrows and lines goin' from here to there all over the place."

"Where ya goin', ta the bookie or the track?"

"Downa track."

"Can I come ta give ya luck?"

"Wid you there's nuttin'. I saw how lucky you were when I took ya ta help me paint the showroom."

"Aw, that was an accident. C'mon, *cumpar'* [godfather]. Lemme come."

"How come ya not in school taday?"

"No school. It's a Jewish holiday."

"I thought I confoimed ya."

"Not me, alla teachers are mostly Jews."

"Ah, ya shouldn't be there anyway. Learn a trade. Go get ya workin' papers, ya could be out making good money."

"Ya gonna be a sport and take me, *cumpar'*?"

"How'd I let them rope me in ta be your godfodder? We gotta

go pick up Jerry and Tardo first."

I knew Uncle Tony would give in. People said he had a heart of gold, which he really needed to afford a nephew like me. The last time I went to help him on a weekend paint job I clumsily overturned an $80 showroom lamp. After gnashing his teeth at me and frantically trying to reassemble the smithereens, Uncle Tony regained his calm and paid for the whole thing himself.

Traffic on the Queens lanes of the Belt Parkway which girdles Brooklyn was light at noon. Long limousines passed us carrying chipper, chattering racing fans. While Uncle Tony's friends reviewed Gelardi's rating in the *Daily Mirror*, I looked out at the Flatland's marsh, Brooklyn's only natural frontier. Along the edge of the road, trees I knew from my science class—sycamore, pine, and maple—were ablaze with autumn-colored leaves that rustled and rippled in the flux of a fickle wind. Running inland, high fields of green hair grass, flecked with gold and yellow, ranged over a stew of life: sweeping over the damp plains where rabbits romped, straddling the catfish creek, continuing through the bird sanctuary bustling with lustrous purple-green pheasants. The grass stopped at the bank of an inlet covered with tacking sailboats, but regrew on the other side scarcely interrupted by the scattered driftwood shacks and God-forsaken truck-body homes of hardy squatters. Out at sea, searching gulls skimmed over the water's swells under pearl clouds. Other gulls scavenged on the garbage dunes along a stretch of beach that belonged to the city dump.

I wished we could have stopped to look around. At a younger age exploring had been my favorite hobby. Attics had always intrigued me. What lay beneath a stone also had mystery for me. I once tried to pry up a heavy boulder in the neighborhood lot, expecting to find a passageway to hell or China. Dredging murky sewers for lost balls, I was always hoping to fish up a bottle with a genie.

We got off the Parkway at Lefferts Boulevard, the Aquaduct Race Track exit. After parking we hopped on a shuttle bus that took us from the car lot to the main gate. Nuns holding out straw baskets covered all the entrances, blessing the bettors who gave them coins. Inside the track we approached a number of newsstands with brightly colored cards, their vendors yelling: "Race ca'ds, scratch sheets, call 'em out." My uncle bought programs for the four of us. As we climbed up to the third tier, a loudspeaker announced: "In the first race, Amber Lips, one pound over." The grandstand was jammed with people, mostly males.

"How come there are so many old-timers?" I asked Jerry.

"What else they gonna do? They can't do sports, and most are retired."

Down on the oval track, a fleet of tractors combed down the dirt surface with tail rakes. A group of Orientals huddled along the fence in the infield. The paddock was fairly well filled with owners and jockeys conferring as they watched the sleek colts being walked around the ring by the grooms. Inside the rail, the green turf insulated a garden of pink and white geraniums around a glassy blue pond the shape of an angel's harp. White swans sailed smoothly back and forth, unmindful of the din. Few people in the stands noticed the ballad setting. Most eyes were riveted on the odds flashing on the tote board.

"Looks like we might hit some rain today," my uncle said.

Jerry looked up. "Yeah, it's overcast."

"Uncle Tony, if it rains do they still run?" I asked.

"Yeah, even if it snows, long as it don't freeze. If it freezes it makes it too hard fa horses' hoofs."

Leaving the paddock, a man in a red suit faced the clubhouse from the track and blew into a long bugle. He then got up on a white horse.

"Whose that man on the white horse?" I asked Tardo.

"Don'cha know?"

"No, who is he?"

"That's the Lone Ranger."

"C'mon, stop kidding."

"I think he's the caller."

The loudspeaker announced, "The horses are on the track."

"I like the t'ree horse," Uncle Tony said. "They took off the blinkers. But it bothers me he ain't got no outrider."

"Wanna hear a joke?" Tardo said. "Lawton picks Bold Marker."

"He's a speed horse."

"So what. He can't close. The four looks like she's ready ta fly." Tardo pointed. "Look at the way she's dancing out there."

"She'll burn herself out. Who does the clocker like?"

"The clocker is goin' wid the chalk," Jerry answered.

"What about Sunsong getting a shift in weight. That'll make up a lengt'. And he's got a good post position," Uncle Tony said.

A bell rang and the lights on the tote board flickered as the final odds were posted.

"It is now post time," the loudspeaker announced. "And they're off! That's Trusdale in the middle of the track getting the lead, Miss Marlow alongside is second, with Bold Marker third, Happy Flyer fourth, Sunsong fifth, Wonderbird sixth, and Amber Lips is seventh. They continue that way in the back stretch with Trusdale opening a gap of four lengths. And as they swing around the turn to the three-eighths pole, that's Sunsong challenging on the outside."

When the horses reached the home stretch the screaming crescendoed, drowning out the announcer. So I listened to the people around me:

"All the way, Trusdale, all the way."

"Keep him out there, banana nose."

"C'mon, boy, c'mon." A man making a kissing sound with his lips whipped himself—"thwack, thwack"—on the thigh with a program.

"Now, Bold Marker, now!" a woman shouted excitedly.

"Bold Marker is out of it, lady," a man retorted.

"*Meta, meta,* Manual."

"Whip him ona prick, Usiree; ona tip of the prick," someone coached, muffling his speech with a program over his mouth.

They passed the wire, the noise subsided, and the announcer's voice returned. "And the winner is Trusdale."

Jerry turned to us in a fever. "Ya believe it, I switched off him the last minute. Look, look, I had him circled wid my best figure. Me and my hunches. What a *stupidole.* I should have my head examined."

"I had 'im. I had 'im." A blustering little man busted in. "Whadda ya think, he was the class. C'mere, let me show ya. Look at the company this horse has run wid." The man shoved a page from the racing paper at us.

"Don't get me sick," Jerry said.

"Look at the money this horse earned last year," the stranger persisted. "He was hot. They just shipped him from Monmouth. He loves this track. And what a price he went off at."

"I told ya ta stop." Jerry was getting angry.

"Twen'y ta one. He's gotta pay $40."

"Good fa you," Uncle Tony said. "Now will ya get outa here."

The man finally turned and joined the other seers smugly making their way to the cashier's window.

Going home, long limousines passed us again, this time carrying gloomily silent racing fans. Uncle Tony and his friends were in the same mood. They dropped me off at home and drove to the trotters at Yonkers "to get even." Dad was a loser too. He was sitting at the kitchen table when I walked in. I put on a down face not to build up his hopes. Right away he knew, but asked anyway, "How'd I do?"

Dad's take-home pay was $44. He had eight dependents—himself, Ma, and six kids. The month's rent took a week's salary. The milk bill for a month consumed another week's salary. The icebox was always empty by the middle of the week except for leftover *pastafazule*. Ma hardly ever bought things cash. Instead, she traded with a bunch of salesmen who came to our house peddling clothes, sheets, carpets—just about everything. They gave her credit and overcharged by twice as much. To pay the bills, Dad borrowed from loan companies, but that made matters worse. They soaked him thirty-percent interest and tacked on late fees. When he got behind they sent collectors to scare him by threatening to call lawyers and have our furniture taken out. Once they sued him to get at his paycheck. Dad's only defense was that he missed payments because he had to pay for an operation to remove Anthony's appendix. He promised to pay the loan company as soon as he could, and asked the judge not to "garnishee" his salary. The judge said he was under oath to do justice according to the law, which meant looking at the contract papers and ordering garnishment.

During my short-pants years, I liked having the salesmen and collectors come to our house. I got excited over grownups paying us a visit; they patted me on the head and said nice things. Later, when I could understand better, I resented them. Money problems made Ma and Dad act ugly and bitter toward each other, which was sad because looking at their early pictures you could tell they were once happy and in love.

That night, we were in bed but couldn't sleep because Ma was bitching at Dad.

"Ya gonna gimme that ten dollars?"

"Stop yappin' and get in bed."

"This light is not goin' off until ya gimme that money. What kinda man are ya? Ya don't even care about your daughter's birthday."

"Can't ya get it through ya thick skull I don' have it?"

"Ya promised me. Aincha got any honesty, ya two-faced thing."

"Pipe down or ya'll wake up the whole block."

"I'll wake up the block if ya don't gimme that money."

"Go ask ya mother fa it tomorruh. She'll give it ta ya."

"It's not my mother's place ta. That child needs a decent dress. Ya're a shirker. Ya've always been a shirker. That's why ya went fa the sanitation instead of the firemen. Ya got no backbone."

"Ya got ya brains up your ass, ya know that?"

"Watch your mouth, ya kids can hear."

"I didn' go fa the firemen cause the list was too big and I couldn't pass the test then anyhow if I tried. I didn' study enough. No backbone, shit. Shut the light, eh."

"I said I'm not shutting it until you gimme the money."

"What'sa matter wid ya? Doncha think I'd give it ta ya if I had it? Doncha think I wanna buy it fa her? I'm up against da wall wid the loansharks."

"But ya can play the horses, can'tcha?"

"Two dollars cause I'm desperate. I'll tell ya the truth, I played it so I could buy it fa her if I won. The only thing we can do is wait a couple a weeks. I'll scrape up some. I'll see my cousin Johnny."

"Tomorruh is her birthday, not a couple of weeks. I don't wanna know nuttin'. Ya promised that money. Now gimme it."

"Whadda ya, simple-minded or somethin'? I jus' got through tellin' ya I ain't got it. How many times I gotta tell ya?"

"I saw ya had money in ya wallet. I want ten from that."

"That money's fa Household Finance."

"I don't care about Household Finance. It's Madeline's birthday. Household Finance can go to hell. They're not gonna stop my daughter from having a decent dress on her birthday. Think about your child. Never mind them."

"Never mind them. There's no use talkin' ta you."

"Ya're a miserable garbage man."

"*Zita !* [shut up!] you bastard."

"Here comes the mad dog."

"You better shut up."

"I'm goin' through ya pants and take it."

"Get away from those pants, ya hear what I'm saying."

"Stop it, stop it." Madeline cried from her room. "I don't want no birthday dress."

"I'm takin' what ya promised."

"I'll belt ya in the mouth, ya touch those." The bedsprings creaked as Dad got up, and then we heard feet moving around like wrestling, and bodies banging against the chairs and bureau.

"Get yar hands off me," Ma said, crying and out of breath.

"Gimme the wallet."

"Leave me alone. I'm takin' ten dollars fa my child."

"Gimme that wallet, Ange. I'm warnin' ya."

Then we heard the smack of a punch. Ma screamed. Anthony and I got up and ran into their room. Ma, in her slip, was standing against the wall. She was having a hard time breathing. Then she fainted, sliding heavily to the floor. Seeing her laying there unconscious, I felt a razor cut through my insides.

\\\

5 Richie coughed up a glob of phlegm and spit it at the back of Mr. Fallin, our eighth-grade Social Studies teacher, who was writing on the blackboard. The mucous splashed onto his shoulder blade and then slowly dripped to the hardwood floor. Snickering rippled down the rows of desks. Mr. Fallin turned around scowling. When the room quieted he resumed writing.

Al leaned forward into the aisle between our seats to whisper, "Let's dry hump June Maywood inna wardrobe when the bell rings."

"Naw, you do it."

"What'sa matter wid you?"

Mr. Fallin turned around again. Al straightened up in his seat. "Eyes up front! I have just listed a number of historical events you should know from the homework I assigned. In the few minutes remaining in this period, I shall call on members of the class to explain why these events are important. Please stand when I call your name. Thomas Meerto!"

"Yeah."

"Stand up!"

"Sorry."

"What is the Open Door Policy?"

"Somebody forgot ta close the door."

"Sit down." Mr. Fallin whacked the blackboard with his pointer to stop the laughing. "Richard Berder! What is the Open Door Policy?"

"Catch me next time 'round. I'm not up on this crap."

"Go out in the hall and wait for me in front of Mr. Washhauer's office."

"Should I bring my jacket?"

"Yes, get it," Mr. Fallin snapped. "And take your books, too."

Shuffling to the wardrobe in full view of the class but with his back to the teacher, Richie balled one hand, clasped the other around his wrist, and then rotated his fist. The class laughed at the slur.

"Joseph Sorrentino! Do you know what the Open Door Policy is or do you want to join him at the assistant principal's office? I don't want any more nonsense."

"I think the Open Door Policy meant that everybody, ya know like all countries, should be able ta trade wid China. I think the leaders of this country were afraid those other countries were gonna take over China."

"Asskisser!" Tommy hissed across the room.

➤➤➤

At the three-o'clock bell students galloped down the stairs like Apaches and charged the vendor wagons camped along the street. Within a short time they had shrunk the snowcone man's block of ice, the Good Humor man was dunking to the bottom of his box, and a single jelly apple was left stranded in the confectioner's glass case. Mooching a nickel from a classmate, I bought a Mello-Roll at Silverrod's. As I gobbled it down I searched for my friends in the crowd. I spotted Richie crossing to the other side. I could make him out from behind because of the slingshot shape of his tall body. His lithe frame was a narrow pole up to his chest and then forked out to wide shoulders. When he reached the other side he propped himself on the johnny pump with his face turned my way. Richie had good features—blue eyes, tawny hair, a compelling jaw—but girls disliked him because he did not know how to be serious. Always clowning, his face seemed cast in a permanent grin that was at its widest when he was being mischievously nasty, like the time he helped me chop down my brother Nicky's clubhouse. As I

33

crossed the street to join him he sat down on the curb to view the girls' legs from a better angle. We both liked muscular legs. I sat down next to him.

"Has Dottie come out yet?" I asked, looking toward the school.

"No not yet."

"Good, we'll still get a shot of her *coscias* [legs]."

"Hubba, hubba." Richie's hand fluttered. "Get a gander o' those gams." He pointed to a girl with the legs of a fullback.

"Yeah, what calves. They're too much."

"Can you imagine her in white high heels?"

"The livin' end."

Soon the rest of the click, still chomping on stale pretzels, congregated on the curb with us. Tommy Meerto, the picador, started it off. "Joseph, what's the Open Door Policy?"

"Yea, fairy, tell us about it," Mappy razzed.

"Faggot, fairy, quite contrary, Joseph Asskisser, how does your door open?" Richie chanted.

"Don't bust my balls. Cut out da shit." I got mad and wanted to hit one of them.

"Faggot, fairy, quite contrary, Joseph GaGa, how does your door open?" They all pranced around me.

"C'mon, you guys."

"GiGi, GaGa, Joseph Shit, Joseph Brownnoser."

"C'mon." I felt like Natie the Jew.

"Who even wants the creep ta come home wid us," Mappy said.

"Yeah, let's leave the leech by himself."

"Goodbye, Asskisser." They took off.

Later in Charlie's Candy Store they froze me out again. Even the older guys made cutting remarks: "I heard ya sucked wind out of ya teacher's ass," I looked up to them too much to answer back; a private can rage at other privates, but must submit to generals. I needed my friends, so it hurt to be shunned that way, and they kept it up for days. The problem was that Miss Lawsen had made me want to study and the habit had carried over into the eighth grade. But the way everyone was acting toward me now, I saw myself as some kind of freak. Acceptance came back on the day I got up and wrote on the blackboard: "Mr. Fallin is a prick."

6 The streets, washed shiny black by rain, still shimmered under the lamplight like patent leather. Stars blazed in the clear night like Fourth-of-July rockets. Walking to Timmy Kelly's weekend party, I gazed up and picked out the Big and Little Dippers. I knew the constellations from class trips to the planetarium. I recalled being fooled by my eyes when the projector beamed a galaxy on the ceiling. After the planetarium show a guide opened a door and said, "This way out to the real world." Walking along now, I wondered whether the sky I was seeing was in a little room, too.

Passing the church my thoughts changed to Timmy Kelly. Unlike the rest of us, Timmy attended parochial school. His St. John's Prep blazer stitched with the Irish name T. KELLY over the breast pocket often got him off with Brooklyn's Irish cops while the rest of us were arrested. His looks protected him, too. Except for four pounds of veal cutlets for ears, he looked like a teenage Paul Newman, with clear green eyes, brown curly locks, and full rosy cheeks. When he was seven, he modeled as a cherub for the ceiling frescoes of Regina Pacis Shrine. As for his body, he was so rawboned Richie nicknamed him Consumption. His lunch every day consisted of five candies: Chuckles, Chunky, JuJubes, Royal, and Clark Bar. Decay had burrowed out cavities in his teeth like the catacombs. For all his outward appearance of innocence, Timmy was the shrewdest, most cunning member of our click. Once when the butcher got into an argument with someone on the sidewalk, Timmy slipped inside and walked away with his cash register. Another time he ordered several charlotte russes from the baker, clutching what seemed like a ten-dollar bill in his hand. When the baker gave him the cakes, Timmy handed him the ripped-off corner of a ten and ran out. One Christmas he cleaned out the stock cellar of Rudy's Tavern—he crouched along the bar all night and carried out nearly 100 bottles right under the bartender's eyes.

Turning up 67th Street I could see his house. Timmy was far from rich, but I thought he lived in luxury because he had his own bedroom with a wall-to-wall closet. His modernized brick house contrasted elegantly with Danny Charms' mud-colored, collapsing wooden house across the way. Danny's place with its upper balustrade looked misplaced from a saloon town in the old West.

Loud music and voices from the party at Timmy's spilled over into the street. I hurried to the basement. Grinning Richie was popping balloons that hung from the ceiling on crepe paper. Along the walnut-paneled wall on one side, girls on folding chairs were talking away, undaunted by the radio blasting rock from the Moon Dog station. Out on the linoleum floor couples—some of them two girls—were lindying. You couldn't miss Mappy, dapper in a black cowboy shirt and flamingo pink pants with the latest style in patch pockets.

"Whadda ya say, Sarry," friends shouted.

"Eh, Sarry." Timmy came over.

"Hi, Tim."

"That was some sad ass game we played this afternoon."

"It was Mappy's fault tryin' ta pitch. He's got a pipedream that he's like his cousin Johnny Tap. How's the party?"

"It's leash now, but it'll liven up. It's still early. I got wine or vodka wid orange juice. Whadda ya want?"

"Gimme some wine. Where's ya mother?"

"She's out working wid the beads. Why don't ya get a girl while I go fa the wine."

"Whose the one sitting next to Concetta? She's nice."

"Ya like that, eh? She's Concetta's cousin, Josephine Tarino."

"She ain't from the neighborhood?"

"No, she comes from Amityville or some other place way out in Canarsie. She's just visitin' fa the weekend. She's older than Concetta. I think fourteen. Why don' ya go over."

"Yeah, I will in a minute."

"I'll get the wine." Timmy pushed through the dancers.

My eyes had been on Josephine all the time I was talking to Timmy. She had a cute chick-pea nose, puzzling brown eyes, braided black hair, and a sun-browned complexion. When I first noticed her standing she looked slender because her face was long and her calves straight and she was wearing a blue ruffled dress that hid her shape. But when she sat down and crossed her legs, her skirt offered a peek of rousingly healthy thighs for fourteen.

Bobby asked Concetta to dance, leaving Josephine sitting by herself. She finished her drink and then looked up at the dancers. Her eyes found her cousin Concetta, the only person she knew on the floor. Concetta smiled over at her but then returned her attention to Bobby. I was standing on the fringe of the dancers, a diving board's distance away from Josephine. I was weighing what I should say to her and trying to muster the confidence to go over.

When she caught me staring at her, instead of turning away she composed a flirting smile. I considered that an invitation and darted over, cutting off Mappy who was about to join her.

"I hear ya from Amityville," I said, sitting next to her.

"Yeah, do you know where it is?"

"It's out on Long Island, right? Near Babylon."

"Have you been there?"

"No, but I was ta Babylon once wid my boss. He has a country place there."

"Dija like it?"

"Ta tell ya the truth I liked some o' the things but most o' the time I was bored."

"That's because you don't know the places. What dija like?"

"I liked watching the Piper Cubs take off and land at the airport. And I liked the fresh jelly donuts they sold on Sunday mornings at the Danish bakery. Ming! They were really full of jelly." I studied her pretty face. Her mouth was set in a slight smile.

"What's your name?" she asked.

"Joe. I know yours is Josephine. I did a little spying."

"Oh, ya did, huh." She giggled. "Do you like your name?"

"Sometimes I think it's too ordinary."

"I feel the same way about Josephine."

"But I always say it's God's fodder's name. And St. Joseph's Day, that's like anudder birthday fa me. My grandfodder bakes me those delicious *sfinges* [Italian pastry]."

"I don't get none of that being Josephine."

"Do you like the Four Aces?" One of their songs, "A Garden in the Rain," was on.

"They're okay. I like Eddie Fisher."

"I'm big on Don Cornell. Let's dance." I got up.

We started off with a fox-trot, and her knees kept me at a distance, but I hoarded her for every slow dance for the next two hours and kept pulling her in closer until I was grinding up against her and could feel her budding bosom getting hotter and harder through both our clothes. After each dance I walked back to our chairs hunching to hide the bulge in my pants. Timmy shuttled back and forth refilling our glasses with wine. Wine loosened my tongue, but it had an opposite effect on Josephine. She was falling into a quiet peacefulness. Her head rested cozily on my shoulder. Before the next record came on I nudged her. "Let's go fa a walk."

"Awright, let me tell Concetta. I want to get her key." Her words made me sure that we would make out. She expected to stay out late. In a minute she was back wearing her jacket. At the door Timmy's cat politely meowed for us to let her out, too. It was a nice night. The streets had completely dried. A sickle-shaped moon balanced on a cloud overhead. We walked up 67th Street holding hands but ignoring each other. My mind was trying to decide where I should take her. I hated to go far. She wasn't drunk but she was in a warm mood with a lazy wildness in her eyes. I was afraid if we went any place too far away the fresh air would bring her out of it. I decided on the Fortway Theater's fire exit; there was a dark alcove at the top. When we got there people were pouring out. The last show must have just finished. I gave up on the alcove and headed for the railroad lot.

"Where're we going?" she asked.

"Not far. Only anudder few blocks. We can watch the trains go by. Once I saw silver circus trains pass."

As we approached the railroad my eyes spied ahead for a place with good cover. There was a long strip of vacant land overlooking the ravine which held the tracks. Most of it was weedy city property with some scattered old victory gardens and tomato plots.

"Concetta's really nice, ain't she?" I tried to take her mind off the surroundings as I led her by the hand through the jungle of weeds.

"Yeah, she's sweet," she answered, following me with no hesitation.

The air was silent except for an orchestra of crickets fiddling their legs, At the end of the weeds there was a stone wall to prevent people from falling into the steep ravine. I guided her into a spot against the wall facing me. A shaft of light from a distant street lamp danced on her face.

"My brother Nicky used ta have a clubhouse here," I said, moving close to her.

"It must have been fun," she said without real interest.

"Yeah." I knew she didn't want to talk and neither did I. I pressed up against her and kissed her.

I continued to straight kiss her, holding my breath for a long time. I thought that was the lover's way. Then to show off my worldliness I kissed her on the neck with a wide open mouth and nibbled on her earlobe. I didn't get a charge out of that kind of kissing but the older guys said it excited a girl. After a long period of necking I teetered on the brink of squeezing her "ninnies." I looked at her face. Her eyes were still in that lazy mood. Like a sneaky coward, I slid my hands up her armpits and touched her breasts with just my thumbs—like curb feelers. I wondered if she noticed. "She must've," I thought. Kissing her again, I moved my hands over her breasts and squeezed them. She didn't push me away. When I looked at her face she just smiled in a mischievous, brazen way as if she'd had it done before. I never knew a girl before who would let me feel her up just like that. Encouraged, I stuck my hand under her dress and felt inside her panties. She didn't say anything, but just closed her eyes like it really felt good to her. I pressed harder with my fingers. She bit her lip turning her head to the side and her thighs closed around my hand like a Venus fly-trap. Excited and out of breath, I got the idea that she would let me go all the way if I wanted to, which I did, but I didn't know how. Up until this moment the farthest I ever got with girls was Stinky Finger with Lisa next door and a hand job from the girl everyone took turns sitting next to during the Saturday matinee. She reached over and did it to you without taking her eyes off the movie.

Clumsily tugging down Josephine's panties and my pants, I tried poking straight at her, standing up. I didn't know if I was entering her. How could I know what doing it right felt like since I had never done it before. I wanted to ask her if I was doing it right, but I didn't have the nerve.

I never knew if Josephine was the first time for me. The next and last time I saw her was months later. I had four friends tag after us as I took her up to the fire exit alcove. All of us were expecting to do it to her, but she was a different girl. She reneged.

7 Mr. DeMeo, who was both my gym and homeroom teacher, sat at his desk handing out the last report cards for the eighth grade. The students were in an alphabetical line that curved around the room and was moving quickly except for an occasional delay when a student receiving a bad report card came to the desk. Richie lingered, being told he was left back. He listened with his head bowed seriously while he flipped the bone behind the teacher's head. I lolled against the back wall viewing the crayon sketches on the wardrobe. When the S's neared the desk, I nervously hoofed

at the woodwork. I really didn't care about the bad grades, and I could turn him off if he tried to belittle me, but I dreaded a long talk on how I had let him down. I never admitted it to any of my friends but I liked and respected DeMeo. He was great on the high bar and tough with his hands. Richie once challenged him to go into the locker room, and only DeMeo came back out.

"Joe, I'm disappointed." His mouth sagged. "It's hard for me to talk to you about this report card."

"Yeah, I know." His mood seeped into me.

"An F in Spanish, a D in Social Studies, a C in Shop."

"I di'nt have time ta study. I was deliverin' orders aftuh school."

"We both know that's malarky."

"But . . . "

"How can you go from an A to a D in Social Studies? I saw the papers for the first test in there. You had one of the highest grades."

"I never got da other book."

"You know you're only hurting yourself with the attitude you have now."

"Maybe I'll wise up in ninth grade."

"I hope so. There's a lot I'd like to talk to you about but there are other students waiting. Can you make it up to the rec center tonight?"

"Yeah, I guess so."

"Why don't I talk to you up there. Before you leave now, do you know yet what you're going to be doing this summer?"

"My fodder got me a job in a bleach fact'ry."

"Well, at least you'll be making good money."

"Yeah, a big four bucks a day."

"That's a lot more than most of your classmates will be making."

"I won't holler if they wanna change places."

"Your family needs the money, Joe. It's not easy for them."

"Can I get the report card now?"

"Yeah, but don't let it fool you. You can be anything you want to be." He picked up the card. "Don't forget the rec center to-night."

"I won't."

Richie was waiting for me in the hall. "Whad the creep say?"

"He wants ta see me tonight."

"I thought you wuz comin' wid us ta get wacked off by Mary

Lapadooley."

"I still am. I'm not going up ta any fuckin' rec center ta get a lecture."

We joined Tommy Meerto at the bus stop. As the next bus pulled out the three of us hitched on the back. The surface was so flat we must have looked like magnets. We latched our fingertips on a metal lip under the window and stood penguin-footed on the slight bumper. I hopped off as my block came up.

"Smoking stunts your growth," Ma was scolding Nicky when I walked in.

"I wasn't smokin'. Those were punks."

"Punks, smunks, I don' want ya smokin' anythin'."

"There's nuttin' wrong wid punks, Ma," I interrupted.

"And you lift ya feet when ya walk around here." She examined the floor. "Ya scuffin' up the carpet. It's bad enough as it is. That man, nuttin' bothers him; fifteen years the same carpet. Get me the steel wool."

"Where is it?"

"On the sink. What'sa matter wid ya? Ya walk like a *mu-shamatelle* [slug]."

"I'm tired. Lemme alone."

"Ya know why ya tired? Because ya not havin' ya eggnog."

"Ugh! Ya call that eggnog the way you make it?—a raw egg in milk. If ya made it like the milkman I'd drink it."

"Well, how do ya want it? I'll scramble it fa ya. Ya gotta have an egg. It feeds the blood. And stop eatin' that junky candy. That ain't nature's food."

"What about farina, Ma? Is that good fa ya, too?" I baited her.

"Farina does a world of good fa ya stomach. It gives new lining ta the system."

Ma was always prescribing for nutrition. Fish gives you brains. Olives put oil in the scalp. Beans clean out the gas. But the omnipotence was *cicoria* (chicory). There appeared to be a direct connection: the more horrible something tasted the better it was for you. *Cicoria* being the bitterest was the best. Once when I was in the third grade I came home from school crying after being drubbed by a bigger boy.

"Ya know why he can beat ya up?" Ma said. "Because ya don't

eat ya *cicoria. Cicoria* makes ya strong."

For the next two weeks I gorged myself on *cicoria* and then met him outside the school. "I wanna fight you."

"Box or wrestle?"

"Eider one."

"Wrestle," he said, clamping on a headlock. Tossing me down like a wafer, he pounced on my chest and pinned his knees in my shoulders. "Ya give?"

I thought. "Awright, *cicoria,* take. Hurry up and do ya stuff."

"Say uncle," He pummeled my face.

"This can't be." I couldn't budge him.

I limped home bleeding and crying.

"What happened?" Ma screamed.

"You and ya *cicoria.*"

The factory of the Potenza Bleach Company was a dreary turn-of-the-century gabled garage with rust-hinged pine doors and soot-blotted windows, assortedly cracked and held intact by adhesive tape. A handful of loyal shingles remained on the roof, but most of the rotten deserters hid in the weeds below. Inside the garage, a garden hose and hundreds of empty wine gallons were in a muddle around a table that was a mess of coffee cans dripping homemade paste, stacks of bleach labels, and the peelings of sundry wine brands. Against the back wall two lidless tanks of chlorine rested on a warped platform of mildewed planks across cinder blocks. To pump chlorine into the gallons we dipped a tube into a tank and started it by mouth suction, mildly burning our lungs in the process. We fed each gallon an inch of the gem-green chemical, and then filled it to the top with water.

From seven in the morning until noon we bottled bleach and loaded the company truck. After a tomato-salad lunch we began the delivery route. There were four of us on the truck, a spoke-wheeled Metro with a crank starter and a horn that hiccuped. I sat up front on a soda box with Mappy on my knee. Komineel, a stubbled, lumpish man in his sixties doddered on the running board wearing baggy pants and a longjohn top. As the truck was in motion his nose driveled a liquid spaghetti. He tried to pinch it off with his fingers but the wind boomeranged it over his ear. Driving at the wheel was Mr. Torrio, the company owner, a lusty white-haired immigrant shaped of three blubbery balls like a snowman.

"*Javella* man! How many today, *signora?*" He bellowed in his operatic voice as the truck turtled up and down the neighborhood streets. "We got only da besta stuff."

Housewives came to the window to call down orders. Others sent their daughters to meet the truck. If a girl was wearing a low-cut dress or loose housecoat, Mappy and I always put the bleach down in front of her. Delivering to stores we competed to see who could carry more full gallons. The first day on the job, while loading the truck, I looped ten on my fingers, and almost reached it. The boss docked the loss from my pay. Trying for the record, Mappy held ten with his contorted fingers and cinched one under his armpit. He tensed like a pallbearer balancing a coffin on his shoulder as he descended the stairs to the stock cellar. When he reached the bottom he found himself in the dark. He forgot to turn the lights on before going down. I thought I might have heard him call to me. I was sure I heard eleven crashes.

One day at dinner time we were still on the route. I pressed the buzzer of a shabby duplex on Thirteenth Avenue. A short, muscular guy in a sleeveless undershirt came to the door.

"Whadda ya want, kid?" he asked, even though he was only about eighteen himself.

"Need any bleach?"

"Hold on a minute, I'll check." Going back inside he conversed with a woman in Italian. When he came back out he had two quarters. "Yeah, gimme a gallon."

"Regular or extra strong?"

"Gimme the strong."

I handed him a gallon with a lion on the label.

"What's the damage?"

"T'oity cents."

"Keep it." He gave me the quarters.

I ran back to the truck excited. "Mappy! Hey, Mappy! Guess what? I think that's Tony Bavimo's house I jus' done."

"Howda ya know?"

"I seen him only once before when he was standin' in front of Infantino Brothers. I'm pretty sure it was him but . . . "

"I thought he was doin' time fa shootin' at the teacher."

"He musta gotten out. His hair was like a prison crew still. Ming, you shoulda seen his neck."

"Big, eh?"

"Ming, like the chlorine barrel. An' he's got some arms. When he picked up the gallon the ball popped out."

"I don't think Whitey of the Rampers is gonna be toughest anymore now that Bavimo's out."

On most days I was peeved when I got home from work. Handling bleach for twelve hours was shriveling my skin. My wages were thirty-three cents an hour. I thought that was slave-cheap to be giving up the summer fun my friends were having. That evening was different. I couldn't get over the thrill of having been face-to-face with Tony Bavimo.

Ma had some ladies over. As I came up the stairs I could hear them griping in the kitchen. I recognized Mrs. Pucci's voice.

"Ya think yours is a *facheam*. My prize sits there all night by the window gawking at his daughter's friends."

"They're all the same. They got an ugly streak in them, these men," Ma said. "Must be bad blood."

"You know, Jenny's daughter married that well-off fella," Mrs. Gargiolo chimed in.

"I don't see how she married him, not liking him," Ma said. "The things ya have ta do fa them. I think the whole business in bed wid a man is disgusting."

"She's the type who gets pleasure out of it, my son told me. These girls taday are as bad as the men; there all *putannas* [tramps]," Mrs. Pucci said.

"Would you girls care for annuder cuppa tea?" Ma asked.

"Not fa me, Angie," Mrs. Pucci got up. "That *modeoole* of mine, if I'm not home ta wait on him hand and foot he raises the roof. Ooh, ya boy is gettin' big," she said, passing me on her way out.

"Ya expect me ta stay five years old the rest of my life?" I thought.

"Angie, I didn't wanna tell ya in front of Helen, but I can't go on anymore wid my husband's family. I slave all day over a lousy stove and they don't even appreciate it. His mother bosses me around like I was her servant. Angie, I'm getting migraines from them." Mrs. Gargiolo broke into sobs.

"Oh, you've been through so much, you poor thing." Ma was the kind of woman other ladies liked. She listened to their troubles with a sincere, sad face. Ma felt sorry for others who had it hard, but she had a tough life herself. As a little girl she started knitting

booties in Grandma's basement factory. By fourteen she was working in a sweater factory in the garment center. She married young
and had her third child die inside of her at three months. She carried the rotting fetus for six more months, always in danger of
blood poisoning, but the doctors were afraid to cut her open because she wasn't bleeding. They feared she might hemorrhage.
After nine months, natural labor extruded the remains of the still-
born infant. Then she gave birth to five more healthy children. Ma
said that after the job of raising us was over, when we were all big,
she wanted to adopt a couple of orphans. To her that would be the
good life, to have nothing to do but take care of two orphans.

At kindergarten age I used to snoop around in Ma and Dad's
bedroom. I had been curious about their bed, whose nighttime
squeaking could be heard through the thin wall that separated
their room from mine. Eventually the crosspiece at the foot of the
old bed collapsed. Dad, who was not handy, never repaired it, so
they ended up sleeping on an angle like on a travois. Above the
head of the bed there was a crucifix, and not far to one side was
my parents' wedding picture. Dad wore a sleepy-eyed Don Juan
face in the photo. Ma looked bashful. During their early dates
Grandma chaperoned them. She gave them six months together,
which was liberal in those days, and then told Dad if he wanted to
see her again to bring his mother and father over to set the marriage. They had a big church wedding in South Brooklyn. To Ma
the second most precious thing in life for a girl was to have a
church wedding. The most precious was to walk down the aisle
wearing a veil. She often nagged me, "You better marry a virgin. It's
a disgrace not to have the veil." By church tradition only a virgin
should wear one. But despite the rule, every girl wore a veil. Had
the rule been obeyed, a wedding would have become an event for
catty gossip. It would have also changed proud parents into furious
ones. "You *putanna* where's ya veil? Whadda ya been doin'? I'll
breaka your face."

Ma's concern was not only that I marry a virgin, but that I be
one too. "Marriage is sacred," she said. "A man should be pure.
That's God's way of life to live." In her prudishness she even got
apprehensive if I remained in the bathroom too long. One night
when she and Dad were in bed she started to shout, "What's that
boy doin' in there so long? You know about those things. Maybe he's
touching himself. Tell him how he can go crazy."

"I don't know what he's doin' in there," Dad shouted back. "I hope he's not doin' that. I hope he knows what it can do ta him."

I didn't think masturbating was wrong but I got angry at them for accusing me. All my friends masturbated. We did it in the basement, and in Al's garage; we even did it in school. I got caught in the act once by Miss Murdock, my old-maid eighth-grade English teacher. I tried to zipper up fast but nicked myself and yowled and the whole class turned around. I finally got the zipper up with my face red and the teacher's purple. After Ma was called to school about it, she stayed up with her rosary beads all night.

8   Danny Charms was sitting at the counter in Charlie's Candy Store using another stool as a bongo drum. What you quickly noticed about Danny was his trimness, how neatly casual clothes fit him without a crimp, like an *Esquire* model, and the stamina of his lungs. Timmy Kelly called him Supermouth. "Charms," his other nickname, was a shortening of his last name, Charmsalupo. I loped up to him.

"Whadda ya sa, Danny! Up fa chins on the high bar?"

"I thought you were deliverin' bleach this afternoon."

"My boss left early for his country place. So whadda ya say? Ya wanna work out?"

"Lemme finish this egg cream."

"Ya been practicin' the giant swing at all?"

"Nah, I had a tooth pulled this week at the clinic."

"Don'cha mention dentists ta me."

"It took him two hours ta get it out. The tooth was so decayed it had no crown left."

"Holy smokes, that musta been somethin'. Ya know, I got a date wid the Nishski you were hot fa at Bobby's party."

His eyes flicked up to a mental screen. "Ya mean the zofty one. Yeah, she's good. But lemme finish telling ya about the tooth. The dentist couldn't get it out wid the plyers they use so he hadda hammer and chisel it out bit by bit. I kept spittin' blood in that bowl and drinkin' cold water. They say ya can't feel nuttin' when ya get the needle. Lemme tell ya, I felt the pain. And it's that funny kinda pain. I can't explain it. It creeps up on ya like, an' it's real stingy. The woist part was when he started to jimmy the root. I was getting real jumpy. Blood was all over the place. Ya shoulda seen it. The dentist hadda call the nurse ta hold my arms down. An' you know me, Joey, I don't get worked up easy."

"Ming, ya really had it bad. You wanna know now how I bagged the blond?"

"I ain't finished tellin' ya yet. There was nuttin' left ta the tooth when he was through. There was all these teeny weeny white pieces wid blood all ovuh 'em. The dentis' gimme the root to keep. I got it on me in my hanky. Wanna see how there's no tooth lef'?"

"No, I take ya woid fa it. Now lemme tell ya how I nailed . . . "

"Do ya know why the dentis' always dips the pointy thing in a flame?"

"Ta kill the germs," I answered, getting irked.

"Ya know, I never knew that until this week."

"Now ya remember Buckeye, right? He's that twerpy lookin' guy Mappy brought around."

"Yeah, what about him?"

"Well, his brother is married ta the Nishski's cousin."

"Speaking about gettin' married, ya should see the shower they're gonna give my sister Julia. The whole flat is decorated. I didn't figure until I saw what goes inta it how much somethin' like this costs. About thoity girls in the neighborhood are comin'—Timmy's sister ChiChi, my cousin Tessie, my Aunt Mariaucche from Mott Street, everybody. Ya figure meals fa alla them, prizes fa the games, plus decorations. It all adds up."

"Danny, I don't give a . . . "

"And ya know what's gonna cost the most, don' ya? The weddin'. She's gonna have a football weddin' wid piles of sandwiches on every table. I love those little pickles they put in coppacola sandwiches, don't you?"

"Danny, will you stop. I could give a shit less about showers and decorations and ya Aunt Mariaucche."

A big Buick Roadmaster pulled up in front of the candy store. It was Mappy's older brother Jackie's car. Tony Bavimo was with him. Danny and I were the only ones at the counter when they came in.

"These kids are a couple of terrors." Jackie elbowed Tony. Bavimo smiled tightly.

"Whadda ya say, Jackie." I greeted quickly to show respect for his age and reputation.

"Whadda ya say, Jackie," Danny parroted. Neither of us said anything to Bavimo because he didn't know us.

"This is Tony Bavimo." Jackie turned his thumb toward Tony like a hitchhiker. Then, like a one-hand card deal, he flipped the same finger at each of us. "This kid is Sarry an' that's Danny Charms."

"Whadda ya say, Tony."

"Whadda ya say, Tony."

"I seen that kid before someplace." Bavimo concentrated on me.

"Yeah, I delivered *javelle* ta your house once, Tony."

"That's it. I was just about ta glom a *jumbota* riceball when ya rang the bell."

"Gee, I di'nt mean ta interrupt nuttin', Tony."

"It's shit under the bridge, kid."

"Do ya wanna shoot some straight pool next door or go get a bite, Tone?" Jackie asked, helping himself to a pack of cigarettes on the counter and leaving a quarter.

"Let's go ta the Greek's and *mange* [eat]. Talkin' about that rice-ball woiked up my appetite."

"I can see it," Jackie said. "I'm arvedstay."

"C'mon, San Diego," Tony called me by a cellmate's nickname. "You an' ya partner come wid us."

"Maybe the kids got somethin' oinggay awready," Jackie said.

"Youse ain't doin' nuttin', are ya?" Tony asked.

"No, we wuz just gonna go work out on the high bar, but we could always do it after," I said.

"Yeah, we could always woik out," Danny said.

"So let's go ta the Greek's." Tony threw his arms over our shoulders. "Give ya *labonza* a little woikout."

▬▬▬▬▬▬▬▬▬▬▬▬▬▬▬▬▬▬▬▬▬▬▬▬▬▬▬▬▬▬

The rear of our building faced onto a long cement yard that caught the drippings from the many clotheslines above. Windows of the dozen buildings bounding the yard were open to the humid heat of summer. At dinner time the concerted clanking of knives and forks of a hundred families could have been a sword battle between two pirate ships. When I entered our vestibule, the aroma of fresh vegetables stewing filled the hallway. I bounded up to our apartment. My family was finishing supper at the kitchen table. Swinishly, Ernie mopped up the juices in Madeline's dish with a slice of bread.

"Your fish is in the oven," Ma said.

"I awready ate. Tony Bavimo bought me dinner."

"Tony Bavimo! Go wan," Anthony scoffed. "What's he doin' wid you?"

"That's right, Him an' Jackie Map took me and Charms ta the Greek's fa roast beef."

"How come ya're eating meat on our Lord's day?" Dad demanded.

"That's only a rule of the choich. It's not one of God's rules," I said.

"It's still a mortal sin."

"It's only a venial sin."

"It's a mortal sin."

"I still don' see anything wrong about it."

"It's not fa you ta see." Dad's face smouldered. "Everyone else in your family obeys it. Only you can't make a small sacrifice fa the Almighty."

"Okay, okay, so he won't eat meat on Friday again." Ma stepped in front of Dad and picked up the plates on the table. The rest of the family got up and drifted into the living room. Madeline swaddled her dolls and played house using a cardboard box. Ernie piddled with his carpet gun. Dad plopped into the overstuffed chair and clicked on the radio. Melodramatically, the voice of Gabriel Heatter announced: "Ah, yes, there's good news tonight." Nicky brought out a Cheerio yo-yo.

"Want me ta show ya how ta make it sleep?" I asked him.

"Here, I'll show ya." Anthony snatched it from his hand.

"I asked him foist. Gimme."

"T.S., you can show him aftuh me."

"I don' wanna show him aftuh ya. God damn it. Now gimme it."

"Shaddap, and stand on the side."

"Don't tell me ta shut up."

"Stop ya yellin'," Dad barked.

"Tell him ta stop. He started it. Ya gonna gimme that son-of-a-bitchin' thing." I snatched the yo-yo out of Anthony's hand, but before I had it free, he grabbed my wrist. We banged against the wall wrestling for the toy. A pair of big hands yanked us apart and then one spun me around and a rock fist pushed my nose in, putting me on my back.

"Mad man, you do nuttin' all the time and then you go overboard," Ma screamed. "*Coma brute* [animal]. Leave him alone."

Blood spurted out of my nose.

"Pick ya head up." Ma stuck a pillow under my neck.

"Why di'nt he hit him? He started it," I said, crying.

▀▀

The pestering hum of mosquitoes awakened me. I swatted at them and stepped over to the open window. Down in the yard a frowsy tomcat humped over a scrap of fish and hissed a warning to an approaching pack. Sweet scents crossed the street from Vito's bakery. I loved the smell of baking Italian bread. A vivid moon lazed in the clouds. The moon hardly frightened me anymore. Until I was ten I would shut the blinds not to see it. The sun caused the same reaction. I couldn't understand how a fireball could stay up without something holding it. If I put my eyes on the sun I would see the sphere spinning loose about to fall. When that happened I ran to Ma. She tried to remove my fear by telling me that God kept everything in its place. So many things frightened me, but barely anything bothered Anthony. He used to laugh at me for racing up the dark stairs at night. Once, when we were both late for school, I sniveled in the vestibule all day, afraid to go into my third-grade room, but Anthony walked into his classroom "like a little man," his teacher told Ma.

Only a little over a year separated us in age. For five years we were the only two children. Dad was doing well as a bandleader in those days, headlining at the Luna Park Casino with Alan Dale. We each had our own nicely furnished room. On Christmas we received brand new toys, although Anthony's always seemed better than mine. One year he got a dashing set of Lionel trains while I got a little sparking tank. Being the first-born son, Anthony was Dad's favorite. In every photo we took as a family, Dad stood behind him and Ma stood behind me.

Luna Park burned down about the time Nicky was born. With the Depression still a vivid memory and a family of five to support, Dad gave up music as a career and took a steady job with the Department of Sanitation. All the sessions of self-teaching and hard practice in music and the youthful dreams that energized them were over for him. Even with Nicky Ma kept me close to her. She took me shopping, had me help with the housework, and if I woke up at night she let me sleep with her and Dad. Ernie was born two years after Nicky, Madeline came soon after, and Camille followed her. I saw less of Ma; Anthony and Dad became even closer. On weekends Dad took him to his season locker at Raven Hall Pool where he taught him how to swim and dive. He bought him a clarinet and gave him music lessons. They went to Dodger games together. Once I asked to go along but Dad refused to take me. He said I was too young for a night game. Running after them in the hall I tugged on his coat, begging him to take me, too. Exploding, he dragged me back in and punched my legs until I ached too much to move. When Ma screamed at him, he told her that was how his father had taught him discipline. Eventually, Anthony also took up Dad's hobby of flying pigeons. Being involved in swimming, the clarinet, and homers, my brother was doing the three things my father loved most as a boy. They were pals.

▚▚▚

9 An Indian-summer sun sliced between apartment buildings, hashmarking the shadowed street. The subway turnstile reeled in a long line of workers. I walked along Fort Hamilton Parkway with my ninth-grade books slung over my shoulder with a belt. It was early so I wasted time, taking care to step over slits in the sidewalk and stopping to inspect store window displays.

"Yo! San Diego!" A voice hailed me from the Fortridge Diner. Tony Bavimo, sitting near the window, waved me in.

"Whadda ya say, Tony." I slid into the other side of the booth.

"Where ya going?"

"I'm on my way ta school."

"How'd ya like ta come up ta the C.Y.O. gym and watch me spar wid Chico Vejar instead.?"

"Ming! That would be great."

"We'll leave in about half an hour. How's ya friend?"

"Ya mean Danny Charms? He's awright."

"That kid never fuckin' shuts up, does he?"

"Awh, he's a good guy. He'll give ya the shirt off his back. Doesn't Marciano work out at da C.Y.O. too, Tony?"

"Used ta."

"Whodaya think is gonna win, him or Walcott?"

"Marciano'll eat 'im up. I seen 'im at the C.Y.O. Clumsy as shit but folds the sandbags. Al Weil put him in wid a coon ta spar once. The foist shot he landed made a noise like a Mack truck."

"Whadda ya think of Chuck Davey?"

"He's a fuckin' douche bag."

"How 'bout Whitey on the Rampers? He's supposed ta be fightin' main events now."

"He's anudder one I'll can."

"Ya gonna have somethin' or else leave." The crabby old Greek in his white apron stood over me with a skillet.

"Gimme a Coke."

"G'head, San Diego, order some breakfast."

"Gee, t'anks, Tony. Gimme an order of scrambled eggs wid home-fries and a glass of milk."

The old Greek stumped back to the sludgy grill.

"Ya know, Tony, I never learned how ta throw a punch right."

"Da main thing is ta get ya whole body behind it, even ya legs." He swiveled his body, pulling back a fist. "And in the street make sure ya throw the foist punch."

"It's hard ta jus' hit a guy right away."

"That's bullshit. Ya know ya gonna be in a fight or else look like a hard-on so ya might as well jap the cocksucker."

The Greek returned with my order. The food jiggled on the plate as his palsied hands put it down. Tony stretched up to speak in his ear. "I'm gonna piss on ya grave ya old fuck." The old man mumbled some Greek curses back at him and left.

"Hurry up and douse them eggs, San Diego."

"I'll polish 'em off one, two, three."

▰▰

After picking up Tony's gear we took the subway to Fourteenth Street and walked over to the C.Y.O. building. On the gym landing we could hear the jangling chains of squelched sandbags, choppy nose breaths, the rhythmic peppering of a speed bag. As we stepped inside, an electric fan blew a breeze of odor at us: the pervading smell of sweat and stale socks, of rubbing alcohol, of oil of wintergreen, and the bitter dry bite of old leather. And then the sights. Fighters clad in sweatsuits in a flurry of shadowboxing before mirrored walls, grizzly heavyweights slamming a medicine ball into each other's gut, a trainer with a towel over his shoulder executing the peekaboo defense for a lightsome bantam, grimacing blacks in headgear and chastity belt-like protectors slugging it out in the corner ring. I remained on the gym floor while Tony went to change in the locker room. A few minutes later he came jaunting out wearing his sparring gear.

A promising welterweight with a crowd-pleasing style, Tony was undefeated in four professional bouts. He looked impressive in his sparring session with top-ranked welterweight Chico Vejar, hooking him to his knees in the opening round. Embarrassed, the contender picked himself up and went to the rosin box, screwing his shoes inside for more footing. At the gong for the end of the fourth round another helmeted prelim boy climbed in to box with Vejar. Tony vaulted out of the ring and put on his bag gloves. "Whapity, whapity, whap," he practiced combinations on the speed bag. Next he shifted to the jump rope. Invisibly the cord swished under his leather footwear as he danced on ball and toe. When he finished his workout we returned to Brooklyn and reentered the Fortridge Diner, wedging into the same booth we had been sitting in that morning.

"Whaja think a that fuckin' hook I decked Vejar wid?"

"You hurt 'im."

"If he di'nt backpedal I woulda . . . " Tony's speech trailed off as his eyes goggled. A bronze-tone Ford with flapping mudguards pulled up to the curb outside. The face of a pretty girl partially blocked the handsome profile of Bobby the Breeder at the wheel. Bobby got out alone and came inside.

"What's happenin' Breeduh?" Tony asked.

"I just banged this broad." He pointed over his shoulder to the car. "Ya want her, Tony?"

"Who is she?" Tony glanced out.

"I picked her up this morning at the unemployment office. She's outa work. She told me she's a receptionist, but she's too scatter fa that. You won't believe her when you get her clothes off. She's got the heftiest lungs, and what a mover, wicked."

"Where's she goin' now?"

"She ain't goin' no place. She's wid me."

"Awright, lemme take her in the back lot. Ya got the keys?"

"They're in the ignition. I left it idling. She's probably gonna give ya a hard time."

"Whaja tell 'er?"

"I told her I was gonna stop a minute ta see somebody."

"Why di'nt ya tell her ya owed a friend a favor?"

"She told me she doesn't go for that. She only lays one guy. When ya get in that car she's gonna panic a little."

"I'll break her fuckin' legs."

"I know you will, but first try to talk her into it. And please, don't smash the windows in my car if ya have to force her."

Tony hurried out. The girl turned her back against the window when he got in. Looking at her hard, he slammed the car into first and peeled around the corner.

An hour later Tony came back on foot, grinning.

"How was she?" Bobby asked.

"Sucked my brains out."

"Where's the car?"

"In the back. Ya not in a hurry, are ya?"

"No, why?"

"Let the kid get his pecker wet."

"Awright, but tell him not to shack up in there all day."

"Ya ever bang a girl before, San Diego?" Tony asked.

"I think so."

"Whadda ya mean, ya think so? Whadda fuck kinda answer is that?"

"I dunno if I done it right."

"Just' go in and do it from the sittin' position. That's the easy way."

"Okay, Tone," I answered, making believe I understood. "Where's the car parked, in the back?"

"It's right near the mechanic's shop. Ya'll hear the guy welding."

The girl was slouched in the back seat with her dress mauled and was sniffling when I got in.

"What'sa matter?" I asked, moving close to her.

"Where's Bob? Who are you? Why did Bob make that other fellow take me back here?" She was very pretty. I couldn't believe a girl with such a sweet face would do what she did to Tony. I was getting hard in the pants thinking about it.

"Bob's got some calls to make. He tol' me ta keep ya company until he finishes."

"When is he coming?"

"He'll be here in a few minutes."

"I told him I don't do these things," she sniffled.

"Are ya upset? Did Tony hurt ya or somethin'?"

"That Tony, he's an animal." She broke into gulpy sobs.

"Here, ya wanna use my hanky?"

"He forced me into it," she said, more to herself than to me.

"I asked if ya wanna use my hanky fa ya face."

"Why did he do that to me?" she cried.

Feeling sorry for her, I reached for the door handle to get out.

"Oh, no! Don't rape me! Please!" she screamed, swiftly sliding flat on the seat and spreading her legs. "Don't do it."

I stood there stunned holding the door open.

"Please don't rape me," she pleaded.

I closed the door and got on top of her. She reached down, undid my zipper, and quickly guided me inside of her. Throughout the act she kept moaning, "Stop, stop it."

▲▲▲

"Bless me, Fodder, fa I have sinned; this is a year since my last confession," I said, kneeling in the dark confession box. The priest was sitting opposite me behind an opaque screen. I wondered who it was going to be. Father Russo always let you off easy with five Hail Marys and five Our Fathers, but the Monsignor was strict. He bawled you out and dictated a long penance.

"Son, has it been so long because you have been living in a state of purity?" the voice of a new priest asked, "Or are you falling away from the church of almighty God?"

"I jus' been a bad Cat'lic, Fodder."

"Tell me, son, what mortal sins you have committed so I may give you absolution."

"Well, Fodder, I've lied. I ate meat on Friday. I've done things wid girls."

"Now tell me, son, what are these things you have done with girls? You know each thing you do is a separate sin. Let's start with the first girl you remember. What did you do with her?"

"There was this girl last month, Fodder. My friend Tony made me go inna car wid her."

"Was she lying there in the nude?"

"No, Fodder, she had all her clothes on."

"What did you do to her? Did you start off petting?"

"No, Fodder, we di'nt pet."

"Did you right off touch somewhere under her dress?"

"Uh, I di'nt start off doing that. I went alla way the first thing."

"You mean you entered her? You know that act is a grave mortal sin outside of the sacrament of marriage?"

"Yeah, Fodder."

"Were there other occasions with this girl or only that once?"

"I went wid her more times. My friend Tony got her ta come around a lot. Alla guys inna poolroom were goin' wid her. They called her the Snake."

"Why did they call her that?"

"Cause she wrapped herself around you when ya did it ta her."

"There were no perverted or unnatural acts committed in addition to intercourse were there? You didn't have her do other things to you, did you?"

"Not da first time, but after that."

"What were those unnatural acts?"

"I made her go down there."

"Tell me exactly what happened, son. To give absolution I must have the full account."

An hour later I stepped out of the confession box. The line of waiting penitents stretched to the altar. I bowed my head piously and clasped my hands, pretending not to see all the dirty looks.

The ones you saw most often waiting on the confession line were the *pomodoros* (tomatoes), the girls who were being plowed by the whole neighborhood. They entered the church looking saintly holding a handkerchief over their head with one hand and making the sign of the cross with holy water with the other. The *pomodoros* were all hoping they could go to heaven, but the odds were against them, six to one. The only time they could get into heaven was on Friday after confession when they were forgiven all their sins. But only a few souls will luck out and die on Friday. One *pomodoro* tried to cheat her way into heaven—she committed suicide on Friday, but that's a mortal sin, they said.

Coming out of confession was a good feeling. You felt cleansed of all the sins you had committed. There were some sins, though, like "no meat on Friday," that never caused any guilt. They seemed too trivial. Other rules were harder to shuck. Masturbation didn't seem wrong, but if I did it alone without my friends, guilt flooded over me. The way drugs can become part of your body, the church was a part of my mind. It had been riveted in my brain at home and at Catechism. From the third grade through the seventh I attended Catechism a half school-day a week. "Don't ever look at yourself in the bathtub," Sister Catherine warned us. "And when you step out, don't dry yourself below the belly. If you feel an impure thought, get out of there fast. If it's strong, do some work right away, work hard, sweat it out of you. And don't ever look at dirty pictures. They're the devil's way of tempting you. You must never touch yourself. I don't think I even have to tell you it's a mortal sin. It's a dirty, slimy act only animals do. A person who is weak with no dignity gives in to that kind of filth. You can always tell who he is, too, because he cannot look others in the eye."

The nuns also taught us rules if we had a non-Catholic friend. We were never supposed to go into his church, read his religious books, serve in his wedding, or attend his funeral service. "The Catholic Church has the special love of God," Sister Cecilia said, "but that love brings responsibility. His true children should be kind and friendly to all people, but a Catholic must never have anything to do with the wrong teachings of other faiths." This principle also prohibited us from marrying a non-Catholic girl. To do so meant excommunication unless she agreed to raise the children as Catholics. The rules were to protect us from being converted.

Sunday I went to mass with my family. It was the first time in a long while for me; the others hardly ever missed except Ma. "God understands I have a baby to take care of," she said. In her way Ma was very religious. The walls and bureau tops of our apartment were blessed by over sixty sacred objects. Religious calendars ten years old were left up because Ma could never throw a picture of her Savior in the garbage can. Catholic missions from as far as Alaska had her on their mailing lists for donations. She sacrificed in our house to send money to them. "Have God in your heart," she was always saying, "that's the most important thing in life."

Walking up 67th Street we saw the Veriglio family gathering in front of their house to leave for mass. There were eleven in the family. They lived one block from the church in a beat-up two-room clapboard shack heated by bonfire. Five brothers and four sisters slept on the floor in one room. I waved to my classmate Al Veriglio.

We crossed the street and walked along the side of St. Rosalie's, the old church. At the corner we joined the crowd going up the steps of Regina Pacis Shrine, our new million-dollar cathedral. Bell tower stacked on top of bell tower reached higher and higher away from the neighborhood and climaxed in a spire touching the sky. Inside the church, creamy pink marble smoothly veneered the walls. Fluted columns were crowned by golden curlicues. Over a thousand candles glowed in red glasses clustered around interior grottoes. The candles were attached to gold stands with coin slots and signs: FOR LARGE VOTIVE LIGHTS TO TAKE HOME, INQUIRE IN THE GIFT SHOP AT THE MAIN ENTRANCE.

Stained glass windows spaced on each side angled in toward the altar, drawing parishoners' eyes to floodlit images of the Madonna and Child wearing diamond-studded tiaras. The jewels came from the women of the parish after Monsignor asked them to donate their engagement and wedding rings. Looking down at the parishioners from a huge painting on the ceiling, was the Monsignor and the Bishop standing near Christ, with Timmy Kelly nestled between them as an angel.

The priest opened the mass with announcements: "The movie 'The Moon Is Blue' is forbidden to Catholics because it has immoral subjects. The Carlucchi family (of Carlucchi Olive Oil) has contributed another thousand dollars for the new wing of the rectory. Wednesday night is Bingo night, don't forget to tell your friends. Monsignor has asked for another silent collection (no coins) so we can get along with our plans to renovate the old church." After the banns the priest opened the Bible. "And now from the Holy Gospel. Jesus speaking unto us in Luke gives us these words: Everyone that exalteth himself shall be abased, and he that humbleth himself shall be exalted."

The priest then moved to the altar to prepare the Host for Holy Communion. Making the sign of the Cross with a gold disk, the priest placed bread wafers on the linen cloth spread on the altar. He removed a chalice from the tabernacle and decanted wine and water into the gold vessel, chanting: "*Deus, qui humanae substantiae dignitatem mirabiliter...*"

After the wafers, representing the body of Christ, were soaked in the red liquid, representing the blood of Christ, the priest summoned those who had been cleansed by confession to come up to the altar. Kneeling on the altar steps I stuck my tongue out waiting for the priest to deposit a wafer. I swallowed the Host without biting it, for **that** would have been mistreating God's body. Looking up I could see the diamond tiaras. It was like having communion breakfast at Tiffany's.

Returning to our bench I noticed the Latero family sitting a row behind us. Their youngest son Jimmy died of leukemia when he was four years old. His bewildered mother collapsed the first night.

Through the presence of Father Russo at the wake, the church became a buffer against mental breakdown. He was at their side all through it, telling them, "God wanted the child. Jimmy is going to heaven to become an angel." That comforted his mother. At least God was going to take care of him. His death was not just a cruel and senseless happening.

The Church did other good works, too. There were a number of Irish and Polish families along with the Italians in the parish. Worshipping together was reducing hate among them and making them feel a bond as Catholics. The Church's holidays brightened the emptiness of time. I think that without Christmas, Easter, or a Feast of San Gennaro, every week would have been just another workweek for my family. Perhaps the Church's most important contribution, however, was giving people a set of moral rules by which to live instead of confusion and whim. They had conviction of what was right and wrong. The Church taught them responsibility, respect, charity, honesty. Ma walked twenty blocks once to return extra change given to her by mistake. But I wished that the Church allowed more understanding and flexibility. I believed in God but I had misgivings about some of the Church's dogma.

▬▬▬▬▬▬▬▬▬▬▬▬▬▬▬▬▬▬▬▬▬▬▬▬▬▬▬▬▬▬▬▬▬▬▬▬▬

10 "Me an' Mappy were playin' packs in Hesson's class this afternoon," I said to Al as we strode into the Wagon Wheel Diner. "He beat me outta' all I had, and then when I wanted ta borrow from him he quit."

"That was weak shit but ya know he's that way," Al said.

"Yeah, he's got that fault," Bobby said, following us in.

"But ya know whose woise?" Al said. "Richie. He won't beat ya in cards or anythin' like that, but he'll let ya treat him all day and won't offer ya a glass of water."

"*Senza faccia* [He's got no face]." I laughed.

We straddled three stools at the crowded wheel-shaped counter. Waitresses shuttled back and forth from counter to chef, lancing order slips on revolving spikes and picking up steaming dishes. French fries crisped in a basket sunk in vintage grease. Music squawking from a ceiling speaker was drowned out by the clatter of dishes in the kitchen and commands shouted by scurrying waitresses. Menus were tucked in a cage attached to the push-button record selector. I took one out and went down the dessert list. A waitress stopped at our place and plunked ice in three glasses of water.

"Whadda you boys havin'?" She flipped her pad.

"Gimme a Wagon Wheel Float," Al said.

"That sounds good ta me, too," Bobby said.

"I'll have a Coke," I announced, making a last-minute switch.

"Anything else?"

"That's it."

As the waitress moved away I glanced around the counter. Six guys wearing orange club jackets were sitting across from us. They looked a couple of years older, about sixteen. The Jello-sheen color of their jackets held my attention. One of them noticed me watching, so I dropped my eyes to the record selections. I didn't want him to think I was looking for trouble. After a while I glanced over and he was glaring, so I dropped my eyes again. To stare back meant a challenge, and I didn't want to take on six older guys. Minutes later I glanced over and he was still staring, I became edgy. I wasn't going to keep my head bowed all night. Finally I returned his dirty looks, thinking, "Fuck it. If he wants to start somethin' I'm down for it."

"What's Richie doin' tanight?" Al asked.

"He's probably wid Concetta," Bobby said.

I wasn't paying attention to my friends. The guy on the other side was pointing his finger at me. "Who you lookin' at?"

"You talkin' ta me?" I stammered.

"You heard me," he said arrogantly.

"Listen, I'm not lookin' fa trouble," I said in a meek voice, sliding off the stool. "I was just curious about your jacket." I moved around the counter. People delayed their next mouthful to see what was going to happen. I was surprised he didn't get off the stool to meet me. He waited, looking relaxed, which scared me. As I got closer his face flashed a goofy smirk. I mumbled cop-outs until right up to him. I wanted the edge of the first punch. If he thought I was quailing I could get it. Instead of lunging at me as I had expected, he froze, moon-eyed. I clubbed down at his face with the heel of my fist. The blow slit his nose, causing a geyser of blood as from a punctured jugular. He tried to block my second punch but it wrenched him off the stool. The next instant something heavy sledge-hammered into my head. My eyes blurred. Numbed by shock I felt none of his friends' fists banging my face. I punched back in a nightmarish stupor. The fight broke off quickly as the frenzied owner ran into the street screaming for the police. I dashed out of the place tasting my own blood as it came down my cheeks in ribbons. A nicely dressed young man sprinted into my path and sank a gun in my gut. I stopped short and my insides lumped up.

"Hold it." He unflapped a badged wallet. Snapping a handcuff on one wrist, he gave me a handkerchief to hold on my head with the other. We sped off in a commandeered car to Maimonides Hospital. By the end of the short trip the handkerchief was blood-soaked. We hurried up to the emergency room where a nurse sat me on a table and prepared my head for stitching. She shaved a patch of my scalp and disinfected it with alcohol. The doctor in the room then stitched up the gap with a hook-needle and thread. From the hospital we drove to a police station on Fourth Avenue.

"What's this one for?" the desk sergeant asked.

"In a brawl."

"Yeah, I can see."

"This way, kid." The plainclothesman steered my shoulder to a stairway. We walked up one flight to a stuffy office with pea-soup green walls. Unlocking the handcuff, he motioned for me to sit.

"How'd it start?" He hung his raincoat on a rack.

"Me and my friends, we went into the diner, minding our own business, an' then this guy tries ta stare me down."

"How about a cup of hot chocolate?"

"Yeah, thanks," I said, rubbing my head. I could feel a soreness now.

"Gawhead, I'm listening."

"At first I looked down at the records ta ignore him, but I couldn't look at the records all night. And I wasn't gonna let him make me do that shit."

"Did your friends get in it?"

"They were there when the bout was on, but it was jus' me and this other guy havin' woids foist."

"Did he do that?" He pointed to the medical dressing on my head.

"No, it was one of his crew."

"Which one? Do you know?"

"How could I know? The guy creamed me from behind."

"Was it a bat? You said they were wearing indoor jackets."

"No, they di'nt have no bats wid them. I think it was one of those sugar bowls. Ya know, the thick glass ones wid a metal point. They got those ona counter there."

"The detectives are gonna talk to you. Just tell them what ya told me."

▗▖

The sole passenger, I was taken by paddy wagon to the Youth House. The police decided a little time in there would do me good. There was no trial, no judge. Getting out of the paddy wagon, I looked up at the building's caged windows and felt a stir of pride, sensing that I was about to take a step into manhood. It gave status in the poolroom to have served time someplace. I felt left out before when the older guys talked about Warwick, Coxsackie, Elmira, and the other prisons they had been in. Now with the Youth House under my belt it put me a prestigious notch above my own friends. None of them had served time anywhere yet.

The first day I gloried in my new surroundings. Besides the glamour, conditions were more comfortable than in my own home. Another boy and I shared a cheery blue room. We each had our own bed and a drawer, the shower worked, and we received three filling meals every day. Officer Burke, the plainclothesman who made the arrest at the diner, paid me a visit. I thought he was a nice guy "for a dunkey cop." He seemed genuinely interested in what happened to me. I told him that since being around Tony I had been getting into a lot of fights. He urged me to stay away from that whole poolroom crowd.

Soon the sour side of the Youth House outweighed its early appeal. We were locked in twenty-four hours a day and the daily routine was empty. At 6:30 in the morning a grouchy counselor pounded on the door to wake us up. Wrapped in towels we stepped out into a frigid hall to get the dungarees and polo shirt we were issued daily. I thought it was stupid for us to have drawers and a closet in the room but not be allowed any clothes. After dressing we were marched to the cafeteria, where we were served powdered milk and eggs for breakfast. When we finished eating, the counselor passed out cigarettes. The rule was one smoke after each meal. Evasion attempts never ended. My roommate had his sister smuggle in a pack on visiting day and then hid each cigarette and match in a separate cranny in our room. Overnight, all were confiscated, even the match he Scotch-taped on the underside of a drawer. The staff were expert searchers.

We attended classes in the morning from nine to twelve. The Science teacher entering the room was welcomed with raucous raspberries. He retaliated with a yawn. Then he put half the class to sleep by drowsily mouthing the lesson from a book. In Math the teacher diverged from multiplication to ask us questions about our sex lives. Some kids spent class time tattooing themselves. First, they diagramed a figure in pen or pencil. Ashes were spread over the area inside the figure. The final step was driving the ashes under the skin by a thousand pricks with a safety pin.

The Youth House was mainly a waiting station, so at lunch the flap was often about where someone had been sentenced to go during the morning. One boy returned from court all smiles because he got a "zip-five" (zero- to five-year sentence) at Otisville, where his older brother was serving. For a number of kids like myself the Youth House was the terminal place of detention. Our offenses were not serious enough to go to court, or we were being dealt with leniently because it was our first time in trouble. In my case it was more the first reason.

On liver-nights at dinner I ate only bread and butter and gave the meat away. "Give it ta me, man." "No, fuck him, man. Give it ta me, man." The Negro guys went ape over my handouts. I laughed at them as freaks. I resented being with blacks. Once I almost got into a fight with one who tried to pull a comic book out of my hand. He was less interested in the comic book than testing to see if he could dump on me. When I rose to fight him I was quickly surrounded by a dozen others. The whites went by turning their heads. If a counselor hadn't broken it up, I would have been mangled. Whites who were strangers to each other didn't stick together as well as the blacks. I had a queasy feeling about fighting a black, too. Because they lived on the other side of Brooklyn, I never knew any personally as people. The black body looked primitive to me, and this feeling was reinforced by the long razor scars I had seen on some black faces.

The ages of Youth House residents ranged from ten to sixteen. The youngest kids were usually in for minor wrongs such as truancy or running away from home. Whatever bad habits they acquired before were increased by the Youth House experience. In the

evening all age groups mingled in the recreation gym. Like preda-
tors, the older boys always picked on the weakest or most sickly
looking of the younger boys to force into their room. One night a
counselor hearing a rumpus, opened the door to a room and found
a mound of boys cavorting in the nude.

The only girls allowed were on pinup photos. Once Madam
Ghandi toured the Youth House and was shocked. She considered it
corrupting for such young boys to be looking at pornographic pictures. We thought so too, and asked the staff if we could have real
girls up to our room. Desperate for thrills, one sixteen-year-old was
caught screwing an artificial vagina made from a roll of liver inside
the head of a bottle.

At the end of the day we returned to our blue-walled rooms.
Lights died at 10:30.

The day my parents came to take me home was a happy one.

"That's some cut he's got on his head," Dad said after he settled in
the kitchen chair.

"Why does this boy always get into trouble?" Ma put on her
apron.

I went into the bathroom and pulled my pants down. Inspecting
my bush I started to sing, "They fly through the air wid the greatest of ease, da daring young lice called the itchy crab fleas." It
seemed a whole troop of crab lice had nested on me at the Youth
House. Resembling ocean crabs in form, these speck-size mites
were incredible trapeze artists. They could swing from a pubic hair
of one person to another's a few feet away. Another acrobatic stunt
they were known to perform was to leap from the shower floor up
to a crotch in a single bound. Once there, they clawed into the skin
and lived on blood.

"Ya never see that boy Donald Pascale cause his family any worry," I heard Ma say to Dad.

"Donald goes to Poly Prep," I thought. "That's a great school.
They got dugouts in their field just like in the major leagues."

"I'll tell ya why that boy Donald is good, mister," Ma preached
on, "because his father puts his foot down. That boy would never
be allowed to go in a poolroom by his father. I always said you're
too easy-going wid yours."

"Ah, you don' know," Dad said. "Ya always quack from the top

of your head. Kids grow up good or bad themselves. My father di'nt
have ta lock me up so I wouldn't go stealing wid that bunch
from my neighborhood. And that was a woist section. Even in Harlem ya got bad ones and some who are good workin' kids."

"Yeah, and that's because the párents let them get away wid everythin' or are firm and keep them outta poolrooms."

"What about your other son, Anthony? We never had a day's aggravation wid him. He's always been good. And they're in the same
house. Why doesn't he go in the poolroom wid those bums?"

"He's got his pigeons, like you were a pigeon bug."

"Whadda pigeons got ta do wid it?"

"Ya know what they say. Idleness is the devil's workshop. The
birds keep him away from bad things."

"Joey works afternoons."

"But at night he's got nuttin'."

"So Anthony has pigeons keeping him busy a few nights a week.
He's not wid them every night. He has free nights. Why don't he
go in a poolroom those times? He stays here on 63rd Street wid the
nice crowd of boys. I tell them both ta stay out a the poolroom.
One boy listens and the other don't. Why do I have ta break one's
skull ta keep him out? Hitting him don't do no good anyway. He
still goes. I tell ya it's the kids themselves, what they're made of."

"Ya boy Ernie eats like a hog," Ma said. "If nobody says anything ta him he'll eat all the Jello. The only way ya gonna make
him not have hoggish habits is ta tell him don' eat more than his
share or else."

"So he's a little hoggy now. He'll straighten out."

"Maybe Joey will keep out of trouble for a while. My mother
wants him to help her make the wine again. At least he'll be busy
some nights."

"Ain't that the bell?" Dad asked.

"I think so," Ma said. "Go see in the hallway. Ya can hardly hear
it anymore."

"Yeah, it's Joey friends," Dad said from the landing. "Press the
buzzer ta let 'em up."

"Ya better do something about the wiring inside the bell."

"It's not the wiring inside. It's just stuck. Youse been pressing it
the wrong way. The button gets caught inside the lip. Look at the
damn thing when ya press it next time. It's jus' a matter of how ya
press it and the thing will work fine."

"Da other people's bells inside the building don't get stuck."

"That's what I been saying. They press them right."

"Is Joey home, Mr. Sorrentino?" Richie asked, galloping up the stairs. I could hear other steps behind his.

"*Bestias, diavolos.* I come uppa wid a hatcha," Grandma yelled from the basement.

"Joey, ya friends are here," Dad said, knocking on the bathroom door.

"They can come in."

"Hey, we hoid ya were in the Yout' House," Richie charged in. "How was it?"

"Awh, it wasn't anythin'. I had my own bed fa the foist time."

"Al says you really ruined that guy at the diner."

"Yeah, but they gimme stitches." I showed them my scalp, feeling like a hero.

"But ya still demolished them. Al tol' us ya laid out three guys."

"I was in a daze all through it. It was like fightin' in a dream."

"Dija get in any bouts at the Yout' House?"

"No, but almost, wid a jig. Where's Bobby and Al?"

"They're in the Fortridge."

"Let's go over," I said.

〰〰〰〰〰〰〰〰〰〰〰〰〰〰〰〰〰〰〰〰〰〰〰〰〰〰

All the booths in the Fortridge were filled. I walked in expecting salutes. Tony stopped me at the door.

"Hey, Rocky, I hoid ya dumped four guys and were in the Yout' House."

"I punched like ya showed me."

"That's the way, kid." He slapped me on the head.

"Thanks, Tony."

〰〰〰〰〰〰〰〰〰〰〰〰〰〰〰〰〰〰〰〰〰〰〰〰〰〰

⌡⌡ The two storefront windows of Pop's Pool Hall were painted black up to a tall man's eyebrows for privacy. Inside the hall four kettle-shape lamps hanging from long chains poured smoky light over four hippo-legged oak playing-tables spaced down the center, with a string of scoring beads for each overhead. A crowd of onlookers sat on benches and empty milk crates along the sides. Behind them on the peeling walls, posters lettered in black and red announced next Friday's boxing card at the Fort Hamilton Arena and a coming pool match between Chinatown Charlie and the Masked Marvel. In the back corner was a Speed-O pinball machine, a few card tables, and a door that opened to reveal a dung-encrusted toilet and cigarette butts littering the sloshy floor around it. Hoary old Pop, wearing a vested pencil-stripe suit, high-button shoes, and a feathered fedora tilted back, sat up front on a high Coca-Cola chair dragging on a corncob pipe that had the same craggy texture as his eighty-six-year-old face. Pop charged a penny a minute for a game of straight, keeping time by a clock on the wall. Usually when Pop wasn't looking Timmy Kelly turned back the clock.

In the early afternoon the poolroom was a noisy hangout. Break shots boomed amid a steady racket. Bells clanged off points on the pinball machine. Jimmy the Rat, named for his scrawny size, raved at the ceiling in his squeaky voice: "J.C., ya gamme looks, ya gamme brains, ya gamme a physique, why di'nt ya gimme luck?" Everyone liked Jimmy but no one trusted him. He was a habitual liar. He never went to mass, yet when he was groaning apparently near death in the street once after a gory accident, a priest kneeled over him to administer last rites and Jimmy squeaked, "Fodder, I been a good Cat'lic. I went ta choich every Sunday."

The older guys were playing cards in the back. Petey One Ball, who had a hernia, was dealing pinochle. His partner in the game was Lefty the Falcon, who resembled the actor Tom Conway, who portrayed that role. Their opponents were Sha Sha Brioni, who lisped with a spit-spraying oversize tongue, and Bushels, an ex-pug who used to catch punches by the bushel. Looking on behind them was Louie Tic Toc, a demented boy whose head always bobbed from side to side.

Cutting ninth-grade Math, I was shooting Danny Madden a game of straight on the first table. A miraculous shooter, freckled-faced Danny wore horn-rim glasses with ice cube lenses. He had such a gangling body that he had to turn his long arm inward like an orangutan to pump the cuestick. Despite these handicaps he rifled in long shots. Danny was my arch rival, and we once played fourteen consecutive hours, breaking only for supper. We started that time intending to play one game, but I lost and said, "Okay, best two outa three." Losing again, I challenged him to another round. I was such a diehard I forced him into a seventeen-game rubber before giving up. It was the longest pool marathon anyone there could remember.

Now Danny moved around the table squinting at balls, continuously poking a finger under the glasses cutting into his nose. I tried to offer a bad shot. "The six looks like a deadie to me."

"It's not even kissing."

We were distracted momentarily when someone shouted, "Anybody know what's playin' at the Alpine?"

"Gee-a-Party," Mappy answered.

"Ya mean Jeopardy," Jimmy corrected. "Ya grammar ain't too hot, is it, kid?"

"Forget the Alpine," Al said. "They got a great whackoff picture at the Fortway. Cyd Charisse does a dance in it that puts *Slaughter on Tenth Avenue* ta shame. I already dropped a pound on it, and I'm goin' again tanight."

"I'll go wid ya," Richie said.

"Why don't we all go when we get back from Klein's?" I said.

"Sounds good ta me," Bobby agreed. "But let's make it aftuh we eat."

"That's what I meant."

"When're youse leavin' fa Klein's, Sarry?" Danny asked.

"As soon as Timmy comes."

Danny brought me back to our game. "Deuce in the side, Sarry." He twisted up to aim and the tip of his stick touched the ball.

"That's a shot," I yelled.

"It di'nt move."

"My ass, it did too."

"I swear ta God, Sarry."

"Ya gotta cheat ta beat him?" Timmy Kelly asked as he walked over to us.

"Okay, gawhead, take it ovuh."

"Awh, bitch," Danny said when he missed making the shot.

"Chinky shows ya mudder knows." I chanted.

"Ready ta go, Sarry?" Timmy asked.

"Yeah, okay, T.K." I shut off the table light. "I'll give ya this game, Danny, but I wanna rubbuh tomorruh."

"Ya a glutton fa punishment?" Timmy said.

"Ah, he's got a horseshoe up his ass. I can't figure how he beats me. I got it all ovuh him in form."

The others who were going to Klein's paid Pop and left with us.

The Fort Hamilton subway station platforms were at the bottom of the railroad ravine. We climbed over the stone wall and scooted down a dirt bank to the northbound platform roof. Hanging from the roof's edge, Richie and I dropped onto the tracks. Mappy and Timmy shook loose next, but Bobby remained dangling, afraid to let go.

"C'mon, jump, you chicken shit, *jooche,*" Mappy jeered.

"That thoid rail makes me leery," Bobby whined.

"Don't look at it. Jus' fall the opposite way. We got ya anyway," I said.

The "To City" sign started to beep, which meant the train was on its way. Time was short.

"Will you stop worrying about the fuckin' thoid rail and jump," I said. The square face of the train was a miniature in the distance, growing larger every second. My heart was bouncing like a pogo stick.

"Jump," Mappy yelled.

Bobby fell, tumbling forward to avoid the third rail. We all leaped onto the platform. Seconds later the train, sparks flying, pulled into the station, its multiton cars rumbling over our footprints.

"Ming! Ya scared the shit outta me," I said to Bobby, getting aboard.

"Outta you," Richie said. "I'm afraid ta touch my pants."

Soon the Sea Beach train was roaring through the underground darkness, and we positioned ourselves around the front window of the first car. Lights changed red, green, and yellow to signal track traffic ahead. Stale warm air rushed through the top slit, tickling our faces. After the Pacific Street Station the train ascended into daylight again on the Manhattan Bridge.

We left the window and, weaving around the poles standees grasp, we promenaded through the cars. Timmy thought we should have a contest to see which one of us would get the most looks from the girls on the train. The game irked Mappy when it was found that most girls favored Bobby. Even mature women had big eyes for him. We got off at Union Square.

Entering Klein's Department Store, we turned our heads away from the guards at the door. The store swirled with bargain hunters. We climbed the stairs to the men's clothing department, where Timmy Kelly went to the rack of motorcycle jackets, found one his size, plucked the tags off, wiped the dusty floor with it, and then put it on. I had a motorcycle jacket already, so I browsed around for something else. A standout camel-hair sportscoat trapped my eye. I tried it on in front of the tripanel mirror.

"The sleeves have ta be taken up a little," I thought, "but what's that? A coupla bucks."

"Forget it, ya'll never get it out." Mappy appeared behind me in the mirror.

"Sez you."

"C'mon, they got nice Eisenhowers dyed black over here." He tried to tug me away.

"Looks sharp, don't it?" I turned sideways.

"Don' get all worked up about it or else ya gonna get blue balls."

"What're ya chalking it off fa?"

"Ya got some clear head, what am I chalking it off fa? Wid them shrunk dungarees ya got on wid *bracciola* stains how ya gonna walk outa here wearin' that dress jacket?"

"I could stash it under my sweater an' suck in my stomach."

"The thing will make a lump as big as ya head."

"Maybe ya should leave it and come back when you're all dressed up," Richie suggested.

"I guess I could do that."

"That would be the best thing," Mappy agreed.

"But they might not have it."

"These jackets are always in stock," Richie said.

"I don't think so. This is the foist time I seen em," Bobby said as he joined us.

"Take a walk, huh, Bongo." Mappy elbowed him.

"Bobby's right. I ain't seen these around."

"That still don' change things. Ya still gonna have ta pass it up this shot," Mappy said.

"Wait a minute. I got a scheme." I took off the sportscoat.

"Ooh, *Marone!* But ya won't listen." Mappy rolled his eyes up toward the ceiling.

"Here, nix these." I handed him the price tags and made a ball of the sportscoat. Then I went into the dressing room with it.

"You're off ya nut," Mappy said when I came out.

He wouldn't walk down the stairs with me, but Timmy and Richie did. As we left the store, the guard at the door gazed at me with pity.

"Good day," he said.

"Good day," I said, passing him bent over, the hot jacket stuffed under my sweater making me look like a hunchback.

Back in Brooklyn I gave Mappy the jacket to hold at his place because his mother never asked questions. "I'll meet youse in Pop's tonight for the movie." I turned and went inside.

▀▀▀

"Close the door. Ya'll let in those ugly horseflies," was Ma's greeting as I walked into the apartment. She was in the bathroom squeezing out a mop and Dad was sitting in the kitchen.

"They turned down the pension again today," Dad said to her between bites of a *provolone* sandwich. "There's no justice in this world. We got the most dangerous job in civil service, yet the cops and firemen always get the best deal. Some guys have been on our job over thoity years and can't retire, but a cop gets his pension in twen'y."

"Why ya think yours is more dangerous?" I asked.

"Don't we gotta be out on the street on rainy and icy days? Cars go outta control. There's pneumonia in the air. Hell, the cop on the beat runs inside fa coffee if there's a cool breeze. And how many of our guys get pulled in the back of the truck and get chopped into mincemeat? There's no reason they should get more than us. Ya understand the point I'm tryin' ta bring out?"

"Sounds unfair."

Dad sauntered over to the cupboard and took down a persimmon, a delicacy he bought once a year. "Had it up here fa a week. Should be sweet as sugar," he said, sucking into the squishy fruit.

Ma came out of the bathroom with a pail of water cloudy with CN and began mopping the kitchen floor.

"The *provolone* was stale," Dad griped.

"I don't wanna hear boo outa you, ox. I got enough aggravation."

"Automatically I'm insultin' ya because I say the cheese is lousy. What's that got ta do wid you? Don' go ta that store no more."

"Don't tell me where ta shop."

"There, ya see. Ya take things too poisonal. Ya too touchy."

"*Pava tain, scurciamens.* [Go, nuisance]." Ma rebuffed him.

"I give ya all my money, I expect a decent piece of cheese."

"All your money! Don't make me laugh. If I wasn't so young I woulda never married ya, ya pauper. Oh, I was crazy not ta marry Michael Gangi. That man thought I was adorable. There's a man wid ideals who amounted ta something. He build that plumbing business up from nuttin'. Ya can't go anyplace now where ya don't see his trucks wid his name on them."

"So why dincha marry him? Ya woulda done me a favor. Whadda ya think, you're a bargain?"

"Don't get me started. If it wasn't fa these kids I woulda packed up a long time ago. I always said it."

"So why don't ya go? I'll take care of the kids. Don't worry about them. I'm tired of ya always throwing up the kids as an excuse. I'm tellin' ya in front of ya son. Ya can leave now. I'll take care of the baby, too."

"You can't even take care of yourself," Ma laughed.

"Why da youse always gotta argue?" I said, getting up from the table.

"Watch where ya walkin'. Can't you see I just mopped that spot? And stand up straight. Ya slouch just like ya father. Ya got good height but ya ruin it wid ya posture."

"Stop, huh," I said, heading for the living room.

"Before ya go, take this water in. I still ain't gotten in there from this morning."

I took the pail and followed her in.

"This room is a disgrace," she yelled. "How can youse stand ta be in such a holy mess. I'll disown youse if I see this place like this again."

"Oh, you're always bitchin' about something."

"Don't talk that way. That's low class."

~~~~~~

After dinner fourteen of us met in Pop's to go to *Singing in the Rain*.

"We don't have ta go through the roof," Mappy said. "Mike da Bouncer is off."

"Good, I'll go ta the Lost and Found and open the fire exit," Bobby said.

"If ya see a nice hat, take it fa me," I said.

"Screw you, I'm gonna say I lost a jacket fa myself."

The manager let Bobby in to go to the Lost and Found. Soon

Bobby opened the fire exit in back and the rest of us slipped in. We scrambled up to the balcony and filled the first row, sitting a seat apart.

"Hey, there's Roniro. All set ta go." Richie pointed.

"Boy that guy's fucked up," Mappy said. "He's gotta see a doctor because he jerks off nine times a day."

"We should sell stock in him for artificial insemination," Timmy said.

"What's that?" three voices asked.

"Get ready, the part is comin' up right away," Al warned. ·

We all shaped our jackets into small tents over our laps.

Then as the leggy dancer in bikini tights writhed around the screen to a sultry rhythm, the zippers in fourteen pants zapped open. At the climax, jackets were removed and semen splattered down around us, ending our tribute to the performance.

12 At the fruit store I stacked the last box of grapes in Grandma's cart and then wheeled for home on the run. Fall was winemaking season.

Each year we made the wine the same way, except that Grandma no longer pounced on the grapes with her feet. We now used an old hand-cranked machine with meshing gears that squashed the fruit as it passed through a funnel. The color of wine comes from the skins. To make red wine we left the skins of black grapes in with the juice. Grandma liked dark wine, so we left them in a long time. For white wine we used green or black grapes, but the black skins had to be separated from the juice right away. If the grapes had been picked too early and were not sweet, we added sugar. Being thrifty, Grandma dumped the stems in the tub with the squeezings. This not only made her feel she was not wasting anything, it also gave the wine more body. After pressing the grapes we drained the juice into a wooden cask to ferment for a few months; overfermenting produced vinegar.

To age the wine we bottled it and then took it down to a rugged room my uncles had picked-and-shoveled fifteen feet below the regular cellar. Inside this subcellar, warped clay and rock walls harbored a chilly damp darkness. Entering it reminded me of a grave. We stored the vintage here because the constant chill temperature and absence of light protected the taste. The bottles were stuffed in niches on their sides to keep the cork moist, so that air wouldn't get into the bottles and turn the wine. We never let the wine age too long. Wine aged past its prime became watery. Grandma brought up bottles of zinfendel, her favorite wine, after aging about a year. In Grandma's house wine flowed at dinner every evening. As she was always telling me, "It putsa nicea pink inna your cheeks."

When I got home with the grape-filled cart, I lifted a crate onto my shoulder and carried it down to the cellar. There, I unshouldered the crate of grapes I was carrying and put it down in the front room. Still out of breath from running, I turned the crate sidelong and sat down on it to rest. I could see Grandma sitting in the back room. She didn't even hear me, that's how big the cellar was. I estimated that the front room ran a pitcher's distance to homeplate. It was simple and stony—a gray concrete floor and walls, with a bone-white metal ceiling. Furnishings were spare—a long table in the middle supported by a block of oak for legs, to the left a foot-pedal sewing machine, to the right a cupboard loaded with plain white dishes. A few steps from Grandma's chair at the head of the table was a four-legged cast-iron stove, a double-duty sink, and an icebox topped by a flap-door toaster. Down by the end of the table where, on holidays, children sat, there was a lone pianola against a wall cluttered with photos of my uncles in Army uniform and religious figurines encased in glass globes filled with snowflaked water. Sunlight slanted into the room through domino-shape windows high on one side.

Having rested briefly, I picked up the crate of grapes and took it into the homier back room where Grandma was sitting on a pillow-softened easy chair near a table on which sat a chapel-shaped radio. She was listening to her favorite soap opera, "Portia Faces Life."

"Oh, it's such a beautifulla stor'," she said, looking up.

"That mushy stuff. I can't stand it."

"By-n-by youa grow up and enjoy."

"You want me to crush the grapes by myself this afternoon?"

"No, I help. Go getta the rest." She got up and took the crate of grapes out of my hands. She handled the heavy box easily.

Grandma was a typical Italian woman. At fourteen she was voluptuous, at twenty-four pleasantly plump, and by thirty-four she had nineteen-inch biceps. She didn't take anything from anybody. If a tenant got belligerent with her she would be after him with a hatchet. Once she clobbered Jackie Map with a mop for lighting cherry bombs on her stoop. She even took on the city when she scrapped the coal furnace and put in a new oil burner. A city ordinance required that a protective wall be built around a furnace in any building with over four families. Grandma thought it was unnecessary and told the "inspect', " "This is mya prop', nobody tellsa me what I gotta put ina." So the matter went to court and Grandma was brought before a judge.

"Do you want a lawyer?" the judge asked.

"My! For what I needa lawy'? Seventy years ama get along wida no lawy'."

"How do you plead? Guilty or not guilty?"

"Guilty! Whadda your face say guilty to me? Shamea you. Ama paya my taxes ever since I be in this countr'."

The judge let her off with a two-dollar fine, but she had to build the wall.

Grandma's first husband died when she was in her twenties. With no means of support, she had to go to work in a coat factory, on a seven-to-seven shift. For ten years she raised eight children by herself, scrupulously attending to their health and cleanliness by such practices as giving them each a hot bath in a wooden tub every night, fine-combing their hair after dousing it with kerosene to kill lice, making sure they each took a spoonful of castor oil before going to bed. She met Peepa, my "arrangement" grandfather, in South Brooklyn. His wife had recently died and he had three children, so he moved in with her, giving each of their children a full set of parents. They never married because Peepa saw no need for such formality. He told her they would stay together only as long as they were happy. Grandma was able to buy the building we lived in by turning the basement into a knitware factory. All eleven children were put to work knitting booties at the oak table.

While Grandma was the whip of the business, Peepa did the cooking. Before coming to the United States he worked as a chef in Naples. An artist in the kitchen, he carved fresh basil leaves into specks in seconds. Coddling his cream blend for *Sfinge di San Gieuseppe,* he threw kisses "um, um, *bellezza* [beautiful]." Once, to show his gratitude to a doctor, he baked him a pastry castle. Ten pounds of painstakingly hand-peeled almonds were used for stones. Sugar was melted into a torrent of hot cement. Then, using lemon slices for a trowel, he constructed the sugary castle walls. When it cooled he twirled towers made of rum cream and then pieced together a drawbridge with cinnamon sticks. It seemed a sacrilege to cut into the walls of this creation. Even with his recipes no one could duplicate his masterpieces. It's sad a chef's genius cannot be preserved like a sculptor's in a museum.

There was another side to Peepa who hobbled around on a cane even though his legs were sturdy. If you pulled on the cane handle it unsheathed a saber. I once found a cache of guns in his scullery. Ma said the Black Hand was after him because he refused to pay protection money.

In his youth Peepa was with the Socialists who were purged by the Fascists in Italy. Visitors from over there said the people were happy with Il Duce in power. They praised him because "he made the trains run on time and established law and order." Peepa spat, "Mussolini isa no good." Mellowing in his seventies, he became only mildly pro-Russia and took to listening to Pasquale C.O.D., the comic, instead of the political news.

Peepa might have been a bold agitator in the old country, but when Grandma got peeved he moused up. The movies portray the Italian man as ruling his family with fist-pounding absolutism; that's often true I suppose—but not in Grandma's house.

13 On Halloween night a strawman and a skeleton, both cardboard, were the companions of a luminous jack-o-lantern in our window. Down in the courtyard Nicky's friends roamed around with eggs, while a younger group powdered each other with flour-filled socks and chalk sticks. I was going to the horror show at the Fortway but it wasn't until midnight, so I lounged around the house. In the kitchen, Ma was dressing Madeline in a princess costume Ma had sewed for her. My sister's friends, masquerading as pirates, flappers, and hobos, assembled as her court waiting to go "trick or treating."

"Okay, your highness, you can go now," Ma said, looping the last button in front. "I want her home by eight," she told Mary, the oldest girl in the group. "And don't go crossing streets. There are plenty of apartments around this block." As they were going out the door Ma added one last thought, "And make sure you don't go to Ginalumens. That woman won't like you bothering her."

Ginalumens was a woman who lived around the corner from us and who read cards and knew black magic. Ma thought she might not like the children's game. In some ways Ma was very superstitious. She got upset if I put shoes on the table or opened an umbrella in the house because such acts were supposed to bring trouble. On the other hand, she didn't really believe Ginalumens could harm anyone seriously with her black magic. "Only heaven has the power to do those things," she said. Grandma never quite accepted Ginalumens' power either. "Anyone who wishesa me harm gets ita back double themaselves."

I knew Ginalumens because I used to deliver bleach to her. She believed in *la vecchia religione* (the old religion). There were no outward signs in her apartment of her worship except that it was oddly crowded with plants. Once she would not let me out of her hallway until a man with pink albino eyes passed on the sidewalk. She feared the *mal'occhio*. Ginalumens was not the only person in the neighborhood who believed in the *mal'occhio*. I was always hearing stories about it from the old immigrants.

The *mal'occhio* describes an eye with the power to cause evil to befall one upon whom it gazes. From ancient times there has been a belief that a malevolent envious mind can project its evil through the eyes, causing misfortune by a glance. Both the witches and the alleged victims believed in it, which made it work. If the *mal'occhio's* curse was supposed to be that a man's insides would rot away, the accursed worried so much that ulcers afflicted him. Sometimes the victim became possessed and acted like a completely different person, as though an alien force had taken hold of him. Death was the extreme effect of the *mal'occhio* and, long ago, laws were enacted in Italy making its use a crime.

There were two forms of *mal'occhio*: *voluntario* practiced by witches and *involuntario* (or natural) an abnormality a person was born with, like pink albino eyes. This unfortunate individual, although not wanting to hurt anyone, was felt to be powerless to do otherwise. Beautiful women and youth were especially vulnerable because beauty and youth attracted the *mal'occhio's* gaze. To ward off evil spirits, the old people wore beetles or agates, or carried salt or garlic in their pockets. *Pietra della croce* (cross of stones) protected a child from the sickness caused by the *mal'occhio* and was worn in a little bag hung around the neck. It was believed that certain hand gestures could thwart the *mal'occhio*, too. The *mana cor-*

nuta encloses the thumb over the second and third fingers with the first and fourth fingers extended. If a person received praise he said, "*Grazio Dio* [thank God]", out of fear that envy prompted the praise.

Friends of Ginalumens went to her if they believed someone had cast the evil eye at them. They said Ginalumens had a gypsy remedy. A jar was filled with water and seven cloves of garlic that symbolized lightning, since gypsies were said to believe that lightning leaves behind a smell like garlic. The brew was heated and stirred with a coarse stick while Ginalumens intoned:

> *Evil eyes now look on thee,*
> *May they soon extinguished be.*
> *May they burn, may they burn,*
> *In the fire of Tana.*

Other superstitions were brought over from the old country. A lemon stuck with pins brought good luck. It was unlucky to spill salt or oil. If I ever spilled salt around Dad's mother I immediately had to toss salt over my left shoulder—over the left because evil spirits congregated on that side. This act was supposed to drive away the demons and to ward off the evil they were always ready to do. For the girl who couldn't decide whom she should marry, there was a ritual solution with onions. She gathered onions on Christmas Eve and put them on an altar, then under each onion the name of a suitor was written. The first onion to sprout indicated God's preference.

Also there were supernatural cures for illness. Once when I was twelve I got hit with a baseball on my small finger. The swelling and pain continued for days; Dad took me to a doctor but the pain lingered. Then someone told Dad that Ginalumens was good at healing aching bones so he took me to her. All she did was wrap a leaf around the finger and dunk it in hot oil while repeating an Italian chant. After I left her apartment the finger was still swollen but the pain had subsided. Within a week the swelling was gone.

Another time when Grandma had pains in her legs Ginalumens advised her to take a bath in hot washing soda. She has been taking baths in it ever since. But Grandma did not accept all of the old Italian folk cures. As a young girl back in her peasant village outside of Naples, Grandma saw people use cures that were primitive. Fried mice were eaten to cure whooping cough. To rid a person of gout, a spider with its legs pulled off was wrapped against the foot.

An earache was relieved by dropping into the ear the froth from a punctured snail. For dropsy, a teaspoonful of powdered toad was taken internally for seven days at the growing of the moon.

The moon has special meaning to superstitious Italians. Cain was supposed to have been imprisoned in the moon. According to *la vecchia religione*, Ginalumens' creed, the moon symbolized God. I was surprised when I investigated it, to find that Ginalumens' creed had a gospel just as Christians have the Bible. Her gospel was called *Vangelo di Strega*, which means the *Gospel of the Witches*. The *Vangelo* says that Tana (Diana) was the first act of creation. At first, she was darkness and then divided herself into darkness and light. The light was her other half and was her brother Lucifer. Lucifer was so beautiful that Tana trembled with desire for him and the desire was Dawn. Tana and Lucifer both went down to Earth at its creation. Tana seduced Lucifer by assuming the form of a cat that crept into his bed and changed back into human form in the darkness. As a result of this union of light and darkness and brother and sister, a child was born, Aradia. She was sent down to Earth as the female Messiah to teach *Stregonerie* (witchcraft) to mankind. The witches were to be taught secrets of magic power and the art of poisoning. After Aradia had performed her mission and Tana recalled her, she gave to her deserving worshipers the power to understand the voice of the wind, to converse with spirits, to change ugly women into beautiful goddesses, to bless with power, to grant success in love, to tell fortunes with cards, and to vex with a curse.

Once a witch has received the power of black magic from Tana, she cannot die until she transfers it to another. This she often finds difficult to do, as shown by a legend. There was a girl in Italy who became a witch against her will. She was sick in a hospital and in the next bed was an old woman seriously ill, but who could not die. The old woman groaned and cried continually, "*Oime! Maaro! A chi lascio?*" ("Oh! To whom shall I leave?") But she didn't say leave what. Then the poor girl, thinking of course that she meant property, said "*Lasciate a me—son tanto poverà*" ("Leave it to me—I am so poor"). At once the old woman died, and the poor girl found she had inherited witchcraft.

Back in Sicily, the cult of Tana met in the cemetery once a month on the Sabbath to adore the Goddess. They waited for a full moon because Tana, as the queen of heaven and darkness, is represented by the greatest object in the night sky. Rites were performed in which a black cat was torn to pieces to summon the dead. The witches were naked at the meeting as a sign of freedom and because clothes hinder magical powers. They prepared an ointment from rat's blood, belladonna, and the fat of a piglet. The fat was set with water in a pot and the thickest part that rose to the top was mixed with the other two ingredients. The ointment was heated until it was seething hot so that when rubbed on the body the pores opened and the flesh absorbed the solution. The witches rubbed until their bodies were red. Rubbing the labia carried drugs into the bloodstream. Once in the bloodstream, the belladonna excited the witches into a frenzy. They danced, shouting chants to Tana and Cain who was in some way related to Tana. Usually a coven of twelve women and one man participated in the ceremony. The man who embodied the devil was dressed as an animal with a mask bearing two fangs. Near the end of the night a love potion was prepared with saliva, sloughed skins, tubercles, and animal wastes. The last ingredient was supposed to give the cult an intimacy with nature. At the end of the ritual the man became a stud to the twelve witches.

One reason for the meeting was to invoke black magic against enemies. (During World War II, witches on the Allied side offered to help the war effort by sticking pins in Hitler.) But the main purpose was to pray to Tana, the Great Mother, for fertility. In the peasant farm lands of Italy, livestock was the people's livelihood. The cult believed that the Great Mother created the universe and ordered the lives of men from birth. Only a woman could bring forth children, so only a female goddess could bring forth the world. To country people whose lives were bound up in breeding animals, a Great Mother made more sense than a Great Father alone. For a long time many believed in both.

With almost everyone else in my family and all my friends and generation skeptical, I took the Italian superstitions and witch cults as seriously as masked children on Halloween. Only once did I come close to superstitious fear. I had always been afraid of the dark and one night in bed I was trying to tell myself that there was no reason for it. There's nothing to be afraid of out there in the dark. Satanic spirits don't exist. If they do exist then God must exist too and he would protect me from them. If there's hot there has to be cold, if there's bad there has to be good. So if there's a Devil there has to be a God. Then, trembling, I wondered why it's necessary that God must exist because the Devil exists. Must everything have an opposite? What if only the Devil exists? I prayed.

The doorbell rang. I went out into the hall to see who it was. My friends were downstairs ready to go to the horror show. I checked the clock. It was almost midnight. I grabbed my coat and joined them. Walking along Fort Hamilton we talked about shocker movies.

"Ya know what was scary? *The Beast Wid Five Fingers*," Bobby said. "Remember the hand crawls down the stairs and strangles the guy at the piano."

"How 'bout *The Mummy's Tomb?*" Al said.

"I ran home after that," I said.

"The way he walked!" Al imitated the mummy.

"What was the one where the guy is half frog?" Mappy asked. "He goes through high hedges and you can't see him. All you hear is sliding and balop! balop! No one could make it out until the end."

Up ahead the Fortway marquee blipped: FRANKENSTEIN IN PERSON TONITE. We slunk around the corner to the back lot. The roof of the adjoining bowling alley was only one story high so we formed a human pyramid and Timmy got on top. He hitched a rope to a brick chimney for the rest of us to monkey up. We repeated the same process to get from the bowling alley roof to the Fortway roof. A removable skylight led to a catwalk above the stage. We crossed the catwalk, shinnied down a rope to a storage room backstage, and then crawled out through the orchestra pit to seats in the front row. The movie was nearly over. A gypsy wagon with its lantern swinging wildly was being pulled swiftly by two frightened horses along a misty dirt road at night. In the distance a castle loomed on a cliff. The driver, with a bandana over his head, whipped the horses harder and harder. Next to him in the gypsy wagon a stone-faced old fortune-teller, Maria Ouspenskaya, joggled up and down clutching her shawl. When a full moon sifted through the clouds and the bay of a wolf filled the forest, she spoke somberly, "Hurry, my son. Even a man who is pure of heart and says his prayers by night may become a wolf . . . " The scene changed to the inside of the castle, zooming in on Ilona Massey descending cel-

lar stairs holding up a candelabra. The movie ends when the bur-
gomaster shoots the old lady's werewolf son with a silver bullet and
the girl in the castle hammers a stake into her vampire uncle's
heart.

The maroon velvet curtains closed and the footlights came
on. Shielding his eyes from the glare, the manager stepped
out from the wings to a chorus of heckles and boos. "The
next portion of our show is live," he announced. "We ask any
members of the audience with a weak heart to please leave.
If you stay it's at your own risk. Please do not go out by the
fire exits when the show is completed. And don't forget, tomorrow night is dish night."

The stage darkened again. Tizzy old matrons rushed around
flashing their searchlights at noisy sections. Everything became as
quiet as the morgue. Five minutes passed and nothing happened.
Suspense gripped the audience. People eating popcorn waited on
the next handful. Girls squirmed closer to their boyfriends. Kids
watched through peepholes between their fingers. The long silence
was broken by bursts of lightning and thunder as the curtains
slowly opened to a dimly lit laboratory humming with electricity,
all the sounds coming from somewhere off stage. Instrument panels
with gauges, switches, and a HIGH VOLTAGE apparatus were set
against a backdrop. Up front on a stand, dry ice foamed in a trian-
gular flask and greenish liquid bubbled in swan-necked bottles
tubed together. In the center of the stage, electric sparks crackled
in the air across two corkscrew coils in glass cylinders. Between the
coils, Frankenstein, suited in ragged black over a woolly sheepskin
sweater and chunk-heel metal boots, was strapped on an operating
table, tilted up, facing the audience. The dimensions of his shoulders nearly outspanned the table. Surgical needlework made his
sphinx-still face a mess of zipper-shaped scars. A white-coated doctor entered the laboratory and started probing the body. After a
brief examination, he fastened leads from the coils to knobs on
Frankenstein's neck and then went around turning on all the dials.
Finally, he tripped the switch on the HIGH VOLTAGE machine,
galvanizing a spasmodic twitch of Frankenstein's whole body. The
electric vibrations intensified, and the obsessed doctor watched excitedly as the needle on the voltmeter climbed to the red danger
zone. Frankenstein's fingers began to move. The vitalizing current
brought a slight movement to his flat head. His eyelids rolled up.

The static charge continued. His hideous eyes rotated from side to side. Suddenly Frankenstein leaned forward and gave a jerk with his shoulder, snapping the upper belt. Then he reached down and ripped out the shackles over his legs. He lumbered off the table with a menacing growl. The doctor fled through a door. Screams penetrated the theater. Knocking over a machine with a brush of his arm, Frankenstein headed for the audience. He stretched his arms out stiffly and walked awkwardly with heavy thumps. The thundering bass bars of "Prelude in C Sharp Minor" accompanied his footsteps. He started down the stairs on the side of the stage. Kids in the front row ran from their seats. Before Frankenstein reached the bottom he was rushed by Tony Bavimo and the older guys. Stunned with disbelief, he immediately turned and tried to get away. Hampered by the padded suit and boots he managed only a few steps before Tony nabbed him by the collar and buckled his knees with a left hook. Real screams let out from the audience. Another punch pumped to his kidney, and Frankenstein lurched off the stairs with an anguished face. The theater rang with the thuds of kicks to the head. The theater lights flashed on and the manager and ushers came running down the aisle. Within minutes a wailing siren was heard. When the siren stopped, two white-coated attendants hurried in with a stretcher. Out cold, bleeding with one knob gone, and his arms loosely dangling, Frankenstein was eased into the ambulance and was sped to Kings County Hospital.

Back in the lobby all of us praised Tony for his great sense of humor. The scene lingered in my mind all the way home. I couldn't get over how that monstrous hulk went flying from Tony's punching power.

14 Honking trucks were backed up to the East Side inching toward their garment-center destinations. Shirtless boys and shriveled old men ploughed rattling coat racks through the clutter. Here and there on the sidewalk, cellar doors parted and an arched elevator popped up. After winching up the truck's tailgate, I went back into the sweater factory where I was working as a stock boy for the summer. In a month I would be starting high school. My ninth-grade report card was dismal, but I eked into Fort Hamilton High.

"*Mach Schnell, mach Schnell,*" the foreman grumbled when the efficiency manager came into view. "We're not paying youse to stand around."

"Kiss my tookus," Harry, my work partner, said under his breath.

Since there were no more loads to make, we grabbed rags and dusted anything in sight.

"Mah sweetbaby Sarah is gonna be at the Apollo this weekend," Jim said, polishing the Coke machine.

"Are you gonna go?" Harry asked.

"Man, I'll be there wid bee-nocu-lars."

"I'm glad ya mentioned glasses," Harry said. "Have you seen *Bwana Devil* yet?"

"Cool it! Brown's coming," I said.

The efficiency manager casually prowled by again.

"I hate that *fekokteh schlemiel,*" Harry said. "Getting back to 3-D. It's really weird. They make you wear special polaroid lenses. One of these Africans throws a spear in the movie and I swear it looks like it's comin' right at ya."

"Crazy jive."

"And this is the best part," Harry cupped his palms in front of his chest, "The jugs of these native chicks are sticking right out there in the audience."

"I have your checks, boys," the bookkeeper's voice broke in.

At five o'clock I punched out and hurried to the bank. As usual, long lines were moving slowly because of Christmas Club and regular deposits. I got my paycheck cashed and joined the hordes draining down into the subway. An hour later I was in my apartment.

"Here, Ma," I threw the crumpled bills on the kitchen table. "Can I have my money now?"

"You're a good boy." She handed me four dollars from the twenty-nine I had been paid.

"Whadda ya got ta eat?"

"I'll heat up some *lenticchia* [lentils]."

"What, *lenticchia* again?"

"Don't complain. The poor people in Europe wished they had it."

"All right. I'm gonna go wash up while ya put them on."

"Don't use the toilet. It's flooded again."

"What am I supposed ta do if I gotta go ta the damn bathroom?"

"Stop bein' a grouch. Go ask your grandmother if ya can use hers."

"Dija get my suit outta the cleaners?"

"I di'nt get a chance."

"You di'nt get a chance! Whadda ya mean ya di'nt get a chance?"

"How many hands youse think I got around here?"

"What the hell am I supposed ta wear ta the party tanight? In this fuckin' house nuttin' is done."

"Don't use that gutter language around here."

"You're hopeless, Ma."

"Ya got a lot ta say for a fifteen-year-old."

"I'm out bustin' my hump all day while all of my friends are playin' stickball and ya can't even get me my suit."

"You're actin' like a *cafone* [boor]."

"How'da ya expect me to act when I don't even have a suit ta wear and Timmy'll be here at eight?"

"Wear ya Father's suit."

"How can I wear that thing. It'll be too baggy on me."

"If you keep ya jacket closed, nobody'll notice. Ya can fold the back of the pants and wear your belt outside the loops."

"Oh, God, ain't it enough I gotta wear two different colored socks every other day and have people laughing at me fa that. Now she wants me to go ta a party inna potata sack."

"Nobody's looking at ya. They're all too busy worrying about themselves."

"Don' gimme that."

"You're flatterin' yourself, Joey. Nobody is gonna notice what you're wearin'."

"How can they help but notice wid the clothes I wear?"

"What time did ya say Timmy was coming by? Eight? Ya gotta half hour ta wash and get dressed if you're gonna go."

"Awright, get the old man's suit."

I was combing my duck's-ass when Timmy whistled from the street.

"Tell him I'll be right down, Ma."

▰▰▰

"How come ya wearin' ya old man's pants?" were Timmy's first words to me as I stepped outside.

"That pisses me off. It's noticeable, huh?"

"No, I just know you don't wear a nineteen-inch peg."

Timmy was quick to pick up things. A prodigy or something, he was a straight *A* student and skipped into St. John's College at fifteen. Other guys in the click were still getting left back in junior high. The owner of the bowling alley nicknamed him "The Fuckin' Genius." His brain seemed to be up close to his eyes the way a jockey rides a horse's neck. He didn't just look at things. He made instant calculations. If the butcher's attention lagged for a second, he would have a steak under his coat.

Timmy was an only son. His mother often said, "When he was born my life stopped. I live for him." To pay for his college tuition she threaded beads and Mr. Kelly worked overtime in the cheese factory. If he was out too late she roamed the streets in her housecoat looking for him.

Timmy was having his cake and eating it, too. He was doing everything we were doing and going to college at the same time. He could excel in Catholic school and not get razzed because no one else from the poolroom crowd attended; his quick wit also protected him. Timmy wasn't a tough fighter but we had another standing for ability to handle verbal cutting. Being so sharp, he was immune in that competition. Only Richie, the Lord High Ballbreaker of the neighborhood, tried to take him on, and he got blitzed.

Timmy was overgenerous to his friends but rude to people he didn't know and merciless to enemies. Once in the park he slapped a bull dyke who got snotty with him and then kicked her so hard that as she rolled down a paved hill her shoe taps gave off sparks.

We joined the rest of the click at Pop's to go to the party. Everyone was there except Mappy, who never went to parties with us; he always had to make a grand entrance ten minutes before a party was over. You never knew how Mappy was going to come groomed unless you knew his most recent movie favorite. After the *Valentino Story* he came around with his hair brushed straight back and his sideburns peaked. From the same movie he got the idea of wearing a pearl stickpin, but since he couldn't afford one he borrowed his mother's hat pin. With his pelican nose the resemblance to Valentino wasn't even remote, but he must have imagined otherwise to go through the agony of having his chest punctured all night. The hat pin left blood spots all over the front of his white shirt. He also borrowed lines from movies. Imitating a Valentino scene, he once trotted out of the water at the beach and stopped at a girl's blanket with a confident smile: "Excuse me, is this the Atlantic or the Pacific ocean?"

"This is Bay Thoity in Coney Island. Where ya wanna go?"

Surprisingly, Charlie Custi, Mappy's sidekick, was ready to go to the party with us instead of him. When they were younger Mappy came around as Captain America with a towel and garbage lid, and Custi, though six inches taller, played Bucky. The time Mappy imagined he was Valentino, Custi became his faithful friend, Luigi. When people wondered about the identity of the lady in black who was putting wreathes on Valentino's grave, we would say, "Only Custi knows."

Custi let his sideburns grow long and combed his black hair in a high pompadour glued erect by clumps of pomade. No matter how recently he shaved, he always had five-o'clock shadow. His body was a gawky six-feet tall, and the pompadour added two more inches. Custi wanted to emphasize his best features, so he rolled or scissored his sleeves above the shoulder caps to show his tattoos, and opened the top two buttons of his shirt to let a crop of his chest hair stick out.

The police had him down as dangerous. He was always getting busted for things he didn't do. An old lady once pointed him out in a lineup as the man who mugged her, and he was sent away for a year. Put any person in a lineup every week and sooner or later someone is going to mistakenly identify him. Though he looked like the mugger type, Custi was a timid guy. Once our click got into a fight at a party and as Richie ribbed later, "Custi didn't know how he got his coat on or what he was doing in the closet." Most of Custi's boyhood was spent in the Angel Guardian Home. Officially an orphanage, it was more a prison, with bars on the windows and jagged glass on top of the walls around the grounds. We heard stories about how the nuns beat the orphans with rods. Maybe that's how Custi became timid. Later, a woman as old as my grandmother adopted him. They were so poor that often his bag lunch at school was an escarole juice sandwich.

The party was on Water Street. We took the train to South Ferry and walked over to the Manhattan quay. River warehouses eight stories high shrouded with black iron shutters walled off the cobblestone street. On top of a storage company a leaking water tank pinged drops off the window ledges down to the sidewalk.

Loading platforms in front of the buildings were corroding away and heaped with damp rags, cans, decaying cardboard, and other dregs outstinking the odors of the Fulton Fish Market around the corner. A fluttering paper nailed to a door notified: MOVED TO 123 TERRY STREET IN BROOKLYN. Lukewarm smoke coming out of the sewers threw silhouettes on an abutment of the Brooklyn Bridge, which dead-ended at Water Street. The Jokers, a gang from the East Side, leased a loft in one of the warehouses for a speakeasy. Prohibition had been repealed long ago, but speakeasies remained to serve the underaged, after hours, and to spike alcohol with drugs.

The stairs shot up to the top landing at the angle of a scaling ladder. We climbed up and Bobby, with Richie looking over his shoulder, rapped on the door. A metal disk moved to the side and an eyeball scanned us.

"Philly Monk invited us," Bobby told the eye.

"Wait a sec." The disk closed again.

"Awright." Bobby stepped back.

"Will ya watch where ya step wid those gondolas." Richie nudged him off his feet.

Minutes passed and then another eye looked out. "Hey, Roberto," someone called excitedly. The heavy bolt snapped back and Philly Monk barged out, throwing his arms around Bobby. "Good ta see ya cousin. I di'nt know whether ya could make it."

"How's Aunt Mary?" Bobby asked.

"Still pullin' her hair out."

"That's the breaks, havin' sons like you."

"How's ya old man? Hey, wait, Bob. We'll shoot the breeze later. Let ya friends come inside." Philly ushered us in. "Play it hang loose, guys. It's free and easy."

As soon as we were out of Philly's hearing, Al the Gopher turned to the rest of us. "Youse dance wid the girls while me and Timmy go through their purses."

"Wait a while," Lefty said. "Let's at least have a coupla drinks before we get in a bout."

"Look, Al, we gotta show respect fa Bobby's cousin," Custi said.

"Ya ever figure how ya got in the closet that night, Custi?" Richie grinned, elbowing me. "He's worried about respect."

"I give him right," Timmy said. "We should show respect."

"You got some pair of *cullionnis*, Timmy. Ya blow up a rubber in front of my mother and ya give him right," Al said.

▀▀

I left the huddle to shop around. The loft was dimly lit by road-block lanterns. Drain pipes crooked across the high ceiling. Low benches were built into the walls, with turquoise cushioning tacked snugly. The walls were decked with watercolor sketches of playing cards. In the far corner, guys clotted the bar talking in loud voices. Softer speech paddled along the benches where the girls sat. From a distance it was hard to tell the girls apart because they all had brunette hair teased up like tumbleweed, two black streaks framing their eyes, and a strawberry smudge obscuring their lips.

Moving closer, I glimpsed a girl whose face dropped my heart like the first hill of the roller coaster. She had downy jet black hair in a bun, a scrubbed complexion with ruddy cheeks and dimples, hazel eyes shaded by naturally long lashes, and a profile worthy of gracing Camay soap. Sitting she looked very short, a compact 5'1". Judging by her fledgling breasts and other features she was probably no more than fifteen. I went over to her.

"Why ain't ya dancin'?" I asked nervously.

"Do ya wanna dance?" She smiled, dimpling her cheeks.

"Not this one. I don't know how ta do it. But if they put on a fox-trot I'd like ta."

"Ya wanna sit?" She moved over on the bench.

"What's ya name?" I said, sitting down.

"Dutchy."

"Dutchy! Whadda ya, French or somethin'?"

"My last name is Giantellini."

"So how'd ya get a first name like that?"

"It was my mother's brainstorm."

"How'da ya mean?"

"Well, she said I was such a cute baby that I looked like a little duchess. So I was baptized Dutchy Giantellini. What's your name?"

"Sarry "

"That don't sound Italian either, and you don't look it wid blue eyes."

"My real name is Sorrentino. I like Sarry better. My friends shortened it."

"I think Sorrentino is a beautiful name. It's like the song."

"Ya know, I'm an original descendent of the family they named that town aftuh in the song."

"Really?"

"Naw, my family's from Naples."

"Do you live on the East Side?"

"Can you keep a secret?"

"Yeah."

"This is on the Q.T. I'm from Park Avenue."

"Come on."

"I mean it. My fodder is owner of a pastry business all over the city. Ya like pastry?"

"Um, love it."

"I'll send ya a dozen *cannoles* tomorrow."

"Are ya serious?"

"Naw, I'm from Brooklyn. My fodder is a street sweeper."

"Oh, you're such a tease. I'm from Brooklyn, too. Do you know where the West End stops on New Utrecht Av...."

The amplified crooning of Tony Bennett cut off her sentence.

"That's a fox-trot. Wanna do it?" she asked.

"Great." I slinked my arm around her small waist.

"Whadda ya doin' here?" She looked up as we were dancing. "Are you one of the Jokers?"

"No, my friend's cousin is."

"I di'nt think so, coming from Brooklyn."

"Dija ever hear of the Lancers? I used ta be on them."

"Yeah, I knew a girl on the Lancerettes. Cookie Nessi. Dija know her?"

"Yeah, but I'm not on the Lancers no more. I'm on the Fort Hamilton Boys now. Dija ever hear of us?"

"No, but my brother probably has. He's on the Rampers."

"Whose ya brudder?"

"Little Tarzan."

"Oh, yeah, I guess you must know Whitey."

"Of course, my brother and all the Rampers think he's God. I think it's crazy the way you go bashing each other up."

"Why don't we go sit on the couch. I'll get a couple of screwdrivers at the bar."

"If that's what ya'd like," she said in a soft voice.

I was only half hearing her because I was so infatuated with her face. Just being in her presence made me ache like I had itchy balls down my back.

▚▚▚

The factory whistle tooted the next morning. Bleary from lack of sleep, with vodka still slogging about in my head, I ran over a woman's toe with the handtruck. Her yell vibrated in my head like a sonic boom. I thought my eyes were going to crack. "Sorry, lady," I yawned, and pushed on. Boxes loaded with yards of yarn were stacked in front of the freight elevator. To lift the pile of heavy boxes onto a handtruck, my foot had to shove the steel lip under them. This balancing maneuver was too hard for me this morning, so the next trip I left the handtruck and gumshoed to the stock room, where I camouflaged a bin with empty cartons and stowawayed for the rest of the day in pleasant sleep.

When I got home Ma was in the kitchen spooning molten brown fudge into empty jam jars.

"My-T-Fine chocolate puddin'!" I roared my relish.

"They're for tonight."

"Can I clean out the pot, Ma?"

"Do it over the sink so ya don't make a mess." She handed me the pot.

"You better hide those others before that hog Ernie sees 'em."

"I'm puttin' 'em way in the back of the icebox this time."

"It's a refrigerator, Ma. Would you hand me the milk while you're there."

"Don't talk with a mouthful. Here."

"Thanks." I uncoiled the wire around the cap and gulped.

"How many times have I tol' ya not ta drink from a bo'le? Use a glass, ya slob. When ya gonna loin somethin' about etiquette?"

"What glass? You took 'em fa the puddin'."

"Then use a cup. Nobody wants your germs."

"Awright." I reached into the cabinet to get a cup.

"What's that on ya neck?" She grabbed my shirt collar.

"It's nuttin'." I pulled away.

"Lemme see."

"It's only a hicky."

"So that's the kind of girls ya go wid—*putannas!* Ya better stay away from them or they'll ruin ya manhood."

"Jus' cause I got a little monkey bite right away I'm goin' wid *putannas.* Ya so evil-minded."

"They'll give a disease, these trash, these dizzy things. Find ya-self a nice home girl."

"I have found a nice girl."

"That's good. What is she? Is she Italian?"

"Yeah."

"Why don' ya bring her around sometime? I'll make *lasagna.*"

"I will when I'm ready. I haven't asked her ta go steady yet."

"Don' get serious wid any girl now. Ya have ya whole life ahead of ya."

"Who said anythin' about gettin' serious. I'm only fifteen, Ma."

"Well, I'm tellin' ya fa ya own good. Don' get yaself tied down. These gold diggers, they'll make ya slave an' take all ya money."

"Ma, I don' need ya ta tell me nuttin'. Here, put the milk away."

"Ya might exert yaself."

"Listen, don't bother waking me up early tomorrow. I got fired today."

"Oh, no! What did you do? You *facheam.* My sisters got you in and now you've disgraced them."

"Ah, I jus' got caught taking a nap."

"You're no good. Twen'y years those girls have been there wid-out missing a day and you can't even last a summer."

"Whadda ya blowin' ya tube fa? So I got fired from that crummy sweatshop that bleeds ya fa a buck an hour."

"Ya've got no consideration. Wait'll yar father hears."

"So I'll get a job downa docks."

The next morning I shaped up on the west-side pier and got put on for half a day.

In the evening I went to pick up Dutchy. Picking up a girl at her apartment was a different experience depending on her nation-ality. In an Italian home I was fed again no matter how much I refused. An Irish father took a bottle down from the cupboard. A Norwegian father greeted my swarthy face with a scowl. And when the girl was Jewish, I was introduced to her mother as Sidney.

That night I asked Dutchy to go steady. It was the fourth time that I had asked a girl.

My first sweetheart was Amelia Toscannini (no relation to the conductor—her father was in lemon ice). We started going together in the sixth grade. I stopped seeing her because she was making a public spectacle of our romance, printing AMELIA LOVES JOEY in three-foot letters all over the streets in colored chalk. My second girlfriend, Kirsten Bensen, though only thirteen, had a body that was a traffic-jam hazard. I used to stroll up and down Fort Hamilton Parkway flaunting her. By the time she started high school her looks deteriorated. She got heavier and her facial features readjusted, making her almost homely. I couldn't believe it because she was such a dream girl in junior high. Joany, my third steady, a gymnast, held the World's Women Punching-Bag Championship at fifteen. Practically weaned by her father on a speed bag, she could keep one rebounding for sixteen hours straight. During the championship contest she ate sandwiches with her left hand while keeping up the bag momentum with her right elbow. I often gibed her about being a punching-bag champion, which hurt her, but I was too dull to know until one day she cried and ran away. After we broke off I heard rumors she was undressing little girls in her apartment building and molesting them. When I asked her about it she denied it, looking down at the sidewalk. I felt sorry for her and asked her to a party, but when we got there the family wouldn't let her in. The next time I saw her she was wearing a man's suit.

When Ma said she wanted me to find a nice home girl she meant someone who could take the marriage vows wearing a white veil. I accepted her virgin ideal because it was also the poolroom crowd's preference. Practically every one of the older guys had a steady girl he saw a few nights a week and on Sunday. She was assumed to be the virgin he would eventually marry. Usually in practice the girl didn't last until marriage. During courtship, from our view, it was perfectly proper to cheat. The only absolute prohibition of the poolroom was that you could not see a girl unless you were having some degree of sex with her. A platonic date was unheard of. It was "put out or get out." To see a girl for her company or to talk was unmanly. It was thought being with females made a male act like them. Conversation in the poolroom was limited to fights, gambling, sports, sex, movies, and crime. We didn't want to hear about what interested females. A voluptuous body was sometimes referred to as a steak. That description summed up our attitude toward most girls. They served mainly as a sweetmeat to fill our sex appetites. Nothing more.

∿∿∿

15 Dewy autumn winds baptized the trees around the Dyker golf course. Cascading russet and faded green leaves became pastel butterflies in the moonlight as they fluttered down. When the wind lulled, the leaves pirouetted to new rests. In the canyon below the curb a thin band of old rain which had washed down from the tar highlands gurgled along, carrying a shiny fleet of cellophane wrappers. The mouth of the corner manhole slurped up the rushing flow.

∿∿∿

I knotted my hands together to help boost Dutchy over the golf course fence. "Watch ya dress on the spikes." I followed her over, and retrieved the blanket and coats we had tossed first. We walked over the mounds and down the sandpits beyond the range of high beams on patrolling police cars. "How 'bout puttin' the blanket down here?" I pointed to the grass around the eleventh hole.

"Okay." She unfurled the blanket to spread it out.

"Why'd ya ask me ta gi' ya the movie stubs before?" I plopped down on the blanket.

"I'm gonna start saving them in a scrapbook. Here, have a blade of grass." She snuggled up to me.

"No thanks, I'm a hedge man myself. How'd ya like that waitress botchin' up everythin' in the movie? Wasn't she funny?"

"That fubsy thing was cuckoo."

"Do you know where ya goin' fa Christmas yet?"

"I think we're goin' around the corner to my Uncle Vito's."

"We're goin' ta my other grandmother's in South Brooklyn. Let's go ta midnight mass together."

"Okay, why don' we go ta my parish?"

"I think we should go ta Regina Pacis. Ya gotta admit it's got it all over St. Bernadette's in looks," I teased.

"Bunk! Just because its got all those jewels?"

"Ya're not serious? There's no comparison. People come from all over ta see Regina Pacis."

"But St. Bernadette has all the famous ones. Johnny Saxon and

Vic Damone went there."

"What's that got ta do wid it?"

"Well, if you wanna compare things," her high-strung voice snipped at me.

"That's one thing I hate about ya. Ya always go off the subject."

"Look who's talkin'."

"Awright, forget which is better. We're goin' ta mine and that's it."

"Are ya gettin' mad at me? I'm sorry, Joe."

"Let's go by the pond."

"Oh, it's so comfortable here."

"I'm goin'."

"Flatleaver."

"Well, then come wid me." I took her hand and helped her up.

"Are there any fish?"

"Ya got me," I said, leading the way. "There's catfish in Central Park. We used ta go fishin' there wid a shoelace and safety pin. I forgot ta tell ya, me and Richie signed up fa the P.A.L. We're gonna be training at the same gym Tony Bavimo used ta train at. You can come an' watch sometime."

"If ya want me ta, but I think I'd feel out of place."

"Tony got started in the P.A.L. What a rep he's got now. Any place he goes everybody knows him. In the bars they fall over each other to buy him drinks and he don' even drink."

"That's how people on New Utrecht treat Whitey."

"Ah, Tony'd take Whitey any day of the week."

"The Rampers don't think that."

"Whadda the Rampers gonna say? That's their boy. Tony's got a better record than Whitey in the ring, don' he?"

"I really don't care about it. Argue wid my brother."

"It would come to blows wid him," I laughed, as we arrived at the pond.

"Joe," her voice softened, "remember the party?" She leaned back against a tree. "Why dija come over ta me?"

"Because I thought you were pretty. I still think you're very pretty and I only wish it were summer now." I moved close to her.

"Why da ya want it ta be summer?"

"Because there'd be lightning bugs out and I'd catch one. No, I'd catch a batch. Then I'd get the light part out from all the bugs and press 'em together ta make a ring fa ya. When you'd go ta bed at night the ring would glow in the dark and it'd make ya think about me."

"That's sweet." Her fingers felt the bony bumps on my knuckles. I parted her arms and scooped my hands under her breasts.

"Don't, Joe." She moved back.

"Whadda ya, still a kid?"

▚▚

After walking Dutchy home, I trotted down to Fort Hamilton to see if anyone was in the poolroom. All the table lights were out but there was a circle of kneeling figures in the back. Someone in a shimmering chrome suit perked up in the center with his hands cupped over his mouth.

"A crap game," I muttered, going inside.

The shooter was Johnny Shira. Only he would swagger into the poolroom on a week night wearing a ritzy Fifth Avenue suit. Occasionally Johnny visited Pop's to see boyhood friends, but Broadway was his bailiwick. He was a con man. Slight, canteen-shouldered, 5'6" tall, his cream-oil–trained black hair, smooth swarthy face, and animated brown eyes contributed to his brassiness. The poolroom crowd considered him a magician—"abracadabra, and he's got gash in his car." Even Tony was awed by the talent with which he could talk a woman off the street. But as an easy-moneymaker Johnny was inept, so he had to work for a living. He was employed by a funeral home where most of the time he acted like a maitre d', directing mourners to the right rooms. Another of his duties was to go out with the hearse and collect the bodies for the undertaker. His chauffeur's license certified that he was twenty-three, but with his suave-cut, $300 custom-made suits, which he considered an investment, and his worldly flair, he seemed more mature.

Shaking the dice in his hand, he chanted: "Nina from Pasadena, pull your tits. Be there seven." With a bit of wrist-flourish he chucked the dice. They cartwheeled a few times, skidded, and then petered out with two ones up.

"Snake eyes, anudder loser," Blackie called.

"Leave it down. I'll cover it all." Johnny said, shucking two tens from his wallet.

"Comin' out again," Blackie announced.

"Nina, ya gotta do it for me this time," Johnny chanted, rubbing the dice on his sleeves.

"Let's go, shoot," Doodles barked.

He sidearmed the dice against the wall.

"Three and three makes six," Doodles added. "Six is ya pernt. Anudder fin says ya don' six."

"You're on." Johnny jiggled the dice while reaching for his wallet again. "Get hot you ivories."

"Ten dollars here says he makes it." Jumbo waved a bill.

"You got action, fat man," Doodles nodded.

"Roll 'em," Blackie said.

"Nina, Nina, Nina, give me that moola." He sidearmed them again.

"Seven, up jumps the devil." Blackie hoed in the money with a billiard bridge.

"Reamed by the rigid rod of reality!" Jumbo said. This was followed by "Foiled by the fickle finger of fate!" in his medley of old-hat sayings of New York gamblers.

"I'm out, " Johnny said and started for the door.

"Wait up, Johnny," I called. "I'll walk down wid ya."

"Hold this raincoat for me, Joseph. I want to count my money."

"How'd ya do back there?"

"In the red."

"Ya lost a lot, huh?"

"No, I know when to quit. I never drown myself. Some of those guys are in to the shys for ten weeks pay already. What's-his-name, the parkie, is going to be workin' just to pay off. He got in that deep just rolling the dice for a couple of hours. I feel sorry for his wife when he goes home and she asks for the money to feed the kids. He blew his whole salary." Changing the subject, he asked me, "Where are you comin' from?"

"I was at Dyker Course."

"Ah, yes, Brooklyn's oasis. The only golf course for three million people. I guess you were playing a one-hole game tonight. Did you get in?"

"She's not that kind of girl."

"For the right man they all are."

"Timmy and me still can't get over the time ya took us ta the YWCA. The way ya conned those girls to come out, it's unbelievable!"

"Ya liked that, huh."

"That was the smoothest scene."

"You and Timmy want to come to the city with me again sometime? We'll go uptown and do in a fornicatress."

"That would be a ball. Just say when, Johnny, so I can tell
Timmy."

"Let's do it this weekend. Come by my digs Saturday morning."
His finger dialed air as he talked. "And I wanchas to leave this
hoodlum element behind. Wear a suit, even if you have to rent
one."

When we reached his apartment, Johnny said "Chow" and
tipped his cap to me before going in.

I thought, "Ming! If he ain't smooth, who is?"

~~~~~~

16 Saturday morning. Timmy and I were in the hearse heading for Harlem with Johnny our guide to adventure outside
of Brooklyn. The adventures were always sexual. We were only fifteen but he was already fixing us up with married women. I felt
guilty for violating motherhood by going to bed with them. Usually
they were mothers, prostituting for a supplementary income.

In another sense, Johnny was our sex mentor, and he was highly
qualified to teach us. At his Broadway hangout, the B&G Coffee
Shop, other guys were hustling girls all the time, but probably none
of them scored as much as Johnny. It wasn't because of his looks,
which suggested a weasel; what he had going for him was savvy
and brass. Girls acted differently with him. I often thought a girl
was a certain type, but Johnny could talk to her in a way that
would bring out another person. His manner was casual and intimate, like a hairdresser and his customer. Girls became more frank
with Johnny because he put them at ease. Johnny pretended to talk
straight, but his seeming honesty was only another part of his technique. He told us that girls have mental buttons; press the right
button and a girl will fall back on the bed.

Johnny's favorite button was a girl's impressionability. As part of
his personal build-up, he claimed to be a close friend of Frank Sinatra, backing up his claim by revealing intimate details about Frank.
Of course, Sinatra didn't know him from zero. However, from his
file on famous people, Johnny could talk with familiarity about
Princess Margaret, famous authors, movie stars, sports figures, and

others on top. Telling lies a mile a second, he projected himself as the ultimate insider.

To elevate himself even more he passed himself off as a surgeon. By reading medical books he picked up enough knowledge for convincing conversation, and he always carried an AMA journal with him. So in addition to being part of the jet set he also represented himself as a man of extraordinary skill who saved human lives. The average girl, in awe of such a character, was easily manipulated.

To clinch his act Johnny would take a girl to a suite at the Waldorf, where he never paid. The dumpy hotels demanded payment in advance and could not be cheated, but the plush hotels permitted a guest to pay when he checked out. Even with only an attaché case for luggage, Johnny never aroused suspicion because of his lofty manner and fine-tailored clothes. Registered under a false name and with no luggage to give him away at the desk, it was easy for him to walk out the next morning.

Few persons could pull such con acts convincingly. Johnny could because he was a skilled actor totally lacking in scruples. Once we were in Orsini's on 56th Street having coffee with a girl. Johnny told her his father owned Medaglia D'Oro coffee and that he was leaving for Rome in a few days and needed the services of a secretary. The girl acted excited about getting the job. "Consider yourself as having it," he said. "But there's one thing—I don't want to offend you, but your clothes leave something to be desired." Then taking out a sealed envelope with a wad of play money inside, he placed it on the table. "Now don't embarrass me. Don't make a scene. Please don't say no," he said with dramatic delicacy. "I want you to go to Saks Fifth Avenue tomorrow morning and buy a new wardrobe, something European." He opened her purse and stuffed the envelope inside. The girl, thinking that she had at least a thousand dollars in her purse, was a willing score for the three of us.

Another button Johnny pressed was a girl's vanity. He said that ninety percent of the pretty girls around would love nothing better than to have their faces plastered across the fashion magazines; a pretty actress jumps into bed with a producer, hoping her face will be shown on a movie screen, and girls with exciting bodies usually have the best tans because they're always on display at the beach. "Did you ever watch girls walk down the ramp in a beauty show?"

he asked. "They love to show off what they got. Therefore, to get a girl's clothes off, press the vanity button and you short-circuit the respectability wires."

Once we were standing outside the YWCA on 34th Street when out came a seventeen-year-old girl with a figure contoured in the same hourglass mold as Sophia Loren's. "Jesus, Mary, and Joseph!" Johnny exclaimed, taking off after her. An hour later, she was in a suite with us at the Statler.

"Let me see you walk to the window and back," he told her, pretending to be interested in her for a modeling job. The girl went through the motions as though we were an audience of buyers.

"Fabulous. You're very poised for a big girl, Jan. You'd be great for evening gowns. Oleg Cassini is a dear friend of mine ... ," Johnny poured it on.

"Is that enough?" she asked.

"No, I want you to take off your blouse now. I want to see you in your bra. I'm thinking of swimsuits."

Although the girl required considerable persuading, he got her to remove the blouse and, finally, the brassiere. Then he signaled us to leave. This girl was too good to share.

~~~~~~

Teaching us how to pick up a girl, Johnny said the main hurdle was to get her to stop and listen. In his own case his neat appearance and disarming smile were tactical assets. Many women were too smart or just ignored him, but his philosophy was to play the percentages, to pitch every pretty girl coming down Broadway. He knew he had to click with at least one. It was this reward that made all the rejections worth it. Even in moments of losing he was living, not merely existing.

Johnny's favorite preying ground was the Sloane House YWCA, where teenage runaways and out-of-town girls lived. He also exploited prostitutes. All he had to do to con a prostitute out of her money was give her a plastic bag of yeast purported to be heroin.

~~~~~~

The hearse came off the FDR Drive and entered Harlem, moving from the periphery where "paddies" lived through the Latin belt, where it got darker, and then into the Negropolis. We parked in front of a liquor store with a sign overhead: REPOSSESSED CARS —$20 DOWN—INSTANT CREDIT.

"You stay out here and watch the hearse," Johnny told Timmy. "They'd steal the nails out of a coffin around here. When Sarry comes down, you come up. It's apartment 5G. And give me the bag of yeast I told ya ta hold."

Johnny led the way into the tenement. The hallway was a shambles, with debris piled under the staircase. Johnny said the landlords around there were conservationists of wildlife. "They don't want to see the *zorklas* [rats] go extinct."

"Ratta-tat-tat," he knocked on the door with his impeccable hand. The door opened a fraction.

"Yeah?" a slice of copper-brown face asked.

"Ruddy the cabdriver sent us."

"I tol' that fuckin' Ruddy I ain't gon' take no tricks in the daytime."

"I work nights."

"Don' gimme that sheet."

"Now, baby, would I come all the way uptown and try to shit a shitter?"

"Come in," she said, unclasping the latch.

The girl was wearing a white terrycloth robe tinged with blue. Her hair was frizzy and short. Curves meandered about her body like those of a *Playboy* cartoon heroine. "Kee-rist what a keesta," I thought as my eyes swilled it in. She sat down in the living room and crossed her legs, letting the robe slide up her bare thighs. I never expected to find such a great looking girl through a cabdriver. I was anticipating someone like the five-dollar whores who swarmed through Broadway after midnight.

At first she was curt with us, but Johnny's wit loosened her up and soon she was in a joking mood. She told us her name was Melrose. Before coming to New York she lived in a small town outside of Mobile, Alabama. In a flattering, teasing way Johnny kept telling her she looked just like Dorothy Dandridge.

"Could I have a glass of water, baby?" Johnny asked. "My throat's dry."

When she was in the kitchen running the water, Johnny turned to me. "This pussy is very young. She can't be more than seventeen if a day. She's probably not played out yet and, the way she talks, still enjoys it. When she comes back we'll play a little music and you dance with her. Dry hump the shit out of her to get her in the mood. Dance her right into the bedroom. If she asks for any money tell her I'm gonna pay."

Flouncing back with the water, Melrose gave it to Johnny and sat down. By rubbing her legs together she let the slit go to her panty line. Within a few minutes a 45-rpm of "Earth Angel" was on the record player and Melrose was dancing in my bear hug. I could tell from dancing with her that Johnny was right. Her senses weren't shot yet from duji (heroin). Her body was getting warmer, firmer, and sending out charges. I danced her right into the bedroom, closing the door behind us. We were both eager. Melrose sloughed off her robe and panties. I tossed my shoes off without taking the time to unknot the laces. As I was about to remove my shorts, Johnny came charging in with a look of panic on his face.

"Let's get the fuck out of here," he said, ignoring the nude girl on the bed.

"For what? I was just about ta mount the broad."

"For what!" he snapped. "Come with me into the bathroom." He grabbed my clothes and dragged me into the bathroom. "Look at that."

"Look at what?" I said. "It's a shirt."

"But that's not all. It must be her boyfriend's."

"So what? So she's got a boyfriend."

"Yeah, but look at the neck size."

"It says eighteen."

"That's right, and you can imagine the fuckin' body that goes with it. Let's get the fuck out of here."

Melrose, who had watched silently, confounded by our exit from the bedroom, now came screaming after us. We brushed her aside and scatted out the front door. She came running after us in the hallway with no clothes on. "Chiseling bastards."

It was five flights down to the street from her apartment. A big, husky Negro who heard her yelling charged up, calling us "ofay mother-fuckers."

"Get back in ya apartment," Johnny ordered, "before I lock you up, too." He held me by the collar and flashed up his wallet with a half dollar pressed against the leather. The large man sheepishly moved to the side and let us pass. Outside we walked to the hearse and then sped out of Harlem.

17 Dutchy and I planned to go to midnight mass together on Christmas Eve, but by the time the holiday came around we had broken up. She told me the week before that she didn't want to see me anymore.

When we had first started going together I played it chilly and put myself on a mountain, leaving her unsure of herself. I forced my will on her and she respected me. Although she would not let me go all the way, she thought me masculine for trying. Then, when I tried to come down from the mountain a little, I found the slope slippery. I began twittering syrupy compliments and let her have her way in everything. I wouldn't touch her body because she seemed too pure and perfect to be treated as other girls. I ended up wearing my heart like a neon sign and she, sure of my feelings, was bored.

Street Italians have a saying, *"Non fattura confidenza."* It has come to mean don't open yourself to a girl. The right strategy is to remain close-mouthed while making her reveal her feelings to you. This makes her the vulnerable one in the relationship and somehow prods her into falling for you. But I couldn't budget my show of feelings for Dutchy.

When she told me she did not want to see me anymore I asked for another chance. As I asked I knew that there is nothing more pathetic than a guy begging a girl for another chance and nothing more certain to turn her off. Sometimes I did things that I knew were going to do more harm than good but runaway impulses acted them out. She refused, saying that she was seeing someone else. He was a much older boy who had a reputation as a big talker. The next night I dragged him out of a car and we fought until I knocked him out. I even slapped Dutchy around. But I couldn't turn things back.

On Christmas day we went to Dad's mother's house in South Brooklyn. Snow covered the street, concealing a jigsaw puzzle of cracks, and the cornices of normally drab buildings were now embellished with the exquisite irridescence of icicles. Garbage cans wore a lush fur coat of snow. Tinseled Christmas trees topped by wanded angels glowed from the windows of cold-water flats.

Dad, bundled in an overcoat, led the family down the block to his mother's. The last time we had been there was for Grandpa's funeral. Dad pressed the buzzer. When Grandma let us in Dad threw his arms around her and kissed her. *"Buono Natale* [Merry Christmas], Ma."

"Buona Natale, Nick. It'sa not gonna be the same withouta Pop." She was sad for a moment.

"It's awright, Ma." He held her gently and she snapped out of her gloom.

Grandma, like most poor people, splurged for the holidays. It did not matter if she spent the bill money; she would worry about that later. Christmas was a time of feasting. As is the Italian custom, on Christmas Eve she had prepared a big fish dinner of pasta with clam sauce, fried eels, calamaio (squid), spiced razor fish, and seasoned cod. Today batches of homemade ravioli occupied the beds, while honey-smeared zeppoles, confetti spangled strufoli, egg-rich pizzagran, spongy rum babas, and other pastries that took days to prepare ornamented the tops of bureaus. Sauce, smelling its heart out, simmered on the gas stove. The bread-tin played host to a platter of finooks, walnuts, figs, fresh fruit, and a new bottle of licorice-tasting anisette. Italian music screeched from an old Victrola and more than a dozen joyful relatives and friends bunched around the kitchen table sampling an antipasto and drinking red wine with bravura.

"Ah, *bellezza* Nicole, *buona fest!"* they shouted to Dad.

"Buona fest!" Dad shouted back, going over and kissing all the women. His sons followed, doing the same, while Ma and the girls kissed both the women and the men.

"How you feeling, Nicky?" Uncle Charlie asked Dad.

"Pretty good."

"Look how big his kids are, God bless them," *Cumara* (god-mother) Millie exclaimed in a falsetto voice.

"Angie, sit down," someone invited Ma.

"Give me your coats." Dad's older sister Aunt Rose got up. We gave her our coats and joined the gathering. Dad sat next to Joe Monti. "Ya lookin' good, Joe. How's the job?"

"Ah, this union is an under the hat local. They're not fa the men, just the buck."

"Givin' ya the business, huh?"

"They keep telling us they're gonna go in fa a new contract, but they never move. I say, don't say nuttin' if ya not gonna do it. Am I right or wrong, Nicky?"

"I give ya right, but I thought your local was holding an election."

Uninterested in Dad's conversation, I switched to the women. Though they were at the table with the men, they communicated in a separate circuit now. Labor, like politics, was men-talk, and women in Italian families of the old ways were not invited to participate.

The women made small talk and gossiped. In time *Zia* (Aunt) Julia brought the subject to *Cumara* Rosa's son Vinny, who was "keeping company" with a girl they approved of. They all wished Vinny well. Ma said, "That boy deserves it. I keep telling mine, 'If ya respect ya elders ya get luck in life.' "

I listened without saying a word. The young were even more restricted than the women. Unless we were spoken to we were expected to keep quiet. In the typical autocratic Italian family, the elders possessed all wisdom and the young were expected to obey and never to dispute their views. Even a young person out of college was not taken seriously. The stock rebuttal to any young person's arguments was: "We've lived. We know what life's about. You won't get that in books. You'll see when you get older that we're right. You'll thank us." Opposing ideas almost never reached their minds. Their set views were shut up in mental fortresses.

Finding their talk dull, I left the table and went into the parlor. My fourteen-year-old cousin Charlie, who must have tired of the grown ups earlier, was going through records by the Victrola.

"Whadda ya say, Charlie?"

"Whadda ya say, zoot zuiter? Where'd ya get the splashy suit?"

"Orchard Street fa twenty bucks. Whadda ya doin'?"

"I wanna put on some other records besides this Italian stuff. Here's an album with some good songs." He opened a heavy book of 78-rpm records with one song on each side and read off the titles: "Yes, We Got No Bananas," "Don't Bring LuLu," "Blues in the Night," "Buttermilk Skies," "Pistol Packin' Mama," "Some of These Days," "Josephina Please No Leana on the Bell."

"They sound awright," I agreed.

"There's lots of Christmas songs too but it's early to play them now."

"What time is it?"

"It's only four."

"Why don' we go fa a walk. By the time Aunt Rose gets the

table set we won't be eatin' fa another hour. I wanna see our old neighborhood."

"Awright, let's go tell them we're leavin'."

▰▰▰

We walked over to the church on Carroll Street where I was christened. Carroll Street was in the heart of South Brooklyn. By 1950 more than a million Italians lived in the borough and the largest concentration of them was living tier-on-tier in this train of red tenements by the stagnant Gowanus Canal. They had settled from other ghettoes on the East Side and Italian Harlem, or directly from Italy. My grandparents went there at the start of the century straight from the steerage section of a steamship. Grandma on Ma's side once told me, "Whena the ship comes into New York I see thisa lady liberty in da harb' with her handa up. I'ma thinka she say, 'Stop, go back.' I never go toa no school. Whadda I know what thisa woman isa doin' in the middle of the wate'? I'ma really havea letdown whena I get off. Back in mya village I hear 'America America, I'ma goin' to America.' I thought it was sucha beautifulla thing. But I finda what I left. Dirta piled and horses dying in the street, no sweepers, everything alla bumbled up. Thisa you call America? We hear it'sa free country. We thoughta you get everything free, but *monga neinda.* You gotta worka here justa the same."

Normally in Italy generation followed generation in the same valley, in the same village, in the same job, following the same customs, repeating the same bits of proverbial wisdom. For a long time Italians likened emigration to suicide, and everyone who left his country was regarded as little better than a traitor. But conditions became so bad for the poor that eventually there was a mass exodus to mythical America in 1870, which continued in a swell until six million landed in New York from 1914 to 1918. They came mainly from southern Italy and Sicily, where there was no industry, no railroads, and the land was monopolized by aristocrats. The reception given these foreigners was familiar: They were spit upon and stoned, and called wops, greaseballs, and guineas. Afraid the purity of the Anglo-Saxon race would be defiled, Senator Lodge of Massachusetts introduced a "literacy test" bill to exclude them. An alarmed South Carolina legislature quickly passed a provision limiting immigration to that state only to people of Saxon origin. Other "statesmen" urged similar measures. Writing in 1904, in *The Italian in America*, Eliot Lord, a U.S. government official catalogued the arguments against integration of Italians with other races in this country. It was believed that: "Italians are of inferior and degraded race stock. Intermixture with prevailing Anglo-Saxon race stock will be detrimental. Servility, filthy habits of life, and a hopelessly degraded standard of needs and amibitions have been ingrained in the Italians by centuries of oppression and abject poverty. They are ousting our American laborers from avenues of employment by accepting lower wages. A large percentage of them are indolent paupers and burden our charitable institutions. They are the main cause of slums in our big cities. The greater part of them are illiterate and are likely to remain so. They are incapable of adequate appreciation of our institutions. The food they eat is overstimulating and innutritious. . . . There is no material evidence of progress or prospect of relief save by exclusion."

The clock on a building showed that Charlie and I had been walking for an hour. We hurried back to Grandma's for some of that overstimulating and innutritious food.

18 I failed almost every subject my first term in high school. I 'd start out for school in the morning but usually stray to the poolroom or a movie. On the days I did go to class I'd often get into a fight. My friends boasted that I was "the toughest, or tied with Mappy for the toughest, in the school." Stories about my fights reached Mr. Sachs, the track coach, who was a boxing fan, and one afternoon he sent for me.

When he saw me standing in the doorway of his office, he said, "Come in, Sorrentino. Have a seat." I thanked him and was seated.

"I hear ya pretty good with your hands. You ever think of doing some boxing?"

"I awready have."

"C.Y.O.?"

"No, P.A.L."

"How'd you do?"

"I went up ta the semis, but got beat by a guy twenty-two in a split decision."

"That's no alibi. What do you weigh?"

"I'm a middleweight."

"Do you have heart?"

"Whadda ya askin' me that fa? Ask any of my friends who seen me fight."

"Do you smoke, drink, or play around with girls?"

"I don' do the foist two, though once in a while I hang one on wid a screwdriver. I'm normal when it comes ta girls—I have ta get straightened out a coupla times a week."

"You're going to have to stay away from girls if you want to be a fighter. They'll make your legs marshmallow when you get in the ring. Forget screwdrivers, too. If you want, you can have a beer now and then. It's better to drink beer than soda—you can burn it out by roadwork. Soda will cut your wind. Carbohydrates, in general are bad for your wind. There are a lot of little things you have to know to be a good fighter."

"I guess so."

"The reason I wanted to see you, I know a good trainer. His name is Johnny Mandello. He was a bootleg fighter. He's looking for a boy to train for the Golden Gloves. You want me to talk to him?"

"He's good, huh?"

"Nurses his boys along. Won't put you in until you're really ready. He handled Bobby DeMontzi. You ever hear of Bobby? He had Johnny Saxton down at the Fort. You want me to give Mandello a call now?"

"I ain't got no time. I gotta go home and then be at work at four o'clock. But I'm interested."

"Okay, I'll talk to him for you tonight. Come by again tomorrow."

"I appreciate it," I said, starting for the door.

"And listen, Sorrentino. I got the word they're going to bounce you from the school if you get into another fight. Quit it."

After dropping my books off at the apartment, I hurried down the stairs. My little sister Camille was on the stoop with her friends.

"Lady bug, lady bug, fly away home . . . ," they sang.

"Get out of my way, ya blockin' the stairs, " I groused.

"Buy me a licorice, Joey."

"Ya not supposed ta eat gooey junk before supper."

"Swing me then."

"Us too," the others cried.

"Okay, one at a time." I took Camille by the hands and whirled her around like a merry-go-round. And then one by one all her friends got their turns.

"Again, again."

"I gotta go ta work."

"One more time, please."

"Awright." I whirled them all again.

"Again, again. Please, come on." They followed me around the corner. My head spinning, I sprinted to the bus.

Riding along I remembered when I was Camille's age how the neighborhood was.

So many things had changed in a short time. For instance, Camille had never seen a horse, but in the 1940s—only ten years before—they had been a common sight in the city streets. Fish, ice, fruit, and even milk were delivered by horse-drawn wagon. Locomotives also chugged down the tracks a block away from our house, but now almost all freight was hauled by diesels. Toys were different then, too. A factory around the corner whittled dolls out of wood, attaching rubber bands for the movable parts. My favorite toy was an old chemistry set given to me by a neighbor. It came in an acid-eaten red wooden box that opened like a suitcase upon eight rows of chemicals. There was always the chance that something amazing would happen by adding another drop of this or that chemical to the contents of a test tube.

I didn't have a bike but I had fun coasting down Bum's Hill on my skate box, which I had decorated with the caps from soda bottles. The box was the class of the neighborhood until Timmy's mother bought him a pair of Chicago roller skates. On our street owning Chicagos with red washers and big clamps was like owning a Lincoln Continental. The only kid we envied more than Timmy was the doctor's son who owned a Schwinn bike with a foxtail, the equivalent of a Rolls Royce.

As a boy, the game I liked best was called "King of the Royal Mountain" in which players wrestled to the top of a snow pile, and the one who threw all the others off won. My thought that strength was a person's greatest attribute was reinforced everywhere I turned. In the comics (THWACK!). Captain Marvel knocked out a bulldozer; The Heap uprooted trees; Submariner swam oceans at supersonic speeds; and Charles Atlas flexed his muscles on the back of every comic book. Most sports glorified strength: football pitted force against force; Joe Louis was an especially popular boxing champion because his scourging jab could snap a head back (fancy boxers relying strictly on skill were not as appealing); steel-legged Antonina Rocca dominated wrestling with his pulverizing dropkick and "The Backbreaker." In the movies, Tarzan splintered rifles over his knee; the "stupendous" scene in which Samson pushed down the pillars of the temple inspired me to see *Samson and Delilah* three times; and when King Kong pried apart the jaws of a dinosaur, cheers filled the theater.

In my own neighborhood, the ability to raise a bus stop sign with one hand earned tremendous prestige. Even more important than strength was fighting prowess. Over and over again I listened to stories about the fights of Tony Bavimo, and of Whitey, the leader of the Rampers.

I would hear about a wizard like Einstein, but being a brain did not seem nearly as manly or as exciting as being a fighter.

I punched in at my job in the A&P at 3:59. Putting on a clean apron, I went into the store. Henry, the assistant manager, was bending in the aisle assorting cans of tuna on a deep discount shelf. I walked over to him.

"Where da ya want me this afternoon, Henry?"

"Did ya tie up the bread boxes?"

"Not yet."

"Tie them up and then go relieve Jack in produce fa coffee. Uh, wait. He's been buggin' me. Make it the udder way round. First give him his break and then tie the boxes. And here, take these radishes back. Damn customers changin' their minds."

I headed toward Jack's station in the produce department. Around a bin brimming with cantaloupes on sale, women elbowed each other and pawed the melons. Jack stood behind them with an empty crate. "Don't manhandle the merchandise, ladies. The ones in front are just as good. If ya're not gonna buy it, don't squeeze it."

"G'head out, Jack. I'll take over."

"Thanks, Joe. Would ya do me a favor? Put some tomatoes up. And freshen up the spinach a little. There's a sprinkle can under the counter. You know where the water is."

An old lady tapped my shoulder and demanded, "Why so mushy these cantaloupes? Maybe its overripe?"

"No, that's a good one," I assured her, pressing the ends.

"Weigh it fa me, please."

"That's two cents over a pound."

"Oh, come on, sonny, that's not even a pound."

"Look fa yaself, lady."

"What about alla dirt in the scale."

"What dirt? It's clean!"

"C'mon, stop worrying about the A&P's money. They got plenty. Think of the poor people."

"Lady, it's over a pound. Ya want me to get the manager?"

"Awright, such a big deal, he's goin' to the manager."

When Jack returned I tied the bread boxes and then went back to the assistant manager. Henry said, "I want ya on the floor now. It's drizzling out. Ya know what that means. Watch them umbrellas."

Shoplifting was heaviest on rainy days. A closed umbrella easily converts into a container, and many a customer is tempted to filch one or two little items. Professional shoplifters always come prepared to reap profits. One fat woman caused a stir in our store for weeks. Eddie, the manager, had noticed her one day wheeling an empty basket around for a long time. Suspicious, he feather-dusted the shelves after her. After a while he saw her squat over a gallon jug of oil. When she stood up the jug was gone. Leaving the basket, she waddled toward the exit. Eddie headed her off, and before she got out of the store he yanked up her dress. A gallon of olive oil, hooked to a chastity belt, was hanging between her legs. She confessed to having stolen hundreds of items this way. Another large woman became a legend in another store after she was caught heading for the exit with a watermelon squeezed between her thighs.

Some employees of the A&P had their own methods of stealing. One basement clerk operated a wholesale coffee business. He smuggled out the coffee by layering the bottom of the trash cans with coffee cartons. His distributor was the private sanitation company servicing the store. I knew it wasn't wise to steal from the place where you work, so I limited my shoplifting to *other* supermarkets in the neighborhood.

In the beginning I was a clumsy amateur, looking all around in a sweat before stuffing a Hershey bar under my shirt. With experience my technique improved. I noticed that the busy checkers at the registers didn't pay attention to anything going on beyond their counter. The only person on watch was the manager. So I figured that any time he was not looking my way I could get away with anything. Rolling a cart around the supermarket, I would pack the basket with cereal boxes. I packed it so full that if I wanted to do more shopping I would need another basket. Instead of taking another basket I would take an empty cardboard box and place it on the bars attached to the wheels, improvising a double-decker cart. In this lower box I threw in meats, oils, sardines, and other expensive items. When the box was full I looked to see where the manager was. If he was away from the exit I just picked up the box of groceries and walked out casually as though I had paid for it.

Although I was never caught, I changed to an even slicker method. From a detective story I learned that an individual can become mentally invisible to others. Take the case of a neighbor who goes on vacation and nobody is left in the house. If a stranger were seen to enter that building he would arouse suspicion. But if a man in a postal uniform, say, entered the same building, no one would give him a second thought. In certain other situations a person can blend with the environment so that he is almost unseen. Applying this principle, I went to supermarkets disguised as a beer man's helper. As though going about my job, I walked in and out stacking beer cases on the sidewalk. The bolder the scheme the more improbable it appears to the beholder that something wrong is going on.

Ma and Dad were too honest for me to risk taking the stolen groceries home. I sold part of the stuff, but most of it I gave away to friends' parents who said my mother was crazy and that they would take all the groceries I could steal. I, too, thought Ma was crazy. Why should she be different? The whole world was dishonest. From what I had seen and heard, I knew that was true.

Once Dad's friends came over to play cards and they spent the whole night talking about New York's corruption. It started when Mac, my father's foreman, asked, "Hey, Nicky, ya know where the police-sanitation game is gonna be played this year? Ebbets Field. Ya know what that seats?"

"Thirty-five thousand," Dad answered.

"They sold four hundred and 'fifty thousand tickets awready."

"Where they gonna put them all?"

"They got no place ta put em. They sold all the tickets figurin' that because it's a week day, most folks won't show up."

Throughout the night the card game was accompanied by the players' stories of corruption in local government—charges of kickbacks from contractors, illegal use of civil service workers in political campaigns, payroll padding ranging from taking names off tombstones in nonexistent jobs to sinecures for departmental chaplains ("four thousand bucks a year for one or two communion breakfasts"). Special rancor was reserved for the "freeloaders on welfare." Mac summed it up, "I gotta break my ass and give part of my earnin's to some lazy crumbs. That's crooked!"

The assistant manager's voice brought me back to the A&P. "Looks like its stopped raining," he said.

"I guess it was just a shower," I said, looking up from my day-dreaming. In the aisles, people walked up and down with closed umbrellas.

19 After work I saw my brother Anthony on the roof giving his pigeons a work out. I went up to help him. We moved in different crowds but got along well together. I asked him once why he didn't like the guys his age in the poolroom. He said he had no faith in them. They were just out for themselves. His attitude probably resulted from a vicious beating he took from Jackie Map. They had been in the same class for six years and were friends, but Jackie turned on him because he told a girl, "Jackie goes crazy when he's mad."

I stepped out on the roof. Anthony was stirring the air with a long bamboo pole, prodding the pigeons orbiting overhead to fly faster. After a few minutes of kidding around he handed me the bamboo pole to prod the flock.

Anthony planned to enter his best homers in the 500 Mile Inter-State Derby, and I was helping him get them in shape. He now busied himself inside the coop, cleaning the floor and washing down the walls with sudsy hot water. Then he mixed cod liver oil and wheat germ with corn in the feed trough. Most of his birds were racers and he gave them the care of thoroughbreds. The coop which measured ten feet long and was almost as wide, had been constructed from old crates and fenced with chicken wire. Cubbyholes honeycombed the inside. The densely populated back wall was an elegant tapestry of cooing plumage. Anthony owned diamond-eyed splashes, sleek blue bars, bishoped reds, black helmets, Boston blues, bronze archangels, apple-headed tumblers, and chico baldies.

To bring in the flock I whistled up to them jiggling grains of corn in a can. One by one the birds shaved off and spiraled down into the coop. The birds touching down from flight mounted the perches and moved in beside their mates. In the deeper nooks immaculate buff and white eggs were cushioned on tobacco stems. The father brooded over the eggs during the day. At night the mother replaced him. If an egg hatched, both parents took turns feeding the squab by inserting their beaks in its mouth and regurgitating a rich milk. They could only produce the milk for six days, but it was so high in nourishment that the squab's weight increased six times in that period. As I entered the coop a hen spread her wings over her young. A mother pigeon is normally timid, but she will protect her young against anything. She will peck at a man, fight a rat, and remain to die with her offspring in a fire. Strangely, if her eggs are placed outside the nest she ignores them. Young birds are weaned at six weeks of age. After that time their parents consider them intruders and drive them out. Brothers and sisters become permanently separated and treat each other like strangers except that they will not usually mate. During the workout the young birds flew with zest and ranged far away, exploring the neighborhood, but the older ones hovered close by to protect their eggs.

In the coming 500 Mile Inter-State Derby, Anthony's twenty best pigeons would be trucked to North Carolina; along with two thousand other entries, where they would be released to race home. To train a bird for the derby, most owners relied on one of three systems. Under the *Celibacy System* males and females were kept separate in the coop. Denied sex, the birds preserved all their energy for flying. As the time for the race approached, owners put them on a rigid diet to strengthen their incentives to return home. Anthony followed the *Natural System*. In this system the birds were allowed to mate as they wished. Mating is quite a ritual. The crowing cock inflates his crop, fans his wings, and struts around the chosen hen. Depending on her chemistry, she flutters excitedly, coyly turns her back on him, or flys away uninterested. If she stays he signals a desire to "kiss" by tucking his head between his wing and shoulder. To "kiss," the hen closes her eyes and places her beak in his. Then their heads go through a jerking and pumping motion. A jealous female sometimes tries to interrupt the pair, barging between them and pecking at the hen's head. The younger the couple the longer they "kiss." The male can copulate at any time, but the female has to be aroused. If a female is not yet ready, she affectionately runs her beak through the cock's feathers. The sex act is quick. The male hops on top of the hen and bends his tail under hers so that their cloacas touch. After it is over the birds fly off together or lie side by side preening each other's feathers. Once mated, they remain inseparable for life, although males are willing with an inviting stranger. Either of the pair could be used for a race. While males are slightly larger, females have as much strength and stamina in flying. The bird selected to race tries to return home to his or her mate no matter how far the distance.

Widowhood was the most elaborate system of training. It required a special coop with separate compartments so the birds could be kept isolated in the dark. Only a male can be trained by the Widowhood System. The night before the derby, a female would be put in his compartment. Craving affection and sex, he would try to copulate with her right away. The moment he attempted to do so, the owner would take him out and ship him off to North Carolina.

Cruelly clever devices were used by a minority of trainers to supplement the main systems. Some placed a plastic egg under the hen the night before the derby. Inside the egg a live worm moving around made the hen sense the egg was about to hatch. She would fly back rapidly to care for her expected baby. Other trainers placed an egg a day under the hen for seven days. Each day her maternal concern grew with the added eggs. By the seventh day she was frantically trying to brood over a nest with seven eggs. That day she was shipped off to North Carolina.

One trainer hoped for a better performance from his birds by inflaming them. "The Tormentor" was a magnificently handsome, knightly white, extra large cock kept segregated in a private coop. On the eve of the derby he was shoved in the nest of a homer scheduled to race. The two thrashed and clawed at each other until the defender was enraged. Then, with "The Tormentor" left in his nest with his mate, the homer was shipped off to North Carolina.

▚▚

On Derby day I waited on the roof with Anthony to help him get the birds in and clock them. We would only be able to see the last lap, but from films and shorter races we knew how the derby would be flown.

The homers are lodged in wicker baskets on a truck. At the starting signal the liberators unlid the baskets. The birds flutter up into the air, sweep around once or twice if it is misty, and then streak for home. Flying parallel to the ground, pigeons are among the fastest birds in nature. With a tail wind they can reach a speed of eighty miles an hour. They navigate over territory they have never seen before. This homing ability has been variously explained as a sixth sense, a sensitivity to infrared, an instinct of direction, a sense of air currents. One certainty is that it is not completely inborn. Pigeons who are confined for a year and then driven from their coop sometimes never return home. Without preliminary training they often cannot find their way.

Stretched out like a string of pearls in the sky, the homers are driven by instinct to fight for the lead. As the miles go by, the weak and unconditioned begin to falter and fall behind. From dawn to dusk they keep going nonstop. A pigeon is the only animal that will push himself to destruction to reach his destination. A few birds collapse en route from the grueling physical stress. If a bird breaks from the flock to go down for water, there is the danger of land animals. Even if he escapes them he is doomed, for when he comes home lagging with mud on his feet, the owner will yank his head off. Trainers will not feed or breed a bird who lacks stamina. Head winds, storms, high wires, and hunters are all dangerous obstacles to the homer, but probably the most terrifying menace is the hawk.

Of all the hawks, the Peregrine Falcon, is the deadliest attacker of pigeons. He has black markings like a brush mustache on each side of his beak. No other living bird surpasses him in speed. Cutting the air with bolt-like velocity, he overtakes the fleeing pigeon and strikes with a closed fist that produces instant death.

Because of a homer's speed, the only way most other hawks can gaff one in the air is by climbing high above the flock and diving down. The hawk's attack will be from the sun which blinds the birds to his presence; |for easier sighting, he singles out a light colored bird. Plummeting at hissing speed he crashes into the target with an explosion of feathers and sinks his claws into the pigeon's vitals.

A large hawk carries the homer off with one foot and takes him down to a carving block where he plucks the feathers and devours the whole body. A small hawk saddles the pigeon in flight and tears out the food sack in his throat.

I saw the first wave of Anthony's Derby birds coming home. After five hundred miles and nine hours in flight, they adroitly skipped tall buildings, never breaking stride until over our roof. They landed swiftly but gracefully, fanning their wings and tails against the wind. (Inexperienced birds would try to land with the wind and then would be hurtled into the wall.) Immediately after our first bird was in the stalls, we grabbed him to clock his time. I removed the band from his leg and Anthony inserted it in a timer. We received five more birds in quick succession. A half hour passed without any more arrivals. The others must have been far behind. Anthony took the bands he had to the racing officials, who compared the times of all the birds and posted the winners. My brother's birds finished close behind the money. Widowhood-trained birds performed the best in this race. The prize for first place was $500, but the betting pool returned $2,500 more. The birds who floundered home the next day in last place were "sent to the soup market," as their owners said, "suffocated fast and painlessly."

I thought Anthony was crazy spending all those hours caring for pigeons. I never understood what he got out of it. He won some local races, which was exciting, but I hardly thought it was worth the tons of droppings he had to scrape up. His dream was to win the Derby someday, which meant beating the best flyers all over the northeastern United States, and to gain the money and recognition that goes with it. It was a form of competition that satisfied him, but was too indirect for me.

2

ON A ONE-RUNG LADDER

20 Before the second term was over Dad and I were standing at the desk of Mr. Geder, the crusty principal of Fort Hamilton High School.

"Mr. Sorrentino, we can't have your son in this school. Either you sign him out or we're going to expel him."

"I've come to take him out."

"It's for the good of everyone this way. He's causing you trouble and he's disrupting the school. Maybe he'll gain maturity with a job."

I listened, fascinated by the principal's speech. It was odd to hear an old man speak without a foreign accent. All the old men I had ever known were immigrants.

"And he's only going to be left back again if he remains," Mr. Geder droned on, taking a set of forms out of his desk. Now and then his eyes flicked at me reproachfully.

"Where do I sign?" Dad asked.

"Right over here, on both copies," Mr. Geder said, putting his finger on the line. "Believe me, Mr. Sorrentino, I know how you feel. I have a grandson his age. I do hope the boy straightens out."

I thought: "The foist thing tomorrow I'll go get a job. After I start working I'll move out of that madhouse and get my own digs. I'll buy a wardrobe of classy clothes. And I gotta get myself wheels, a big baby, maybe a cream-colored convertible, an Olds 98 or a Roadmaster. No more being widout scratch. I'll have money on Friday nights. I'm gonna be binging on cloud nine being out of school."

▰▰▰

Exiting the subway, a flow of people swept me into the rapids at Times Square. Honking taxis made us scurry across the street. I was on my way to agency row. Though the sun was flaming, high buildings shadowed the street.

Outside one building I saw a shingle that read:

LEADERSHIP EMPLOYMENT SERVICE

MALES   FEMALES

(HOMBRES)   (MUCHACHAS)

1 FLIGHT UP

(1 PISO ARRIBA)

I walked up to a musty old dance studio that still had waltz steps tracking up the walls. A lone man with a slim face was sitting at a desk putting quarters in paper rolls.

"What kind of job ya looking fa?" he asked.

"Shipping clerk." That rang more respectably than office boy.

"I got a better job. Guarantee up ta sixty bucks in a year."

"Doin' what?"

"Assistant manager in a shoe repair chain."

"What would I do on the job ya're talkin' about?"

"Ya don't do no fixing. Ya try ta make the customers buy little extras. Like they got all kinds of heels. Sullivans cost more. Ya try ta sell accessories. 'Need a polish kit, mister?' Get it?"

"How much does it pay?"

"Start ya in the vicinity of forty, spring up ta fifty in a month if ya do a nice job. If ya stay wid them they got shoe stores all over the city. Figure in three years ya'll get transferred ta ya own place. Won't look at the clock anymore then, huh? Ha, ha."

"It sounds awright."

"Minute I looked at ya I sized ya up fa it. I put a lotta guys in these places. Never a squawk. They bring me cigars. They're tick-led pink."

"Could ya tell me a little more about what I would do?"

"Say fa instance a lady comes in and she wants heels in two min-utes. The place is busy so you say, 'Five minutes, please.' Ya gotta make 'em take the easy way." He sealed the roll of coins. "What's ya name?"

"Joe Sorrentino." I put my hand out. Confused for a second, he put the roll down and limply shook my hand.

"Joe, we charge ya thirty-five dollars. Most places take at least a week. We do more volume so we give ya like a five-buck increase in pay. Never know when a friend of yours might need a job. We take the deposit in advance. There's a ninety-nine percent chance the job is in da bag. But suppose the one shot happens. We get ya another job. The deposit is fifty percent."

"I don't have that much on me."

"How much ya got?" He made a face.

"Only some change."

"Can ya go home and get $17.50 and come back?"

"Yeah." I lied to cut things short, and left.

I went into a nearby building, newly sandblasted on the outside but filthy inside. The antique elevator huffed up to the fifteenth floor. I got off at the All-Collar Employment Agency. When I walked in a pudgy agent with a Skeezix forelock came out of a stall to receive me.

"You've been here before, haven't you? I never forget a face."

"No."

"Then you got a double in this city." He ushered me into his stall. "How did you find us?"

"I saw the sign outside."

"Fill out this application." He handed me a form. "Graduate from high school?"

"No," I answered, taking a pencil from his desk.

"How old?"

"Nineteen." I was just sixteen.

"What's ya draft status?"

"I did a year in the Marine Reserve." I lied again to help my chances.

"Were you overseas?"

"No."

"What kind of a job you do before? Can you handle office machines?"

"I worked the addressograph fa a week once."

"Want a yogurt, Bob?" The agent in the next stall asked him.

"Please," he answered, his stubby fingers flipping through cards. "I got an address downtown I'm gonna send ya to. Ya know Speed-O-Mat?"

"Ya mean pinball?"

"No, it's a rapid processing machine used by direct mailing houses."

"Whadda they?"

"They mail out stuff, for say *McCalls*. These magazines don't mail out their own stuff. They turn it over to a direct mailing house. What's ya name?"

"Joe Sorrentino."

"Joe, we have two different fees. If ya get a clerical job we ask two weeks salary. If ya get a nonclerical job we ask only one."

"Why the difference?"

"Beats the shit outta me. The state sets the rates. Maybe they feel there's more opportunity."

"Is that why the applications are blue and white?"

"Right." Yogurt dribbled down his chin onto his tie. "I got an opening for a ship chandler. Ya interested?"

"What would I do?"

"Supply ships. Depends on what department on what ya supply. If it's cabin and steward it'd be things like sheets, pillow cases, towels. This outfit may cooperate on the fee. Do you drive?"

"Yeah." I didn't say without a license.

"Fantastic. If they put ya in a vehicle ya get more money."

"Got a part-time kid, Bob?" Another agent interrupted. "Must have legible handwriting. Didn't you have a girl?"

"She doesn't want to work above 42nd Street."

"What about the Yeshiva kid?"

"Must have gotten a switchboard. Hasn't been around for a few days."

I brought the conversation back to me. "Why are there so many agencies on this block? Don't it hurt business?"

"No, the more the better. If you want to buy a diamond you go to the diamond district, right? Same thing here. It brings more traffic. Tum, tum, deetum," he hummed, leafing through cards. "I got a rate clerk opening. Can you make out a check?"

"Yeah, at the garment center I saw how she made them out."

"Fantastic. Ya gotta pay the truckers when they pick up. Are ya fairly decent in math? You can multiply nine times five, can't ya?"

"Sure."

"Fantastic. Let me get on the phone and set up appointments for you." He held the phone with his chin. "Mr. Howard, please.

"Mr. Howard, Bob Lace at All-Collar. In reference to the addresso position, I have the ideal man here. He's had a year's experience with the machine. Very mature, very responsible. Engaged, sir. The wedding is all planned. They have the hall. Just out of the Marines. He was at Inchon. Purple Heart winner. No, sir, just a piece of shrapnel in his knee. He's very agile. He'll have my referral slip. That's Rector Street, last car, IRT."

The IRT was unfamiliar to me. Trains with different destinations pulled into the station.

"Excuse me, sir, does this go ta Rectuh Street?" I asked a man getting off. He brushed by, ignoring me.

"Excuse me, sir, do you know if this train goes ta Rectuh Street?" I asked another man.

"Huh?" he shrugged without stopping. I jumped inside before the doors closed. I approached a man in a suit and eyeglasses who looked intelligent. "Excuse me, sir, I wanna go ta Rectuh Street."

"This goes to Wall Street. That's all I know," he answered brusquely, then added, "There's a map on the window, if you can understand it."

"Where ya wanna go, sonny?" A woman next to him asked.

"Rectuh Street."

"Ya're on the wrong train. Get off at the next stop and take the train on the other side."

"Thanks, miss."

At the next station I got off and waited on the other side. When the train pulled in I hurried aboard, confident I was on the right one. After five stops the conductor came inside the car to sit down. To be on the safe side I rechecked with him.

"This train goes ta Rectuh Street, don' it?"

"No, you want the Broadway. Get off at the next stop and change over to go back uptown. Then catch the Broadway line at 14th Street."

Rush hour began just as I boarded the right train. People jostled into the car, forcing me against an old lady in a black coat. As the train pulled out and rocked along, my knees touched her varicosed legs. Mumbling some remark, she kicked me in the shins. The rocking crowd continued to shove me up against her and she, glowering, kept kicking my shins. I blew my top. "Whadda ya outa ya head, lady? If I was gonna be a degenerate I sure as hell wouldn't pick you." She acted mute, and kicked harder.

The addressograph place was closed when I got there. The next day I returned but the position had been filled. Nothing else came through at All-Collar. Every place I went they said my age, or my lack of experience, or no diploma disqualified me. I tried shaping up in a paper mill but couldn't get on. Mappy told me they were hiring men wringing necks at his chicken market, but it made me nauseous to look at the birds flapping around in the barrel without heads. "Get *The New York Times*," Timmy advised, "they got plenty of listings." I scoured the classified section for openings available to a sixteen-year-old dropout. The only jobs were a few stock-boy positions in scattered parts of the city. After waiting hours to be interviewed I was politely told at each place that my application would be considered and that if they decided on me I would be called. Sometimes I could sense the person rejecting me as soon as he saw my manner or heard my speech.

The weeks ticked by and no calls came. Dad got on my back, saying I was a lazy bum, and my uncles started frowning the same message at me. Easter arrived and I was hired for two weeks in the smelly factory of Taniello Cheese Products. Wearing white coveralls and boots, workers stirred mozzarella balls in a huge vat filled with milky liquid. We made different grades for different customers. Housewives bought the premium quality. Restaurants also ordered premium, although some of the most expensive places used the cheapest—a slab of reprocessed milk bulk, almost the size of a loaf of bread, which sold for a dollar and could be used to make fifty pizzas.

It was June before I landed another temporary job, unloading freight in the railroad terminal. The slaughterhouse was only a block from the tracks, so every day I watched both fascinated and repelled, as cattle from the Western plains descended from the cars into a long pen, where a massive Brahmin bull led them into the braining room. Steam from hot blood gave the tiled chamber the illusion of a sauna bath. Each cow was brained as it entered by a butcher who bludgeoned a vital part of the head with a heavy hammer. If the lethal spot was missed, the wounded animal tensed his muscles for the next blow. This animal, when he finally died, produced gristled meat, buyers said. Near closing time the tired butcher missed frequently, and shrieks penetrated the steel doors.

Glad to leave the freight yard, I thought my luck was changing when I was hired for a job advertised as a "management trainee." The training turned out to be adjusting the wheels on reject tea carts. I tinkered with joints and tightened screws on the wheels until the wobble was gone. The factory was located on Box Street near the Greenpoint pier, so after closing time I sat by the water in the industrial hub of New York and looked across at the East Side's housing projects with their rows of punchboard-size windows; at the Navy Yard's skyscraping cranes and expansive aircraft carriers decked with diminutive bombers on their flightdecks; at the sprawling stretches of factories with high smokestacks belching up clouds of smoke; at the bridges proudly spanning the river; at downtown's glass, stainless steel, and aluminum buildings stretching up into the dusk-reddened sky. I felt so small and unimportant in the city.

Tired of nursing wobbly wheels, I quit the furniture factory in a month and began looking for another job, but my efforts were becoming half-hearted. I was sick of running all over the city to fill out forms for nothing. In mid-summer Danny Charms got me in as a mailboy at Rockefeller Center. I had to ride the rush-hour subway to work in a suit everyday, and it was a miserable ordeal. The train was unbearably hot as the humid temperature soared up to the nineties. Standing passengers swayed back and forth like zombies with their eyes open or closed. They held onto nothing; they were so squashed together that other bodies supported them. Horny men jockeyed for cheap feels, and women squirmed to elude or accommodate them. Sweat streamed down my face, armpits, and between my legs. My hair fell in front of my eyes but I couldn't budge my hands to brush it away. When I got off, my drenched clothes clung to me. Out on the sidewalk the summer heat continued to beat down upon me. Entering the building I was instantly chilled by the air conditioning.

On a typical day, Marv, the mailroom head, stood with his hands in the air orchestrating the mailroom sections. One boy was on the postage machine. Another sorted. I delivered. Marv had been with the company since he left high school seven years back. He knew all the executives by their first names, and talked to them about baseball scores. Imitating them, he dressed conservatively and smoked a pipe. If an executive told a joke in the corridor, Marv would be in on it, laughing the loudest. It irked him to have to return to the peons in the mailroom. But no matter how much Marv pushed us, he was always bypassed for a college graduate when the company promoted a new executive. At the end of the summer I told him where to shove the mail, and then moved on to a job in a printing plant.

This job lasted just a day—the work was a drag. They had me carrying trays of type back and forth between the presses and the racks for eight hours. It was a pendulum motion.

Weeks passed before I had another stopgap job as a messenger on Wall Street with a benchful of retired old men. I felt nowhere on a one-rung ladder.

Coming home from Wall Street one night I stopped off at the

McKinley Recreation Center. There was a scrub game on the bas-
ketball court. Mr. DeMeo, my old eighth-grade teacher, dribbled
from side to side, dodging by Mr. Cella the rec coach, and then
lunged in with a spinning layup. After sinking the basket he ran up
to me at the gym entrance.

"Nice shot," I complimented.

"Wanna get in, Joe?" he asked, wheezing.

"No, it's not my game."

"What are you doing with yourself these days?"

"Tryin' ta find a decent job mostly."

"No luck, eh?"

"Never nuttin' permanent, or else the pay is crabs."

"You know what I think you should do? I think you should go
back to school. Night high is just starting its fall term."

"I packed that scene in fa good."

"Then get used to zilch jobs. You're not going to get a good job
without an education."

"Whadda ya mean? I know guys who knock out four bucks an
hour as bricklayers wid no schooling."

"That's different. You can make good money if you can get in a
trade like that, but it's father and son. You don't get that union
card unless somebody in the family brings you in."

"There are other t'ings I can get inta."

"I'm telling you, things are different nowadays. Ya need that diploma. Five nights a week for a couple of hours at Bay Ridge and
you got it before you know it."

"Couple of hours, eh? Ain't Bay Ridge a girl's school?"

"Not at night. I'm telling you, it's a breeze. They know you
work in the day, so they make it easy on you."

"Why don't you give it a shot, Joe?" Mr. Cella, overhearing us,
came over.

"Uh, maybe I will."

"You got nothing to loose," he shrugged. "And once you graduate you can put in for civil service: the firemen, the cops . . . . "

"The cops!"

"Awright, whatever you want," Mr. DeMeo said.

"What about my grades?"

"They don't even look at them. Anybody is accepted."

So I enrolled in Bay Ridge Evening High School. Classes were
from seven until ten, five nights a week, and regular textbooks

were assigned with homework every day. On the way to the school I passed the poolrooms, the candy stores, and luncheonettes on Fort Hamilton where things were jumping. In a class with foreigners and old people, I squirmed in my seat all night waiting for the bell. After classes Timmy would tell me about the fights, the lineups, the trips to Broadway with Johnny, and all the other excitement I missed. I could have taken a different path to and from night school, but I chose to tempt myself. Most of the guys laughed at me. "What's he tryin' ta prove? What's he wasting his time fa, as if he's gonna go three years ta finish. He'll be back on the corner in a couple of weeks."

They were right.

▬▬

21 No longer attending night school, I was making up for lost time with girls. I had free rein now since I was no longer dating Dutchy. My only interest in girls was for sex. There were three kinds of girls available for that purpose: the ones you had to "work your points with," prostitutes, and communal nymphos.

The first kind were abundantly in bloom on Fort Hamilton. In Charlie's Candy Store alone, which was just one hangout, there were the fifty girls of the Lancerettes. Originally these girls, who wore jerseys with Gothic lettering, were a sort of auxiliary of the Lancers, but that gang had disbanded and hooked up with what was known as the Fort Hamilton Boys (an informal alliance of seven hangouts unified by Tony Bavimo). The Fort Hamilton Boys pooh-poohed club jackets as phony, but we did rent a clubroom for parties and as a place to bring girls. In three months time I must have brought over three dozen girls. Some were fast company. Others were prim and straitlaced, especially one religious Catholic girl from Fon Bonne Hall who sat with her legs as rigidly closed as a bear trap. And then there were the girls with idiosyncratic "alibis" for sex. Gail Swensen was this type. Sixteen years old, the eldest of eight children, Gail's appearance was out of tobacco road. She had Swedish blue eyes, auburn hair, and a freckled face almost the shape of hands in prayer. Tall, a few pounds over slender, she walked around stockingless in ageworn loafers and a cotton dress that gave full leeway to her large breasts flopping braless underneath. Whenever she passed she derailed everyone's line of thought.

129

Knowing her reputation, I did not waste any time. As soon as we got to the clubroom, I led her into the back where there was a bare mattress on a bedspring.

"What's back here?" She asked innocently, scanning the walls but ignoring the mattress.

"Feel how cushy this bed is." I flopped back on the mattress. "It's homemade."

Within a minute she was lying beside me, remarking, "It's so peaceful I could go to sleep right here."

"It is quiet, ain't it?" I said, as my hand spidered for her breasts which were standing up solid like two mosques.

"Um." She acted drowsy.

"I like the dress you're wearing" I said, pulling it up so that light from the front room shone on freckled legs and dirty cotton panties. With her eyes closed she rolled to the right and then to the left to help me get down her panties. Throughout the act she pretended to be asleep. When we finished her eyes opened and she remarked, "I had a nice nap."

I thought, "She's gotta find an out."

I found it novel but not surprising that a girl would use sleep to absolve herself from guilt. Another girl once pretended to be in a drunken stupor after two beers. The next day she asked me "Did we do anything?" Johnny Shira was always denouncing girls for their rationalizations. There was one girl he was sure "was no angel," but she was giving him a hard time, saying she was a virgin and crying for him to "please not bust my cherry." Johnny got her to give in by saying, "I won't bust your cherry. I promise. I'll come in on the side of it."

With prostitutes sex was less complicated. I went to cathouses all over the city with Sally Spaghetti. If he was flush from a tip given by someone who hit the number, Sally would treat one of the younger guys to a New York whore. He took us to places where the girls paraded out and you took your pick. The best-looking girls were at those fancy terraced apartments in the East Sixties and Seventies. A lot of them were models, cocktail waitresses, and secretaries earning side money. I liked the "new-girl-a-week" place, but I was not as particular as the customer who insisted that he had to be first with her. This man reasoned that the girl still had a virgin quality because even though she may have whored all over the country, it was her first time in New York. To get our money's worth, we used erotic preservatives like "U-last" which had chemical properties that numbed the nerves and mummified an erection for hours. Nubercaynol, which was marketed as an ointment for cuts, could be applied to create a plaster of paris effect.

Most girls went through the act mechanically, but some faked sighs of ecstasy to gratify the customer's ego. The girls I asked said they were in prostitution so they could afford nice things like clothes, skiing, and beauty salons. One admitted she loved sex so why not get paid for it. Practically all emphasized that they were only doing it temporarily. I never asked the poor Times Square hookers why they were in the love-for-pay business. They came out after midnight, the late hour calculated to snare the servicemen and other single men who had tried the dancehalls and cabarets earlier and still were without partners.

Prices varied with geography. The lowest prices started around 38th Street. As you moved north they became higher. Around 90th Street they began falling off again until you reached Sugar Hill where the price rose once more. The style of business depended on price. Two-dollar streetwalkers rendezvoused with you in Central Park. On 49th Street lesbians sold group sex. Enterprising pimps organized outings at mountain resorts or dude ranches, and I even heard of one to an island Shangri-la. The customer made a package deal for a girl, booze, and the accommodations. So commercialized were some places they were set up like a dentist's office. The customer sat in a waiting room reading a magazine until his name was called.

With the advent of nude art studios, a man could look at a menu with photos of girls and their prices alongside and make his selection. Ostensibly he was selecting a girl to pose for him, but in several places he was really picking a bedmate. Sally took me to a place off Sixth Avenue near Bryant Park where for ten dollars a girl goes behind a curtain with you for a private sitting. Behind the curtain another deal is made. Upstairs there is a girl posing for a group of "amateur artists" who had paid five dollars to paint her in a public sitting. Scores of these studios have cropped up in New York. (At no time in history since the Renaissance has a society shown such interest in art.) The public sitting for five dollars is another form of voyeurism, or secondhand sex, which is the biggest prostitution.

Considering the vicarious participation in events our society

131

seeks through TV, magazines, newspapers, movies, spectator sports, records, and books, one wonders if this century might not be called the Age of Secondhand Living.

Communal nymphos were girls who would go to bed free with twenty guys in a night. Among the regulars on Fort Hamilton were Dirty Dotty, Carol the Nibbler, Little Annie Rooney, and the Lapadoolee Sisters, sometimes called the Lee Sisters: Beastly, Ghastly, and Ugly.

In a typical "gangbang," a car would be parked in the dark lot behind the Fortway Theater. The lineup might start off with six guys but it usually had a jamboree effect as favors were returned to gangs in other neighborhoods. Sharing a girl was a form of diplomacy. When the girl was a stray—someone passing through—the event mushroomed into unbelievable numbers. In most such instances the girl was a sleepy-eyed, yellowish, stone-cold creature strung out on drugs who would sit half undressed on the backseat of the car like a limp rag. Weird events occasionally happened at a lineup. The strangest I know of was when Joe Luxe followed five other guys, then took the girl out of the car and eloped with her.

‚‚

22 As the cold weather came I spent more time indoors playing pool. Usually the poolroom was empty at supper time and then gradually filled up as guys finished eating. One evening Bobby and I were the first ones in.

"Ya wanna put your ass on the green?" I challenged him to a game.

"Let's play eight ball." He squatted down to rack up. With one scoop his cow-catcher hands had all the balls on the table.

"Ya know, Mappy made ya look bad yesterday in fron' of your girl," I said as I grabbed a cue off the wall.

"Ya mean wid the names?"

"He ran the crap in the hole. I wouldna' took it if he did that when I was goin' wid Dutchy."

"Ya right, I should . . . "

His voice trailed off as four strangers walked in. Bobby and I looked at each other flashing the same thought: These gees got some pairs of balls coming in this place. If they were older men it would be different, but they were our age, and I could tell they knew the score. You didn't go into a poolroom on another turf unless a regular took you. Because it was still early, Bobby and I were the only ones in the place. If I had to be with only one other guy I was glad it was Bobby. He might not have known anything about boxing—instead of punching straight he pounded on top of the head—but he was so big and strong he drove guys to their knees like a piledriver. We put our cuesticks on the table and went over to them.

"Lookin' fa somebody?" I asked.

"Has Teddy Bascone been around?" One of them stepped in front of the others.

"Whadda youse want him fa?"

"Just I want 'im. He's got a big mouth."

"Ya got a hard-on fa him or somethin'?"

"He told some chick, if we had it out he'll gimme my lumps. I want him ta prove it now," he said in a cocky tone.

"Awright, we'll go call him and you and him can settle it."

We found Teddy eating at home and called him out. He and this guy, whose name was Garcicco, faced each other in the middle of the street as the rest of us watched from opposite corners.

"She's fulla shit, that snatch. I never said that," Teddy tried to dog it. "Ya know these broads, how they like to blab to cause trouble."

"I didn't think ya'd say it."

"It's just a misunderstandin'. Wait'll I see her."

"Sorry if I took ya away from ya meal." Garcicco turned as though leaving, but it was just to get more leverage for his "jap," as sneak punches were called. Teddy got suckered into it thinking Garcicco was falling for his cop-out. The sneak punch paralyzed him for an instant. It didn't knock him down, but it ended the fight as a fight. I could see Teddy's eyeballs roll up and his whole body go slack. There was no fear, only a dumb dazed look when another swing headed for his face. The punch drove him reeling against a parked car near where Bobby and I were standing. Garcicco swamped him, pinning his head down on the car hood and hacking down on it. Each blow reported twice, from the fist smacking into the face and then the bang of the skull against the hollow hood. Blood welled from Teddy's nose and the corner of his mouth. He was helplessly out with his arms dangling, but he remained on his feet, bolstered by the fender as Garcicco bashed his blood-smeared face at will. It was more painful for me just watching than for unconscious Teddy.

At first I didn't care who won. I only knew Teddy to say hello. We never did anything together. But then I started thinking he was from Fort Hamilton. If Teddy got dumped, Garcicco would be crowing about it all over Bay 15, a real bring-down to Fort Hamilton. And it would be my loss, too. Garcicco's friends were already gloating, looking over at Bobby and me like rooters at a football game signaling, "We're kicking the shit out of you out there." I was getting angry. I turned to Bobby and said, "Enough is enough. Let's drop these scumbags. I'll take care of fucko here making *majinada* [mincemeat] out of Teddy. You stick behind me fa when the other creeps jump in."

I started around the car with Bobby following. Garcicco caught me in his side vision and pivoted. No words were spoken but his look said, "I'll ruin you, too." Flushed from conquering one opponent, he felt he could take on anybody. Before his telegraph swing got around I rammed a fist to his jaw. He bolted backwards and his head crunched against the concrete curb. He just lay there. His friends pounced on me right away. A punch clipped me on my blind side, jarring my head. It struck too high. A little lower and I would have been out cold. "Japs" in the street are brutal, far more punishing than punches thrown in a boxing ring. One obvious reason is bare fists. In the ring, twelve ounces of padding soften the impact. Too, a person in the street is in no condition to take punches and wilts fast; a boxer trains for months to build stamina and resistance to punches. Street fighters throw wild haymakers from the floor; a boxer measures his punches for accuracy. But the most crucial difference is in the state of readiness. A sneak punch doesn't give you a chance to brace yourself. If it lands in a sensitive spot it almost always puts you in a daze, or completely out. It was the advantage everyone tried for in the streets. Garcicco pulled it off with Teddy. I was hoping to do it to Garcicco; his friend tried it on me.

Before I could regain by balance, Garcicco's friend collared me around the throat and pulled me down. As we were scuffling over a sewer someone yelled, "Chicky, the bulls." We both got up and ran in different directions.

I was back in Pop's the next night playing gin rummy. The place was packed. It was hard to concentrate between the richocheting balls and boisterous babble. Gagging cigarette smoke, having no other place to go, hung stagnant in the air. The vents over the door were dammed by dust fortified with grease. A spear of fresh air shot through when Ralphie Shades opened the door. Thirty-year-old Shades got his nickname because he always wore dark prescription glasses. His home base was Pop's but he journeyed around Brooklyn and up to the streamlined billiard parlors on Broadway, making money with his skillful game. Surgically precise, he could graze a full rack without disturbing a ball, or scalpel off a single one to butt the cushion, or sink a consecutive string of a hundred. Along with the other hustlers in Pop's, he had a private cue locked in a cabinet under the time counter. With his own key he unlocked the cabinet and removed the leather satchel containing his dismantled cue. He unzipped the edge, took the sections out, and screwed them together.

"Time on the first table, Pop." He arranged the balls for practice.

"How's it goin', Shades?" Lefty helped himself to a cigarette from Shades' shirt pocket.

"No kicks."

"I hoid ya roped in some stiff from Joisey last night. How many'd ya make him win?"

"Couple."

"How much ya beat 'im fa?"

"One big one. Is the kid Sarry around?"

"He's back there ona bench."

"I got somethin' ta tell 'im."

"I'll get 'im." Lefty backpedaled over to me, all the time watching Shades make incredible long shots.

"Shades wants ta tell ya somethin'."

"I heard. What the fuck could he want?" Shades wasn't the type of guy who talked to you first.

I went over to him. "What's up, Shades?"

"Lemme make this shot first." Recoiling his elbow in a smooth groove, he made the final check on position and then stroked forward with a true bead.

"Nice shot."

"I saw De De Madeon this afternoon."

"Yeah, is he still workin' at the bunking car place?"

"He tol' me that kid you hit yesterday is gonna die."

"How does he know that?" I swallowed hard. My cheeks and ears felt warm.

"It was in the papers."

"Did he say which one?" My throat was dry and I was shaking. Anger at Shades mixed with my fear.

"The *Brooklyn Eagle*. On the bottom of the front page."

"I'll go see."

TEENAGER INJURED IN STREET BATTLE

There was another teen-aged fight in the Fort Hamilton area last night, the second in two days. When it was over, a 17-year-old Grady Vocational High School senior lay in critical condition with a possible skull fracture in Coney Island Hospital.

The boy ...., of .... St., was talking with some other boys at 94th St. and 4th Ave., according to what police could learn, when along came another group of teen-agers. Words led to fist-throwing, and young .... went down from a heavy punch. His head struck the pavement and he lay there. Everybody else fled.

The night before, a gang of teen-agers jumped two lads in Dyker Beach Park, and beat them up badly, hospitalizing them.

I had to cut out. I had to hide before the cops came to my house. I entered the subway in a trance. My mind left my eyes on their own to avoid the poles and get me to a seat. "I'll stay on the Bowery," I thought. "That's cheap and nobody's gonna come there. I'll go home when he comes outta the coma. I know he's goin' ta come out of it. I know he's not gonna die. Die, oh, God."

I got off the train at a local stop after Canal Street. As I hiked up the subway stairs I could hear conga drums. A group of Puerto Ricans sat bandying on a tenement stoop. I went over to a woman watching them from her window with her chin on a pillow.

"Where's the Bowery from here."

"Two blocks up."

On the Bowery I came to a building with a sign: UNCLE SAM'S, A LYONS HOUSE, ROOMS 50¢   I stepped in. The hallway was checkered with peeling black and white tile. Everything else was loosening too except a pair of sturdy rails skirting the stairs.

"How are ya?" A man greeted me as he came tottering down.

"Okay."

"Goin' in for the night?" He clutched the rail to steady his uncertain footing.

"Yeah," I said, starting up on the other side.

The door was open on the second landing. Inside, winos were warming themselves around a potbellied stove. Black grillwork up to the ceiling divided the room in half. It reminded me of the vulture cage at Prospect Park Zoo. Behind the grillwork a clerk was sorting keys on a rack.

"Ya got a room?"

"Be right wid ya," he grunted, looping the last key in his hand onto a peg.

"I'd like ta get a room."

"What's ya name?" he asked in the gravelly voice of a chain smoker.

"Uh," I hesitated, "Joe Sorren." I didn't want to give my real name. The police might come there. But I was also worried that he might ask me for identification, so I made it close to my real name. I could tell him I shortened it. Then I realized what I did was stupid. The police would still follow up on Joe Sorren. I was still in a trance and not able to think clearly.

"That'll be fifty cents." He gave me a card to sign. "Room 312. One flight up through there." He pointed to a heavy fireproof door on wheels, and handed me a key with the number 312 on a metal plate. Another fireproof door almost as thick as a bank vault sealed the next landing. Rolling it to the side, I stepped into a pitch dark place, which sounded like a TB ward. Men I couldn't see were coughing, choking, and spitting. My stomach curdled. When my eyes adjusted to the dark, I saw that I was in what looked like a stable with closed stalls on each side. Red exit signs glimmered in the rear. Relying on the faint light they gave off, I located 312. Inside the cramped stall there was a meager mat on a wooden slab with a vermin-infested army blanket balled up in a corner. Clothes hangers hung from an overhead security screen.

Alternately I was having chills and cramps. To knock a guy out was nothing, but to kill a seventeen-year-old boy was a completely different thing. I never even considered it could happen when I punched Garcicco. I could feel what it would mean for him to die.

I was also afraid for myself. If he died I would be facing twenty or thirty years in prison for manslaughter.

"Thirty years," I thought. I would come out when I was as old as my father was then. I'd have gray hair, all my sisters would be grown women with kids. Life would stop and I would age till the thirty years passed. I'd have nothing: no wife, family, or trade—a blank. Him, he'd just be a body rotting away in a coffin.

I got down on my knees to pray. I didn't know what else I could do, and I had to do something. "Oh, God, please don't let him die. I'll try ta be good after this. Please, God. I di'nt mean ta hurt him that bad."

Exhausted, I finally fell asleep sometime after midnight. In the middle of the night I was awakened by the jiggling of a key in the door. "The bulls, they found me," was my first frightened thought. I visualized two big, beefy-faced dicks in plain clothes standing behind the clerk opening the door. When the door did open a raunchy character was startled to find me up with my fist clenched.

"Oh, are you in here? I'm the night-shift clerk."

"Yeah, I'm in here," I said, knowing if I wasn't awake he'd be going through my pants.

"I was just checking." He stepped back out.

The next morning I joined the winos downstairs in the bleak Confidence Bar and Grill. Some were having pickled pigs feet for breakfast. Others started the day with muscatelle. They all wore frozen looks; eyelids didn't blink, they crept down. One frazzled man, stoned out of his mind, was sitting at a table with his face in a dish. Without having the energy to raise his head he challenged a drunk opposite him.

"Right here," he mumbled.

"Fuck you."

"Right here. I'll kill ya."

I ordered a bowl of chicken gumbo soup. It was hard for me to get a spoonful in my mouth. "Oh, God, I wonder if he made it through the night?" I felt a pressing weight on my head. "The papers would have it if he died." I left the soup and hurried out to a newsstand. I checked all the papers, but nothing more was mentioned.

I walked up and down the Bowery until it got dark. Men were

lying in the gutter in contorted positions. Vomit puddles, bodies, and empty wine bottles littered the sidewalk. I used to call all pint bottles of wine by the same name—Sneaky Pete—but now looking at the labels I saw they were different kinds like tokay, port, apple wine. There were more Lyons' houses along the way and a hotel with SPRING BEDS, HOT AND COLD WATER, FIREPROOF, ONLY 75¢, SPECIAL RATES TO SERVICEMEN.

"Whadda you doin' here, baby?" A Negro woman stopped nipping her beer as I walked up. She was along in years and asked the question like a mother.

"Nuttin'," I answered, shutting off an impulse to bury myself in her arms.

Outside of the Old Dover Tavern a group of winos were singing "America the Beautiful." They weren't trying to be funny. They were doing it straight, but somehow it seemed wrong, and sad. I continued my wandering talking to myself, trying to decide what I should do. I wanted to stay away from Brooklyn, but I had to know what happened to Garcicco. I was responsible. Twice I headed for the subway but turned back. Crossing windy Houston Street I noticed a glowing light in the West Side sky. Curious, I changed directions toward the light. Up closer I saw that it was an incandescent cross on top of a building, flanked by the sizable letters "V." and "A." "What does V.A. mean? Veteran somethin'," I guessed, "but why the cross?" Satisfying one curiosity created another. I kept going. Emblazoned above the portal of the building the symbols were spelled out: VOLUNTEERS OF AMERICA TABERNACLE—OVER FIFTY YEARS OF SERVICE TO MANKIND. In the storefront window a Bible lay open on a wooden stand with a ribbon marking the place. As I started to read, a haggard man with a face full of scabs sidled up next to me. He was holding an empty box of chocolate pudding in his hand.

"Are ya gonna stick around for the services?"

"What services?" I answered.

"They got a bunch of long-winded gassers in there ya gotta hear before ya get a meal."

"Yeah?"

"Don't believe nobody who tells you we get fed chocolate pudding. Damn staff minority only gets that. All the people pitching in the bucks for this place should know we ain't getting it."

"How's the food, any good?"

"Good and done. Damn navy beans cooked for seven or eight days. Are you on the stem?"

"Stem? Whadda ya mean?"

"On the mooch, on the stem, tramping it."

"No, Why? Are you doin' it?"

"If I can answer that I can tell you why I'm an alcoholic. I been an alcoholic since I was fourteen. Got sick on alcohol and cherry syrup."

"Cherry syrup?"

"Sure, ain't gonna drink alcohol straight. You know they're eye-balling you in there."

"What fa?"

"They think you're gonna cop something you're not supposed ta cop."

"I'll see ya."

"Taking off?" He looked down at his empty box. "Sure wish they'd give us some of that chocolate pudding."

I had made up my mind. I was going to give myself up. It was self-defense. He tried to hit me. It was just a matter of who landed first. I didn't mean to hurt him that bad. "I'll just tell the truth."

I headed back to the Bowery and the subway. Conga drums punctuated the night quiet of the condemned block. As if hoarding up sights for future recall I built a store of impressions. Building after building, uninhabited, windows sealed with tin. A wrecking ball hanging over a public school awaiting morning to pound the school into powdery rubble. Abandoned autos minus wheels sitting lame and mutilated in the street. One car was impaled to the spot by an icebox that must have been dropped from ten stories. A bill-board, in shreds, superimposed the face of a Barnum and Bailey Circus clown over that of a candidate for Congress. At the corner a twitching wino slept in an empty furniture carton. I punted a beer can into the gutter which awakened him.

"Hey, Mack, can ya spare a nickel?" he begged, putting out a spindly arm.

"Get lost," a man walking ahead of me sneered.

"How lost can ya get?" I thought as I entered the subway.

~~~~~~

The sergeant rolled my ink smudged thumb in the lower box of the fingerprint card. My attention wandered to a collection of F.B.I.

"Wanted" posters tacked to a bulletin board. Bobby, who had been picked up earlier, was handcuffed to a chair facing the wall in a corner. Teddy, who had also been picked up at his house, was sitting in another corner of the 64th Precinct anteroom staring at the drab two-tone green wall. Behind the slightly open door to the adjoining room, Detective Adams revolved in his creaky swivel chair. In back of him at the grated window, his chief, Plainclothes Lieutenant Tulo, stood peering down at the trolley tracks. From time to time he plucked the lobe of his ear. He looked too scrawny to be the third-degree type. I was glad Detective Reeter wasn't on the case. He used a blackjack when he questioned suspects. Once he told me he was going to break a chair over my head and then report that I had a little accident falling down the stairs.

From having been picked up a lot of times I knew the cops were different from borough to borough, from precinct to precinct, and from individual to individual. In Staten Island, a nice residential community, they treated us civilly. The tougher the neighborhood, the more cynical and crude the cops.

"Awright, get Sorrentino in here, Ed," Tulo ordered. Detective Adams slapped his knee and got up. All eyes went in his direction when he stepped into the anteroom.

"You, inside," he said, coming over and grabbing me by the neck. Shoving me in the office, he closed the door behind us. I stood in front of the lieutenant's desk trying to act calm, like a person who has done nothing wrong. It was hard to act that way in front of the police at this precinct. To them we were just punks always in the wrong and they could push us around without second thoughts. They knew our fathers were nobodies.

"You hit him wid a brick, didn't you?" Tulo snapped.

"Brick!" I felt woozy. "Whadda ya talkin' about?"

"We got witnesses who said ya sneaked up from behind and conked him over the head wid a brick."

"I di'nt hit nobody wid a brick."

"A brick is a deadly weapon. Ya know even if this kid doesn't die we can book ya fa assault wid intent ta commit murder."

I thought, "Murder! Brick! What is he talking about?" Everything was getting hazy.

"We're gonna put you away for a long time."

"Believe me, I jus' hit him wid my fists. My friend Bobby saw it. Ask him."

"Both of them out there are gonna be sent away, too."

"I'm tellin' ya, it was just my fist. Would I come ta the station myself if it was the way you say? It was just a fight and his head banged against the sidewalk by accident. He went ta hit me and I landed first. It was self-defense."

"Don't gimme that self-defense horseshit. I'll break ya fuckin' jaw right here, ya little hood."

I thought, "My own kind and he's trying ta railroad me."

We spent the night in a precinct cell and the next morning we were taken in the paddy wagon to the police gallery for mug shots. Teddy was being charged as an accomplice even though all he did was get wasted. Bobby's father was able to get him out of it and take him home. Before trial or any verdict both of us were photographed for the permanent police file of known criminals. I was sixteen. After another round of questioning we were taken for detention to Raymond Street Jail.

Raymond Street Jail was built in 1836. Coarse gray stones mortared together formed a medieval block of masonry three stories high, with arched bars over the windows and castellated turrets. A yard in the back was surrounded by an age-blackened wall twenty feet high mounted with a gun tower.

My first day at the jail I went through processing.

"Take everything out of ya pockets," a hack hollered at us as we waited in line.

"What's this place like Daddyo?" a colored guy behind me asked.

"It's supposed ta be the woise."

"Shaddap over there." A hack with a billy looked down the line.

We gave up our valuables and marched to our first meal: a wad of scummy liverwurst, some pap made from mashed turnips, and a slice of stale, moldy Riker's Island bread. I left everything on my plate. As we were bussing out trays someone burped.

"You fuckin' lowlife." One of the hacks hit him on the head with a ladle.

Leaving the mess hall we marched to the cell block. Hardened murderers, rapists, arsonists, addicts, and youthful offenders were all herded into a dimly lit dungeon. Our cells were cubicles with two iron beds, a toilet, a tin mirror, and zoo bars. We were locked in for twenty-three hours a day. That other hour was supposed to be spent outdoors in the yard, but a half hour was lost in moving us from our cell and back again. At night the cell block stunk from the diarrhea of junkies wailing in cold-turkey agony. The best deodorant in the world—the only one allowed in jail to combat the stink of your cellmate's diarrhea—was toilet paper singed with a cigarette.

I didn't know much about drugs before Raymond Street. Only a few guys in the neighborhood were addicts and they were looked down upon as freaks. You couldn't rely on them to show up for a rumble or to hold up their end "in stepping out." Their one obsession was to get "shit" to shoot in their veins. Bobby's cousin Philly on the Jokers flipped out once on horse. He fell asleep nude on a steaming radiator, which scorched his skin into bubbling blisters. Later I heard of another guy whose brain disintegrated at the autopsy. In jail I was learning the different types of drugs and the kinds of high they kicked. My cellmate, who got busted for pushing, had dabbled in everything. He started sniffing glue in the seventh grade. "It's hard ta describe the feeling ya get," he once told me, "but it's like being the tillerman on a hook-and-ladder truck going to a ten-alarm fire." Someone else said, "It's like jerking your mind off." His supply of horse came from a big trader who, he claimed, had a couple of airline stewardesses bringing the stuff into the country from France. It was smuggled from Istanbul to Paris, where the stewardesses repacked it in capsules concealed in belts worn under their uniforms. Custom officials seldom inspect members of the flight crew.

I also saw men who had been straight before entering jail become perverted. The sex tug was like gravity—it had to be obeyed, but there was no natural outlet. It was frightening to see tough, masculine guys turn to homosexuality, and you worried that it would happen to you. There was one who came in engaged but ended up groveling around under the mess hall table, going from lap to lap. Inmates risked getting billied on the head to "swap spit and cross joints" with each other. Most of the sex went on undercover, but one couple carried on their romance in the open even with bars and a floor separating them. The man on the second tier unraveled his blanket and dropped a line down to his lover below. After noosing it around his penis, the inmate below gave a signal for the one above to begin his affectionate tugs. They closed their eyes for privacy, but eyelids were no obstacle to the guards. The two were caught and beaten severely. I had my overtures but no-

143

body tried to force me into anything. The grapevine reported that I had almost killed a guy with a punch. The one bothersome thing was having to watch other men rolling all over each other in heat.

Contrary to narrow opinion, masturbation was a mind-saver, but sometimes even masturbating was carried to degrading extreme. Raymond Street's blackmarket charged astronomical prices for pin-up photos. Men were starved for just a look at a female.

I was hoping Dad would raise the money to bail me out. If he didn't I would have to stay in jail until the trial. That was a dread in itself, but there was something that worried me more. I would have to come out of the security cell in back of the court. From hearing others talk, I knew that being led out of the bull pen into court by a marshall taints you as a criminal in the eyes of the jurors. Often you are in need of a haircut and shave and you are dressed in the same shaggy clothes you were picked up in. A person on bail can make a much better impression. He comes into court from the front entrance neatly dressed in a suit and with a fresh haircut; he is indistinguishable from the other respectable citizens sitting in court. The percentage of convictions for bull-pen prisoners is much higher than for bailed defendants. An accused on bail has a better opportunity to prepare his defense. He can confer with his lawyer, locate witnesses, and otherwise help his case in ways a person behind bars cannot. The detention period in Raymond Street varied from weeks to years. One inmate, Joe the Barber, was in his third year of waiting for trial. If you were sent to a reformatory by the judge, the time served in detention was not credited against your sentence. If you were convicted of a minor offense not carrying a sentence, or found innocent, there was no reimbursement for working-time lost in detention. It was just the state's mistake at your expense.

On the day Dad was able to bail me out, thanks to Timmy's parents and Aunt Rose, a number of men came down with food poisoning. Everyone was examined. There was no central medical room. It was done in the cells, a hundred and twenty men in two hours. Dr. Welf, the jail physician, eventually resigned because the commissioner refused him better facilities. The commissioner was a little lady in white shoes who it was alleged appointed her relatives to good positions in the city jails. The newspapers reporting Dr. Welf's resignation said that he called Raymond Street "a disgrace to civilization."

144

I had to appear before the grand jury charged with felonious assault and battery with a deadly weapon. After three days in a coma, Garcicco came out of it and recovered fast enough to be on hand to testify. He didn't want to press charges but was pressured into it by Detective Tulo. I tried to tell my story to the grand jury, but the assistant district attorney kept interrupting me. Every time I said I punched Garcicco, he would insinuate that I had a brick in my hand, stressing how the boy had suffered a concussion and almost died, as though the seriousness of the injury could only be explained by a brick. I tried to explain that Garcicco hit his head against the pavement when he fell, but the prosecutor cut me off, bringing in the brick again.

"I don't fight wid any brick," I said angrily. "I boxed in the P.A.L. and they taught me ta fight fair."

"You boxed in the P.A.L., but weren't you expelled from high school as a troublemaker?"

Primly sitting in the rows of churchlike benches, the grand jurors, who all appeared elderly to me, listened intently to the prosecutor as if he were their preacher. My lawyer was not allowed in the chamber. Rules of evidence did not apply. The only witnesses permitted to testify were members of Garcicco's gang. Charges for their involvement had been dropped. After its deliberations, the grand jury returned the foregone indictment. The main count was felonious assault, but they excluded the deadly weapon. They must have believed me. Even Garcicco's gang denied that I had used a brick. The whoe story had been invented by Detective Tulo. He and the prosecutor must have figured that the more they could charge me with the better their chances were of winning. They left the court building together and pretended not to see my mother, who was crying in the hall. I thought: "Those two bastards. They don't give a shit about what happens to me."

The lawyer Dad retained was a real estate man who at one time was Assistant Deputy Commissioner of the New York Department of Water Supply, Gas and Electricity. Because of the lawyer's former title, Dad, who was civil-service–oriented, thought he was a big shot. "All the judges must know 'im. Wid my attoiney they'll throw out the case."

Dad liked to say "my attoiney"—it made him feel important. The lawyer briefly asked me to tell him what happened. I did, and then he told me not to worry. No witnesses were questioned.

After several postponements the trial got under way and my lawyer went into action. "Your honor, this boy wishes to plead guilty." I shot a hateful look at him, and then stepped up to the bench for sentencing, with Ma and Dad on each side of me. Dad was choked up and could hardly speak. Ma pleaded with the judge, "Please, don't send him away, he's a good boy. He washes the woodwork spic-and-span when I go out." For Ma time never passed; I was eight years old when I used to scrub the woodwork for her. I guess a mother will always find something good in her son.

The judge looked down at us with his hands clasped together, lording his high and mighty power over us and loving it. I hated the idea that I couldn't answer him back. I could be sentenced the maximum if he got offended. It was a crime—contempt of court— to even raise your voice to him. I felt like saying, "Fuck you, Judge, you don't own me."

He declared me a youthful offender because of my age, sixteen. That meant I wouldn't have a felony on my record. He imposed probation for two years and made me promise him that I would return to night school. I was full of promises hearing that I was going to be free. In that moment of emotion I even promised him that I would not get into any more fights. By the next day I forgot exactly what I told him, and within a month it was all beginning to fade.

Detective Tulo and the prosecutor forgot about me after the trial. I was no longer of concern to them. They proceeded to get another conviction with Teddy. He received a suspended sentence, but he still had a mark against him, being ineligible for youthful-offender treatment because of his age. I thought it was crazy. All he did was get a beating. Indifferent to Teddy's innocence, the prosecution figured they could nail him too because of Garcicco's serious injury. I suppose such an attitude is almost inherent in a system that advances men on the basis of the number of cases they win.

23 "Getting off, getting off."
I pushed out of the elevator. The entrance to the Youth Division was crowded as usual. A handful of probation officers were responsible for hundreds of offenders. Probation is the status of an offender who has received a suspended sentence. During this period a

probation officer by close, personal supervision is supposed to rehabilitate him, but a study by the U.S. Attorney General reports that two-thirds of probationers go back to crime.

After an hour's wait I made it to my probation officer's desk. "Hi, Mr. Mirgon."

"Have a seat, Joe."

"Thanks."

"How's ya boxing progressing? Ya ready for the Golden Gloves yet?"

"It's coming up. My manager's been talkin' about enterin' this January."

"Conditioning is the main thing in the amateurs. Half of those guys lose because they run out of gas."

"Yeah, I know. I saw a guy quit once because he was tired. He wouldn't get off the stool fa the last round."

"So you know you have to train hard. Did you ever hear of the Michigan Assassin? That was Stanley Ketchel. He used to climb trees with boulders tied to his feet when he trained."

"Ketchel is the one who got mobilized by Johnson, ain't he?"

"Yeah, but look at the weight difference. Ketchel was only a middleweight. And another thing about the amateurs, ya got a big advantage if ya have a stiff left jab."

"I'm working out wid the pulleys a lot ta develop mine."

"Good, keep at it. How are things at home with your family?"

"Awright."

"Are you still going to night school?"

"I dropped out."

"Oh, why did you do that?" His voice showed concern.

"It was hard goin' ta Bay Ridge from where I work out. I don't get outta the gym until close ta seven and class starts at that time. I'm gonna enroll in Washington Irving which is nearer."

"What about meals?"

"I eat late at night."

"You still have your job?"

"Yeah, but I might be gettin' a better one wid a movie company."

"As long as you work I'm happy. Okay, I guess that's it, Joe. I'll see you next month. Make sure you get in that school."

My car was parked in front of a bail bondsman's office a block from the court building. Twinkling in the sun, the big Lincoln Cosmopolitan was a quilt of different shades of green mismatched by different body shops. Most of my salary went into the car. In addition to costly body and fender work for accidents, the maintenance was high for an old car its size. I also indulged in heavy frills, lacing it with chrome, spinner hubcaps, dual mufflers, curb feelers, sun visor, and a superjuiced engine that could haul the 4,700-pound hull faster than a Ford in a pickup drag. A menace on the road, I was involved in several accidents, but fortunately they were all with inanimate objects like a fence, a parked car, a tree. Once a girl I wanted to impress asked for a ride. Mappy, who was sitting up front with me, got out to let her sit between us. As he held the door open on the sidewalk, I raced the engine in neutral to make her hear its power. I became so absorbed that I forgot about Mappy. So as soon as she sat next to me, I slammed it into drive and gunned out, leaving one of my doors folded around a tree.

Owning a relic of luxury gave me an illusion of importance. I almost always rode with the armrest down in front to cushion my elbow. On a Saturday night I'd pull up in front of my date's apartment, with the big baby glistening from Simoniz. I'd be wearing my classiest threads, a canary yellow suit, and I had visions that the whole building was oohing about the tycoon out front.

Now as I walked around the car to the driver's side, my thoughts changed back to the probation officer. I had only seen him three times but I liked him because he talked about things that interested me. He was such a friendly man my mind separated him from the court.

"Sorry I took so long," I told Danny Charms as I stepped into the car.

"It's about time."

"We talked about fighting."

"Did you tell him about last night's bout?" He laughed.

"No, and I didn't tell him I drive widout a license, either." I revved the engine.

"Why don't we take the streets home?"

"Fa what? This big baby likes ta move out on the open road."

"My stomach don't feel so hot."

"Then it's better if we take the Belt. We'll get home sooner. We won't catch none of the traffic."

"But the brakes are shot, Sarry."

"Charms, will you stop being a snatch. Ya forget I'm Johnny

Dark behind the wheel?"

"Johnny Dark?"

"Don't ya remember Tony Curtis in that racin' pi'ture when he says, 'the fastest po-ta-to-on-the-road'?"

"Lemme sit in the back." He climbed over the seat.

The car bucked out with Danny bouncing up and down like a camel driver. We zoomed onto the Belt and accelerated on the straightaway. I pushed the pedal to the floor. The motor hummed and the speedometer needle plunged past 90. We sheared the banked curves almost at the angle of a bobsled.

"Danny, what the hell ya doin'?" I asked, looking in the rear-view mirror.

"I'm laying down on the floor. It's not as bouncy as the seat."

"You guys are all chicken shit."

The wheels screeched careening down the winding exit of the parkway. Speeding up 67th Street, I pumped the brakes for two blocks and brought the car to a stop in front of the Fortridge Diner.

"Ya comin' in?" I asked Danny as we got out.

"No, I'm goin' home."

"Okay, see ya later." I walked into the Fortridge.

"San Diego, over here," Tony waved to me. He was sitting in the last booth with Twinny and Cord. I slid in next to him.

"Man, ya better say ya Hail Marys ya don't get Judge Leibo-witz." Cord said to Twinny. "He raps out tens and twenties like they were goin' out of style."

"Whose ya mouthpiece?" Tony asked.

"Goldbim."

"He's good. He's got a lotta connections, but he'll put ya in hock."

"Why doncha go see Riolo?" Cord said.

"Stick wid Goldbim," Tony said. "That Riolo will bleed ya just as much and he ain't got half the Jew's connections."

"It pisses me off no end that I even gotta go through this shit. If it wasn't fa that fuckin' wheelman. I shoulda banged him out on the spot."

"Look at that," I nodded toward the front door. A willowy plati-num blonde swayed in with a stocky gray-haired man.

"Ya better keep lookin' straight ahead," Twinny warned. "He's a good fellow."

"What's wrong wid jus' lookin'?"

"It's disrespect," Cord said. "And the one thing ya better never do, *spootsy* [crazy], is raise ya hands ta a good fellow. Those people will bury you. Fast."

"The guy who just walked in wid the piece of tail is Mikey Dum Dum from downtown. They stopped counting the notches he's got," Twinny said with admiration. "He's from the old Murder Incorporated crew of *a bon anima* (departed) Al."

"Ya ever see Dum Dum's car? He's got a custom-made Caddie. The seatcovers are all zebra skin. Beauteeful. I'm gonna get my button someday," Cord said.

Cord then went into a long spiel on why he thought it would be great to become a "good fellow." There was the money. He had heard that Vito Genovese was worth forty million dollars. For Vito, raising a million in cash was as simple as stuffing a suitcase. The most beautiful women in the world, high-society ladies and famous actresses were attracted to them because they were romantic figures.

"They're exciting to these spoiled broads," Twinny said. "They won't take an ounce of shit." They have the status of being celebrities. The newspapers and magazines write them up. Movies are made about them. Wherever they go "in the knockaround world" they're treated with respect. "And don't kid yaself," Twinny added, "the legit world might not love them but they got a lotta respect for them. And the F.B.I. respects them the most. They stand up to the feds and take twen'y years before they'd say a word. Ya think the F.B.I. gets a charge goin' after yappin' dogs? To the F.B.I. they're like a lion is to a hunter."

What Cord and Twinny said added to what I already knew about the "Good People," as the Cosa Nostra was known in the Brooklyn streets. They were a secret cult sworn to the code of *omerta* (silence). In public places they acted as though the Cosa did not exist. I never knew any members well because they were much older men. I used to say hello to one of them who bowled in the Fortway League with a car-wash team. Everyone liked him. He was a devoted family man who attended mass regularly and played Santa Claus for his children on Christmas. He was a warm, loving person within his own circle, but it was said that he could sink a cleaver into a stranger's head without blinking. The old order had my section of Brooklyn parceled out like a feudal kingdom. At the top of the hierarchy a *Don Padrone* received tribute from all the neighborhoods. He commanded everyone's allegiance; if a new element tried to take over a niche, he marshalled the whole family to stop it. Under him *Don Signores* controlled large districts made up of several neighborhoods; they settled any disputes within their jurisdictions. At the base level a *Caporegime* was in charge of a single neighborhood. His group included workers and soldiers—button men as they were called. When a person became a Mafioso it was said he was "made." An official initiation of some kind took place, comparable to dubbing a man a knight. Nicknames were often informally bestowed, and usually the name was related to the member's region—Johnny Rockaway—or a personal feature—Three Fingers Brown.

Once "made," a Mafioso became untouchable to all outsiders who knew of his status. If a working man got into a fight with a Mafioso, he would be let off. But for a "knockaround guy," who knew better, to raise his hands was a capital offense. It was almost as fatal to slander one; and no insolence was tolerated. Courts were held and warnings issued to persons violating Cosa rules. The trial was described as "calling him up on the carpet." Areas of leniency were slight. A debtor who tried to run out on his obligation was taking a mortal risk. If he was caught he was garroted with a piano wire. Garroting was the form of killing chosen when the Cosa wanted the victim to know he was going to die. Killings weren't just to punish. They were to support authority. Beheadings and mutilations were a message to others, just as in earlier times when heads were spiked on the London Bridge as an example to lawbreakers. To the zips or mustachos, the old-timers, killing was an honorable rite of manhood. A Mafioso experienced no guilt for his acts because he grew up in a home where it was a way of life. His grandfather, father, and uncles were all involved, and the women were also committed. That sons were expected to carry on the family business seemed natural.

The Mafia arose four centuries ago in Sicily as a guerrilla band outraged by the injustices of foreign rule. Over the years it changed into a government unto itself, living outside society by its own laws and with its own sources of wealth. Mafioso consider themselves royalty and are proud of their code of honor. From noble beginnings as a cure for oppression in Sicily, the Mafia in time became parasitic and eventually encircled all of Italy like a giant tapeworm. Around 1900 a sliver of the tapeworm broke off and came over with the millions of Italians emigrating to the United States. For decades the Mafia barely subsisted in New York, extorting from the impoverished immigrant communities on the East Side, in Harlem, and South Brooklyn. But then Prohibition provided the struggling Mafia with circumstances for growth. And it continued to grow until it spread across the land. Still flourishing, today it is estimated that the "Good People" siphon off thirty billion dollars annually from the American economy.

Originally only a Sicilian could be "made." No one else was trusted. In time, exceptions were made for other peoples. Today, of the twenty-two million Italian-Americans, a few thousand perpetuate the Mafia along with corrupt elements in the Establishment. Attitudes in my neighborhood toward the Mafia varied to extremes. The poolroom crowd held them in reverence. An aspiring Mafioso would gladly kiss the hand of a Don. To an old Socialist like Peepa, they were scum. Certain church people regarded them as benevolent knights. They contributed heavily to Catholic charities and protected the church from criminals. When the diamond tiaras in Regina Pacis were stolen, the Mafia, not the police, got them back. The thieves were found later, their corpses bullet-ridden. Even nightclubs in the city paid them to police their premises against troublemakers.

The average Italo-American family looked upon the Mafia as a bunch of criminals who should be behind bars. But older *manuáles* took a perverse pride in the Mafia. Few of these immigrants ever heard of assimilation. They felt Italians were second-class Americans. They had never seen an Italian in the governor's office, or the senate, the cabinet, the Supreme Court, or the Presidency. The Mafioso who drove a Fleetwood was seen as successfully defying—and making—it against the W.A.S.P. aristocrats who monopolized everything. Among this group there were also apologists who said the Mafia is no more evil than the first wave of English who slaughtered the Indians and Mexicans to get established here. When angered, I had a recklessly defiant attitude toward the Mafia. There have been spats where I yelled at their relatives, "Go get ya fuckin' ginso uncles." In more sober moments I respected them the way you would a battleship. But I never admired them. They were dictators who valued power above human life. They preyed on human weaknesses. They killed without emotion. And they destroyed lives with narcotics.

Cord harped back to the problem he started with. "I wish I could get their help now to put the fix in. Only Jesus knows who they own in this city."

Tony, who had been listening quietly, suddenly pounded his fist on the table. "I don't need them. I don't need no fuckin' body. What they got I'll get, and the day will come when I take over this neighborhood."

"Tone, those people don't use their hands," Cord warned. "They got an army."

"Bullets fly both ways," Tony snarled.

Saying, "I'm gonna go, Tony," I stood up. His mention of bullets reminded me that Al had asked me to go shooting.

"Take it easy, kid."

I picked up Al and we drove to the outskirts of Brooklyn to Bergen Beach. People rode horseback along the sandy flats near the ocean. Inland, thickets of tall grass that could hide a car provided the gangs with their raping grounds. "Let's take her to visit Mr. Bergen," was the hint for rape. Al thought it would be a good place for shooting. We found a clearing and set up cans for targets. I had a .36 snubnose I had stolen from Peepa. Al aimed a mail-order toy gun he had converted into a live .32-caliber piece. Originally the gun was designed to project model airplanes.

"I got this drug store in Bensonhurst all lined up," Al said as we loaded the guns. "Gotta be at least a couple of balloons in the till, and it'd be a cinch. Ya interested?"

"I may be *spoosty* but I'm no jerk. Ya think I'm gonna go flirt wid ten years fa Kotex? If I step out wid a piece and risk having shots thrown at me, it's not gonna be fa a measly hundred bucks."

"Maybe you ain't got the balls for this action."

"Don't hand me that shit. I got the balls. If everythin' else falls through, I'll say 'fuck it' and go into a bank. Right now I still might make it in the ring. And like I told you, if I ever do step out it won't be for no asshole score. It's still armed robbery if ya take a couple a hundred or a couple a thousand."

"Ya sure ya don't wanna get in?"

"Yeah, forget me. Let's go up to the Jokers Club."

I got home at two in the morning. Ma was still up waiting for me.

"Where've you been?" she asked, trying to sound stern but coming across as worried. "Why didn't you come home fa supper?"

"Listen, Ma," I balked. "I work, I give you twenty dollars from my pay. I don't wanna hear nuttin'."

"Don't give me that big-man talk. Ya still a kid."

"Stop calling me a kid, damn it."

"Dija see Mr. Mirgon today?"

"Who?"

"Dija go to your probation officer?"

"Oh, yeah, the probation officer. Yeah, I seen 'im," I said, almost forgetting that I had.

vvvvvvvvvvvvvvvvvvvvvvvvvvvvvvvvvvvvvvvvvvvvvvvvv

24 The personnel department of 20th Century-Fox was not what I had pictured. The entrance was tucked away in a hall corner like a porter's closet. The office inside was more of a letdown. Where I had expected a llama-carpeted suite luxuriantly upholstered in leather and muraled with star portraits on Riviera-blue walls, there was a small, dull brown room with a gray metal desk and a rug that belonged in the lobby of a three-feature movie house. I had confused the hiring of employees with the signing of movie stars. No one was ahead of me in the office; at least if I didn't get the job I would be out quick. One last time I practiced my opening in my head, and then walked up to the personnel manager sitting at the desk. He looked up.

"Can I help you, young man?"

"My name is Joe Sorrentino. I'm here in reference ta the expediter position you have open. My friend Al Bagella who woiks fa ya recommended me."

"That's right, Al came by yesterday and said you were coming in. Have a seat." He gestured toward the chair to the side of his desk. "Here's an application. Do you have something to write with?"

"Yeah, I brung a pen."

"Why don't you borrow the corner of my desk to fill it out?"

The form included the usual questions: "Have you ever been arrested?" Naturally, I filled in "no." Nobody was going to hire me if I put down "yes, four times." It also asked: "Have you ever been convicted of a crime? Please indicate even if expunged because of youthful status." I answered "no." If it was expunged it was none of their business.

I was hired for a position with the publicity department. The personnel manager gave me directions along with a map of the building so I would be able to find the right office. By stairs, an elevator, and a ramp following a series of turns, I came to a dark corridor about a block long. My steps echoed in this chamber like a dripping faucet in a sleeping house. Imposing iron doors lined the walls. The one I sought, PUBLICITY, was at the end. I opened the door only to find another corridor. This one had high opaque glass partitions on each side with open doorways showing people at desks in various-size quarters. I reported to Ed Connor, the manager, whose office was at the end. He welcomed me to the department and said I would be taking over as expediter for the department. The dictionary defines an expediter as "one involved in hastening urgent government affairs." I ended up alternating between message hops and deli trips for coffee, Danish, lox and bagels, and such other urgent affairs of 20th Century's government.

Being with a movie company I had a chance to get at my friends. My first victim was Joey Map. He had recently changed from the Valentino look to a handlebar mustache and a part in the center of his hair. He had been impressed by Marlon Brando in *Viva Zapata*. Using stationery with the company seal, I wrote him a letter as vice-president of the talent division and sent it special delivery. In the letter I said that one of our talent scouts had seen him with his shirt off at his job at the chicken market and thought he was perfect for a big role in a script we were in the process of casting. If he was interested we were eager to hear from him to set up a screen test. He ran out in the street with the letter, yelling to neighbors, "I've been discovered. I've been discovered." A limousine was supposed to pick him up after we received his answer by mail. He spent a couple of nights indoors waiting for the limousine before he got wise, remembering that I worked at 20th. I pulled the same trick on Timmy. In his case his mother got the special-delivery letter. When he came home from school she had his bags packed.

Publicity launched a premiere my second month there. The staff felt evangelistic. Typewriters tatted and tinged, phones jangled, people scuffed in and out. Hal Rand, the trade editor, sprung out of his chair into the expediter's cubby.

"You busy, Joe?"

"No, jus' got a few more of these synopses ta staple."

"When you get a chance could you please mail these for me?" He handed over a coverless box stuffed with silken envelopes. "Be careful with them. They're the invitations for the premiere next week."

"Sure, Hal, I'll get on it right away."

"Thanks, buddy." He went back to his desk.

I spun around at the department exit and kicked the door open with my heel. Tracing over the tops of the envelopes, I estimated, "Has ta be at least 500 in here. I'll bet they're all fa Park Avenue people." Curious, I leafed through the envelopes, reading the addresses out loud: "Sutton Place, Tudor City, Garden City, Fire Island, Southhampton, Gracie Mansion. Oh, here's one, The Regency Hotel, Park Avenue."

"Going down," the elevator operator interrupted my roll call. I glanced at his white golves and stepped inside. As we were riding down the thought struck me: "How would these people ever know if I didn't send them their invitations? I mean, how would they know if they were invited? None of these snobs with their pedigrees is gonna have the face to call up and ask." I got off the elevator and made a detour into the men's room. I took twenty-five invitations out and made a list of the names. Then I signed the acceptance cards for them. When the others came back in the mail it would be easy to mix in the phony acceptances. Instead of sending out those tickets I would give them to the people in my neighborhood.

The rest of the week, Publicity's expense vouchers quadrupled as cocktails were poured into New York's columnists and prime steaks sated the hunger of prestigious reviewers. Studio chief Darryl Zanuck jetted into town to assist the promotion and caused a nervequake in the department. I cabbed all over the city on important premiere business—rounding up babysitters, delivering horoscope predicitions, buying cigars for Mr. Zanuck. One starlet had me take her black poodle, Othello, to a grooming parlor on Fifth Avenue for a medicated shampoo and an individually styled poof hairdo (that cost thirty dollars).

▚▚▚

Kleig light beams crisscrossed in the ebony night over the city. Police barriers buckled as the ogling throng surged toward the royal blue Rolls Royce pulling up in front of the Roxy Theater. Photographers rushed up to the vehicle, and their flashbulbs blazed as the passengers got out.

"I think it is," yelped a hoarse radio broadcaster. "It's Christine Jorgensen. She and her escort are stopping now for the photographers. Jean, would you describe her fashion." He handed the microphone to his female assistant.

"Ladies, Christine is wearing a stunning, form-fitting white gown . . . . She's the most radiant we have seen tonight, Bob."

"Indeed she is, Jean," the announcer answered.

The Roxy lobby was abubble with celebrities waiting to be interviewed by Dorothy Kilgallen on television.

The publicity staff in tuxedos welcomed and chatted with the telegenic stars entering the lobby. I had a badge pinned to my lapel which said EXPEDITER, so very few stars stopped to chat with me. Rudy Vallee, one who did, facetiously mistook me for Julius LaRosa. I retaliated by asking him for his autograph, for my grandmother. Phil Silvers, who was waiting to go on TV next, griped to me confidentially about Kilgallen talking too much—he had to get to the john. Janet Leigh was courteous and friendly. Monica Lewis had the sympatico of a neighborhood girl. Naturally I was eager to see what my favorite actresses looked like in person. Grace Kelly's delicate beauty magnified up close; Merle Oberon seemed gracious. Linda Christian wasn't as much a goddess as I had expected. Some actresses were disappointing off screen, looking as skinny and alike as mannikins. But not Mitzi Gaynor, whose plunging neckline and windblown hem were adventures for the eyes. And not Marilyn Monroe. I got a better view of her earlier that day at the St. Regis Hotel. I had been sent there with a message for Earl Wilson, the columnist, who was up in her suite. Instead of leaving right away, I told Mr. Wilson I was being trained to be a publicist and it would be good for me to meet Miss Monroe. He said she was out but he would introduce me when she got back. I waited an hour before she swept in. I couldn't decide whether or not she looked better than on the screen. Her face seemed heavily rouged, giving her cheeks a red patina like a child's doll. With her blond hair, honest blue eyes, and hint of freckles, I thought that minus the makeup her face would be that of a local Irish girl. As for the rest of her, she looked very sexy in a blue dress that barely contained her sinuous body. With all those curves she had to weigh in the 125-pound division. Joe D., all class, walked in with her, followed by a batch of reporters. The group wedged between us and I never met her.

High-society notables and famous fashion designers outnumbered the stars in the lobby. I circulated among the Beautiful People, unnoticed, eavesdropping.

Once again the radio announcer was getting carried away by a new arrival.

"Can you tell who that is, Jean?" he asked his assistant.

"I believe it's the Maharajah of Sopolm."

"You're right. I can see the Eastern costume now that he's out of the limousine."

"Yes, and there is his wife."

"Do you want to tell our listeners what she's wearing, Jean?"

"I would love to, Bob. The Maharanee is in her native dress, a flowing, plum sari brocaded with gold fawns. On her forehead is an exquisite teardrop gem. I think it's striking, Bob, don't you?"

Photographers jostled each other to get at the royal couple. In the crush, a *Herald-Tribune* reporter's eyeglasses were knocked off and broken. The royal couple posed for the front pages and centerfolds of the morning newspapers and then hurried inside. No one from the press asked the Maharajah where his kingdom of Sopolm was. It would have been an embarrassing question because there was no such land. The Maharajah was a publicity hoax concocted by a member of the staff.

"Hold this for me a second, sweetie." A woman handed me a gold-sequined purse as she tidied her face one last time in her compact mirror. For the Beautiful People the movie to be shown was only the minor feature. The momentous event for them was this brief period in the lobby when they could exhibit themselves. The women had been primping for days. Cream, steam, ointments, lotions, potions, jellies, rouges, and juices were summoned to bring out their facial beauty, along with capped dentures, color contact lenses, eyelashes, eyeshadow and retread skin. Helped by an elite fraternity of fashion designers, cosmetologists, gynecologists, and plastic surgeons, they were harnessed to wigs, wiglets, falls, fingernails, padded bras, inserts, girdles, nylons, gowns, furs, perfumed lace, and jewels, and then on premiere night they paraded into the lobby like floats at the Rose Bowl pageant.

The males in their circle were often the rugged leading men on the screen: the actors who played chiefs of commandos, rangers, and frontiersmen. Their deeds on the screen were not make-be-lieve to people in the crowd. Swooning girls ran up to one, "What-ever happened to the baby? Whatever happened to Tina's baby in *Fury Wheels?*" A number of actors puffed up as though they couldn't distinguish make-believe either.

In my eyes and to the poolroom crowd it was ridiculous to glorify as he-men these playboys with bleached hair, sunlamp tans, and manicured fingernails, who fought with fake bottles and toy knives and whose only scar was probably from an appendix operation.

At times the Beautiful People were snide about the poor. I heard one prissy heiress say, "If they had anything they'd waste it. They don't know how to handle it." This same woman was said to own ninety-seven pairs of shoes and wallow in perfumed milk baths.

And then they came, percolating out of the subway and breach-ing the line of limousines—all the old ladies of my neighborhood, with Grandma at the front capturing everyone's attention with her robust gestures and shouts to the people behind the barriers: "Thatsa my grandson inside." She was dressed in her favorite white polka dot dress, a crocheted gray shawl, and black-laced Oxfords. Clasp-ing her shawl, her cracked hands looked like a rigger's who has been out to sea all his life. The others who followed her in had natural aging faces and gray hair. "*Que bella theate'* [What a beautiful theater!]" they exclaimed, awed by the Roxy's plushness. I waited at the rear of the red carpet to escort them in. "*Gracia, gracia, Guiseppe,*" they thanked me with gusto. Ma was there too with Timmy's mother, and I heard her say, "He's with such refined people. It's such a wonderful job. I thank heaven for it." They all thought I was a big shot because of the EXPEDITER badge on my lapel and all the tickets I gave away. Timmy's father walked up to me, "Ah, Joseph, it's a fine thing you've done." In the middle of the celebrity-packed lobby, my boss was too beset with premiere chaos and starlets to notice the procession of old ladies. Grandma sat next to Debbie Reynolds during the movie. It was the biggest thrill of Grandma's life. How much could it have meant to the per-son whose ticket I gave her?

25 The faded beach-cloth awning of Charlie's Candy Store slanted down over the two front windows loaded with "back to school" displays. The regular early evening crowd was loitering out in front. Attention was divided among different games. A couple of guys were playing the finger-matching game, Sayee. Others were engrossed in "Steal the Old Man's Pack." Home from a leisurely day at 20th Century-Fox, I organized a game of Buck Buck.

"Buck, Buck, how many horns are up?" Mappy yelled, pouncing on the anchorman of my team.

"Two," I answered.

"One." He held up one finger to the kid playing pillow.

Tony Bavimo and the older guys were watching our game laughing until Frankie Tung crossed the street. Frankie was shirtless except for a leopard skin vest. The buttons were open in front to show off his shaven pectorals which had ballooned from exercising with barbells, and were glazed with salad oil. He strutted around like a matador, his muscle-bound arms stiffly arched at his sides. All heads followed the weight lifter's path into the candy store.

"Whadda ya gettin'?" Charlie lackadaisically stepped behind the counter.

"Gimme five loosies," Frankie said, patting his wave in the mirror.

"Old Golds or Lucky Strikes?"

"Luckies. Ya gotta couple of nickels fa a dime, Shorty? I wanna get some sounds outta ya jukebox."

"It don't take nickels no more, only dimes now."

"Dimes! What, is everythin' a rook."

"Don't look at me. They did a mistake raisin' it."

"Gimme change of a quarter."

Charlie handed him the coins.

"When are ya gonna get some new tunes in this thing?" Frankie scanned the selections.

"Ya got new ones in there. E2 is 'Why Doncha Believe Me?' the big hit by Joni James."

"Big hit when? Last Christmas?"

"It still gets a lotta play."

Frankie played a Bill Haley record. "We're gonna rock around the clock," Haley wailed, accompanied by blasting brass.

"Howda ya turn this thing up, Shorty? Is the switch by the socket?"

"Yeah, but don' make it too loud. I got a sick kid sleeping in back."

As he trailed after the melody with a nasal hum, Frankie began doing dynamic tension exercises with his arms.

"Look at that scumbag," Tony sneered.

"Leave 'im alone, Tone, he's in love," Blackie said. "And if he ever meets a girl it'll be a triangle. She'll love him and he'll love him."

Shaking to the rhythm and snapping his fingers, Frankie came outside where everyone was standing. "Hey, Tony!" he greeted. "I didn't know ya were out here."

"Aincha cold like that?" Tony asked, nudging me.

"Naw, it's not that cold out yet."

"Where'd ya get the tiger vest?"

"Orchard Street. It ain't tiger, Tony. It's leopard skin."

"Oh, leopard. Ya really gettin' up in the woild."

"C'mon, stop banging me up, Tony."

"Ya still liftin' weights?"

"I don't lift. I just do push-ups."

"How'd ya get such a pair of titties then?"

"Whadda ya banging me up fa, Tone?"

"Whadda ya doin' around here anyway?"

"I decided I'm not gonna stay on 11th anymore. There's nuttin' happening there."

"Yeah, so whadda ya doin' here?"

"I figured I wanna start hanging around wid youse guys."

"Hey'd ya hear that?" Tony put his arm around Frankie and turned to us. "Tung says he wants ta hang around wid us. San Diego, go get a rope." He motioned for me to bring the rope off the park's flagpole.

"C'mon, Tone, what I ever do ta you?" Tung pleaded.

"Shaddap, or I'll fuck ya where ya breathe."

I ran to the park across the street and cut the rope off the flagpole. After a violent struggle we tightened a noose around Frankie's ankles. Tony and Blackie then forced him up to the top of the Fortway Theater fire escape. Blackie fastened the rope to a steel girder and Tony tossed the weight lifter head first over the side. Walking away, Tony glanced back at the upside-down body dangling overhead. "It's a good thing ya didn't say ya wanted ta stick around." Tony said, as though he would have knifed him to a wall.

Muscles, on Fort Hamilton, were an asset or liability depending on how you got them. If a guy inherited his build or acquired it from hard work like Tony, it brought him prestige. Muscles developed from high-bar work or calesthenics were less masculine but still a plus. A borderline case was a physique hewed from working out with a crude homemade barbell. The crude implements to a degree paralleled heavy objects on a job. But to consciously go about building a body beautiful with barbells, and flagrantly exhibit it as Frankie did, was a sin and a reason to be lynched.

We kept looking back as we returned to the candy store. We were walking in small groups. Bobby turned to me, "Ya know he could get leprosy if nobody takes him down."

"How'd ya mastermind that?"

"The rope is tight around his ankles and it's gonna cut the circulation off."

"Ya *mamaluke*," Mappy butted in. "That's got nuttin' ta do wid leprosy."

"Well, if his feet ain't gettin' no blood they're gonna rot, ain't they?"

"Ya know, I think you got leprosy." Mappy sneered. "Leprosy of the brain. Yer fuckin' brain ain't there no more. It musta fell out."

When Tony left, Bobby went over and released Frankie.

The next morning I moped into the kitchen scraping away sleep flakes in my eyes.

"Why doncha ask him where he was last night until two o'clock in the morning?" Ma shrilled.

"You ask him," Dad mumbled, circling a name in the racing paper.

"Even on Thanksgiving he was out wid them friends, always wid them rough friends on the street. Find out where this boy goes."

"That's your job. "

"The young ones make a cyclone in here all day and the old ones are out gallivantin' ta all hours of the night. All you do is sit there wid your nose in the horses."

"Listen, numbskull, my mother used ta grab the razor strap of my father, may his soul rest in peace, and beat my ass until I had blisters if I got outta line. She didn't bother him every time. I'm out sweepin' streets fa the city all day, and at night I gotta go blow the horn wid the band. I got no time fa your kids."

"Fa chrissake, Ma, ya're always trying ta start somethin'." I brushed by her to get to the icebox. "Just because I come in late, right away I'm doin' wrong. None of the other guys mudders bug them the way ya're always on my back."

"I don't want you comin' in those hours, understand?"

"Yeah, sure, Ma. Ya better get some more peanut butter. This jar is almost empty."

"He's hanging around wid that bunch that shot at the teacher. Put your foot down, mister. Tell this boy you don't want him in that pool hall."

Dad thought that kids grew up by themselves, and that it didn't matter much how you treated them, their inherent nature would eventually come out. When there was talk about how one child was pampered, or not as strictly dealt with as the next, he dismissed it as immaterial. Nothing mattered from the outside, it was all within the person himself. Ma was fervently of the opposite view. She thought that the parents were responsible for how a child turned out. They shaped him the right way by teaching him the church rules and keeping him away from bad influences like the poolroom crowd. At times, Dad contradicted himself, and conceded that the kids needed disciplining, but if they did it was the mother's job. He was too busy trying to provide for us. Sometimes Ma provoked Dad into hitting me. "Are you afraid of this boy? Can't you control your own son?" That angered him more than anything I had done. Intuition warned me when Dad was going to get up from the chair. If I could make it out the door I would run away from home. By the time I was ten years old I was sleeping all over the city—on a park bench, in someone's hallway, on the subway. I would get up before dawn to steal the milk and bread stacked on the sidewalks before the stores opened.

Once I decided to become a beachcomber to escape a beating. I was going to unlock life's mysteries sifting through all the sand by the ocean. Hopping on a train to Coney Island, I imagined the sweetness of sleep under the stars on soft sand with summer air as a blanket. Pompom bursts of fireworks rocketing off the pier kept me sleepless until midnight. Then all the people left for home and the insects came out. Diggers gnawed into me, sandfleas tickled my nostrils, and mosquitoes raised itchy lumps on my face. The warm air went out with the tide and a chilly wind came in. I packed up and moved into the cab of a wrecked truck in the junkyard. By the third day I assumed Dad's anger had changed to worry so I went back home.

▸▸

26 Dutchy was at the Rec Center dance that night. She had broken off with the big talker. It had been over a year since I last saw her. Butterflies fluttered inside me as I waited for a fox-trot so I could go over and ask her to dance. She was even more angelic looking now, but that was not the main reason I was still hung up on her. Having been cut off so quickly I never saw her flaws. Also I could not forget that she had "dumped on" me. It was like losing a fight and wanting a rematch.

Her face dimpled a warm, friendly hello when she saw me. My butterfingered tongue asked what she was doing at the Rec Center. She smiled again instead of answering, as though she found my floundering amusing. I belatedly apologized for slapping her the last time we were together. I think my real motive was to mention something I had up on her. She shrugged off the incident as nothing. Dancing with her I exaggerated my job at 20th Century-Fox to impress her. She was hardly moved. I tried to be witty, straining for funny things to say. The pressure dulled my mind. I shifted into an overly sincere voice, hoping she would see me as a great personality. Before the dance ended I asked her for a date. She said she did not think of me that way anymore. She thought of me as a friend and a "nice guy" now. Flustered, I masked a stunned feeling and walked away.

"Nice guy," I fumed. "Where the hell did she get that?" Richie noticed me sulking and started goading, "Dutchy dump on you again?" I warned him to cut it out. He kept it up and egged on Neil Tarabino to do the same. I warned him too. As we were leaving the Rec Center, Neil clucked another sarcastic remark. I missiled my fist into his face. He fell back and his head crunched against the pavement. I had heard that terrible sound before with Garcicco. I ran, leaving him there with the others. The next morning I picked the *Journal-American* out of a trash can in the office to read a banner headline about a gang war. In the first paragraph I was jolted by the statement that "Neil Tarabino, one of the boys in the gang war, was near death." I began shivering, "Jesus Christ, what am I gonna do?" I felt like climbing the walls. I checked again to make sure. They must have made a mistake, I thought, there had been no gang war last night. Maybe I had mis-read the name. But when I rechecked, the paper continued that there had been a gang war on Fort Hamilton Parkway outside the McKinley Rec Center and that one of the victims, Neil Tarabino, had suffered a concussion and was in critical condition. My friends must have given the cops the gang-war story to cover up for me. I started going through the same nightmare that I went through with Garcicco. This time it was worse because Neil was a good friend. I didn't know what to do. I was not going to surrender myself to the police again. I called Richie at the lens foundry where he worked. He told me he was going to get a tattoo on his lunch hour and to meet him at Broadway Artists.

"Bizz, bizz, bizz . . . " the tattoo shop was a roused beehive of stinging electric drills. Richie leaned forward facing a tattooer. His left arm rested on a perch. The rapidly thrusting needle shot black ink under his skin. From time to time the tattoo artist wiped away drops of blood. A blue-black panther with exaggerated red claws was nearly finished. I called Richie outside.

"Whadda ya think I should do?"

"If he dies it's gonna be manslaughter. Ya know how many years dat'll be in the can? I'd cut out."

"That's what I wanna do."

"Ya better split now. If somebody opened up they might be waitin' ta bust ya at work when ya get back. How's the bread situation?"

"About twen'y-two bucks."

"I got about ten on me minus four fa the tattoo. I got anudder balloon in the bank, which we can draw out now. That'll give us . . . let's see . . . that'll give us a hundred and twen'y-eight bucks, right?"

"I wasn't figurin'."

"Yeah, that's right. It'll give us a hundred and twen'y-eight bucks. Let's grab the next bus ta Miami."

"What about ya job?"

"Fuck it. I was goin' ta pack it in anyway. I awready have enough weeks in ta start collectin' checks again."

"Thanks, Rich."

"Fa what? You'd do the same thing fa me, wouldn't ya? So that's how it's gonna be."

Sailors shouldering sea bags swung out of the New York Greyhound Terminal. Inside, on the main concourse, opposite flows of hurried people sieved through each other. A loudspeaker garbled off a salvo of towns en route to Philadelphia. As I waited outside a phone booth, a woman getting off a bus came up to me. She pointed to a message scrawled on a piece of paper pinned to her blouse. "I cannot speak English. Please take me to the nearest welfare station."

I shrugged and she walked on. Minutes later Richie stepped out of the phone booth. I tightened up.

"The hospital got him off the critical list. He's gonna be awright."

"Wooh! Thank God, that's a ton."

"Ya can stop worrying. We're gonna have a ball in Florida. It'll be a vacation now."

"What else they tell ya?"

"He's clamming up. He won't tell them anything. Ya gotta give him credit. He's a stand-up guy."

"I hope nobody else squeals."

"I think it's still smart to take off till things cool off."

It was going to be a violation of my probation to leave the state. I was also going to miss my appointment with the probation officer. To prevent a complaint to the court, I sent a bottle of Haig and Haig Scotch to Mr. Mirgon; I knew he enjoyed his whisky.

▼▲

Hissing air brakes punctuated the delays as the Greyhound faltered in traffic at the Lincoln Tunnel. After crossing under the river, the bus swerved onto the turnpike. We passed out of the gray smog over the city into the clean, fresh air of the countryside. It was our first time away from New York, and as the bus approached some foothills, Richie nudged me. "Look, mountains."

Riding along we talked about Richie's boxing matches. The whole neighborhood had turned out to see him in his P.A.L. debut. His opponent was a former Olympic champion. It was a kamikaze match. The guy flattened Richie five times, but Richie was game— he popped up like Rasputin every time.

"Come on, Kraut." We had cheered him on until the referee finally stopped it.

Richie really didn't fit in with a bunch of Italians. Bobby was Polish and Timmy Irish, but their mothers were Italian. Richie was German on both sides and he looked it with his light hair and blue eyes. To make up for his lack of Italian blood, he adopted the name Carmine Tillelli, the real name of boxer Joey Giardello. Coming from an all-Italian neighborhood Richie felt inferior being German (which is a switch; Hitler is reputed to have said, "When we finish with the others we'll send the troops into Italy for two hours"). No one ever called Richie by his adopted name. It irked him, but it was too hard to change over after so many years.

Richie was further out of place because he came from a show-business family. While our fathers were laborers, his was a comedian who had played the Palace. His mother and aunts had been chorus girls, and his sister Janet was in a chorus line in Las Vegas. Richie's mother told us that her husband helped Milton Berle get started in vaudeville. None of us believed her until she showed us a scrapbook with a photo of Berle with his arm around Richie's father. The last doubts were removed one night on Broadway when Richie went over to Henny Youngman as he was getting out of a cab and told the famous comedian whose son he was. Youngman took us all into Lindy's for cheesecake "for old times sake."

Before Richie finished the second grade his father took off. Her income gone, Mrs. Berder was forced to leave the suburbs of Chicago with her four children and move in with Richie's aunts above a pizza place in Brooklyn. Growing up in a household of women made Richie a soft kid. Once Whitey, the leader of the Rampers, slapped him and he cried. But Richie changed when Tony came out of prison. He and I were shadows to Tony, competing to be his protégé. Both of us tried to show him how much we wanted to be like him. He boxed in the P.A.L. so we entered the P.A.L. He walked as though he were carrying barrels under his arms so we walked that way. No one else among the younger boys copied him as much as we. Mappy was completely independent of him. Timmy was more impressed with Johnny Shira. Bobby obeyed his mother too much.

At first Tony snubbed Richie because he was bigoted against non-Italians. But Richie had some of his father's talent, and he got Tony to like him by amusing him. He did a vaudeville act in the poolroom, complete with a soft-shoe routine, a cuestick under his

arm for a cane. He could also do great imitations and had a match-
less tongue for ridicule, a main source of entertainment in the poolroom. Richie often came to Bobby's rescue against Mappy. One
time Mappy was putting Bobby down for boasting he had more
girls.

"Go see where ya gotta go, huh ishgabibil," Mappy mocked.
"You ain't got half my harem."

"What harem?" Richie moved in. "The only harem ya got are
those five fingers on ya right hand that jerk ya little hurdy-gurdy.
You couldn't get laid in a women's detention home wid a handful
of pardons."

"Shaddap, Kraut. Ya wish you could score as much as me."

"Mappy," Richie grinned, "lifting weights did wonders fa ya
body. It's too bad they don' have barbells ya can lift fa ya face."

"I'll make out better than you any day."

"Wid who? Zazu Pitts? She's about your speed."

"Ya not serious that ya think ya make out better than me?"

"Is a pig's ass pork?"

"Ya wanna compare the last month?"

"Mappy, we all know you're errychay. Why do you have these
great dreams that ya think ya're a big lover. It's a wonderful thing
ta save yourself. Remember in *The Egyptian*: 'A man's greatest gift
is his innocence.' "

▄▄

We were sitting in the second row of the bus behind the driver.
In front of us a girl's head and milkmaid breasts stuck out as she
leaned in the aisle to chitchat with a friend across the way. A salesman in the window seat next to the buxom girl intruded in their
conversation. Anger amplified their remarks so I could hear what
they were talking about. The buxom girl believed that religion was
the key to happiness. She felt fortunate being close to the church.
Practicing the true spiritual life she had found inner peace. Earl,
the salesman, criticized religion, saying it stifled natural instincts.
"If you read your Bible," she told him, "you would know that the
human race is being punished for Eve's evil desire. We would have
been allowed to live forever if it hadn't been for her sin, which
wasn't eating the apple. That was only symbolical for you know
what." Throughout their argument she harped on how vile it is to
be a slave to the senses and how happy she was living the spiritual

life. I was drawn to her words because I thought any girl who talks
so much about the "sins of the flesh" must be obsessed with sex. I
had seen the movie *Rain* in which a preacher hurled fire-and-brim-
stone at a whore for her lustful ways and then raped her. Any
fanaticism about virtue aroused my suspicion. I rummaged about
for an excuse to sit next to her.

At the next rest station when everyone left the bus, I plumped
myself into the salesman's seat. He pouted but granted my plea to
uncramp my legs for a while, there being more room to stretch out
in the front row. Soon I was giving the girl a snow job about my
stint as an altar boy. I could detect a fondling instinct welling up in
her. Stretches of land and time passed and I kept slinging it about
my religious devotion. At night the country darkened and the bus
driver shut off the cabin lights as we rolled along through a dense
forest. A gentle rain pattered on the roof. I took Earl's coat down
from the rack overhead and put it over us. Silently our bodies re-
sponded to the warmth. We were so close our hands lightly
touched and then they joined. We moved on to kissing and whis-
pers. In a gradual sequence her face came down to my lap. In the
morning she resumed her pose as a madonna. It was as though
nothing had happened during the night.

After twenty-nine hours on the road we arrived in Daytona. She
got off for the stock-car races. I told her I would look her up on the
way back because I enjoyed talking to her. I don't think anyone
knew what happened between us with the possible exception of
Earl whose coat may have been marked.

We continued on to sunny Miami. At first it looked like a para-
dise with the grand hotels, palm trees, tropical fruit stands, and
lush beaches. But after a while my attitude was that perhaps Miami
was a nice place to visit but no place to live. I missed the close
neighborhood feeling I had known in Brooklyn.

Richie was sincere when he said he would withdraw all his
money from the bank, but spending it was another matter. I used
up all I had for the bus ticket so I had to rely on his generosity to
eat. He bought us chocolate malts for breakfast, lunch and supper
every day. A boil formed at the center of my behind giving it the
profile of a Prussian helmet. We slept on a college campus known
for its basket-weaving course. For recreation he bought us a softball
so we could play catch. I wrote Timmy to wire me money at the
Western Union office. He replied with a telegram saying that he

was going to come down with Al, Bobby, and Charms. They would be arriving the next day.

They rode down in Timmy's new Olds 88. His mother had bought it for him a few months before when he turned eighteen. She was giving him his graduation present early. In June he would be graduating from St. John's University with a degree in philosophy.

They brought good news with them. Neil was being a loyal friend. The police couldn't get anything out of him. Mr. Mirgon was happy about the Scotch and wasn't going to report my absence.

We checked into the Blackstone Hotel near Collins Avenue and then went to Wolfie's for a pastrami supper. Timmy swiped a waitress' checkpad and made out another check charging us only for Cel-rays. It was easy to get away with in a large restaurant where you paid at the cash register.

We traveled up to the beach at Fort Lauderdale the next day to meet coeds. There were plenty there but they shunned us. Only Timmy could converse with them. The rest of us had to be content enjoying the suburban landscape.

In the evening we drove over to the Hurricane Club to see a striptease show. After the act the strippers sat at our table. They tried to guile us into buying them drinks by giving us the same "I'll meet you later" line that we had been onto since age fifteen after being fleeced by dime-a-dance places in New York.

The next morning we threw our suitcases out the back window of the hotel and left. We headed northwest for Hallendale. Al had relatives who owned a cottage there and he was given access to it. On the outskirts of the town we stopped at a newly erected housing tract. Inside a model home a mannikin family occupied the furniture in normal family postures. Before leaving Timmy rearranged everyone so that an incestuous orgy was taking place.

In Hallendale I got a letter from Ma who thought I was in Florida on vacation. One of the things she mentioned in her letter was that Anthony was preparing to take the policeman's exam. I thought it was strange; here I was running away from the police and my brother was on the brink of becoming one.

Nothing much happened the remainder of our stay, aside from more Timmy Kelly pranks. He pinned a beetle on the back of Danny Charms' neck one night while he was asleep. When Danny woke up Timmy told him not to move because there was a scorpion on his neck.

When we returned to New York I was given a friendly reception by my probation officer. My only wrong insofar as he knew was a frolic to Florida. Neither he nor anyone else on the side of the law knew that I had gone to escape arrest. Neil never opened up. Everything was much the same as before, except that I no longer had a job at 20th Century-Fox. I found a new job as a pinboy at Fortway Alleys.

◥◥

171

3

NOTHING CHANGES AT ROSELAND

27 The heavy black ball rolled down the smooth alley and scattered the ten wooden targets. I hopped off the backstop, reset the ten pins, and returned the bowler's ball. Within a second there was another burst of pins in the adjacent alley. I hopped over the guard rail and repeated the same process. Being a pinboy was proving to be a sweaty, wearisome job. I bounced back and forth between lanes all night setting upended pins. I dreaded setting up for spares because you had to retrieve the same man's ball twice. To make things easier for myself I would kick over the seven or tenpin to give the bowler a strike. It was a common practice with pinboys.

Our pay was ten cents a line. On a busy league night I would pin a hundred individual games and think during the effort that those dimes were really adding up, but at three in the morning when I was paid it only came to ten dollars. The place was open seven nights a week. Our only break came on ladies' night. We strung out one pinboy per three lanes to recover their gently swirled balls, which rolled down the gutter or sometimes whisked off a pin or two while the rest of us played cards in the dressing room. Sometimes I would go to the office, which was up steps and had a window overlooking everything like in a gambling casino. Paunchy bow-tied Nick Marotta, the owner, was often up there scheduling leagues. I liked Nick and enjoyed talking to him. Whenever any of the men needed dues money for a union book to get started in a trade, Nick donated the money. He was always advising me to go back to night school, but I had no will to do so. I had already tried four times and the longest I ever lasted was two weeks. Nick, who was an immigrant from Italy, believed that education was a poor man's best opportunity to better himself. Not many others in the neighborhood shared his attitude. They thought a craft or a business were the ladders.

There was a bar in the rear of the bowling alley and a lot of the guys dropped down on cold nights. They brought their drinks to the spectator section behind the players' benches. One night Tony Bavimo was sitting by himself with his foot up on the bench for my two alleys. He wasn't bothering anyone, but one of the bowlers doing badly turned around irritably and barked, "Hey, Jocko, ya mind getting ya prima donna feet off the dam' bench."

"Who da fuck are ya talkin' ta?" Tony leaped to his feet and chopped him across the windpipe with a forearm. The bowler fell to his haunches, gasping and coughing blood. Hurdling the back-rest, Tony slashed at the man's face with kicks. Well-intentioned members of the bowler's party and others from nearby alleys intervened to restrain Tony. Snarling "you cocksuckers," he crumpled the first man who tried to hold him, but they swamped him and latched him to the floor with a dozen arms. I zipped up the bowling alley stairs and across the street to Pop's for help. "Tony's havin' trouble in the bowlin' alley," I blurted in the doorway.

Card games stopped cold, money was left on the tables. Guys dropped their cuesticks on the floor. Others carried them out, disregarding Pop's protests. An avalanche of Fort Hamilton Boys descended on the bowling alley. The sight of our leader being roughed up by strangers provoked us to a massacre. The frightened Mr. Marotta, who tried to talk back the onslaught, was the first to get cracked on the head with a cuestick. A spearhead of the boys broke apart the clump over Tony, and the rest of us fanned out over the twelve alleys. I swung wildly because of slippery footing at a faceless man in a yellow bowling shirt. More nimble in rubber shoes, he wrestled me around trying to hold my arms. I could tell he hadn't been in many fights because he was afraid to close his fist and hit me with it. My habit was to punch, not wrestle. I caught him a shorty to the temple. He yawed out of the lane stumbling to the floor. His delirious wife raved at me. I turned away to see who needed help. Tony smashed a heavy beer bottle on a man's forehead, drenching him with foam and blood. The man floundered into a wall with puddles of blood trailing him. Bleeding like a ruptured main, he began to convulse. I felt a spasm to puke. Another maniac member of the gang was hurtling bowling balls at the ducking bartender and shattering the bar mirrors and bottles.

Thieves in the gang didn't bother with people. Using a portable coat rack as a rammer, they ravaged the jukebox to get at its coins. When someone yelled "law," we ran, leaving the place devastated, with bodies strewn all over the lanes. All the police could do when they arrived was call for ambulances.

The bowling alley was padlocked for repairs; the costly damage would take days to clean up. With the place closed I was at least temporarily out of work. Maybe I could go back when it reopened, but I had a feeling I wouldn't bother. Being a pinboy was like a tire spinning on snow. You didn't get anywhere. Manager was the only position to be promoted to, and Nick's cousin was securely ensconced in that position. The next evening Nick came to the pool-room to talk to us. With his head in bandages, he told us he was willing to forget everything if we gave him our word we would never start trouble in his place again. "I don't mind you coming down to hang out," he said in his sentimental voice, "but I want you to act like gen-tle-men." We found out from him that a number of the people hospitalized were hurt seriously but no one critically. One of those hurt badly was from the Avenue U Boys. It was on the grapevine that they were coming back with the Bath Beach Boys and Rampers to waste us. Over the years a vengeful rivalry raged between Avenue U and Fort Hamilton. During the 1940s the sections rumbled twice, once at Coney Island and another time on the trolley tracks outside of Pop's. They creamed Fort Hamilton both times. Dicky Boy, their leader then, was a New York heavy-weight champion in the Golden Gloves. Stories circulated around the borough about what a powerhouse he was. They said he could punch holes in a garage door with his fist.

By the 1950s a new generation had taken over both gangs. Angelique, Dicky Boy's younger brother, was the new leader of Avenue U. A dedicated professional boxer, he didn't get involved in rumbles but brought glory to the neighborhood by his victories in the ring. Another tough street battler, Kya, led the gang in rumbles. Before Tony, the leader of Fort Hamilton was Augie Chief. When he quieted down to become a family man, the neighborhood splintered into a half dozen smaller gangs. Tony put them all together again when he came out of Elmira. The gangs of the new generation skirmished once at a dance hall. Tony left Kya and four other guys laying on the floor.

If the rumor was right that Bath Beach and the Rampers were coming too, we wouldn't have a prayer without help. Bath Beach was one of the toughest sections in Brooklyn. The Rampers had Whitey, who a lot of people thought was more than Tony's match. The older guys had gang connections all over the city.

New York had about two hundred gangs. The ones I had heard of were the Shamrocks, Overlords, Commanches, Copians, Tigers, Hatfields, Garfield Boys, Robins, Nits, Mulberry Boys, Rockets, Greene Avenue Stompers, Bristol Friends, and the Canarsie Boys.

Calls were made to Coney Island's Madeon Brothers and Louie Talessy in South Brooklyn to stand up with us.

Everyone figured if the attack came it would be around eight o'clock when most of us would be on the corner. We were ready for them. Bombardiers lurked on the rooftops with garbage cans loaded with bricks. The hallways bristled with crude clubs. I saw car jacks, cement-filled pipes, bus-sign bars, bats, and cuesticks. Some guys were packing zip guns of two types, a .22 caliber hand piece and a .22 rifle. The small hand piece was made from a snippet of lead pipe—about the length of a stogie cigar—cut from a curtain rod or a car's radio antenna. The tube from the latter provided a truer bore for a .22 bullet. I also heard of guys ripping out the pipe in a street lamp for the barrel. The pipe was fastened with wire and tape to a whittled block of wood. For the hammer and trigger the square metal rod that connects door knobs was used. The end of the rod, which served as the hammer, was filed to a point. The parts were attached with small rubber bands. Then a heavy rubber band was stretched from the forward end of the block, underneath the pipe nozzle, to the lip of the hammer. Releasing the rubber band forced the firing pin into the cartridge, exploding the bullet out. The gun was very inaccurate and only had a range of about two blocks. It lasted for maybe three firings before it wore out or exploded in your hand. A homemade rifle was put together the same way except for the length of the barrel. The most feared guys in a rumble were the puny runts who had the lunacy to shoot a gun in your face.

I felt alone in the quiet hall, I guess because I had never seen many of the faces around me. They came from as far as the East Side. Most were in their early twenties. The Avenue U gang was supposed to be that age range, too. I was only a few years younger at seventeen but still felt like a kid compared to a guy of twenty.

The sides were clear now. Our troops were in the hallways and the invaders would attack in cars. I wondered how I would know our allies once the rumble started and everything turned topsy-turvy. I regretted coming around. If I had decided to do something else I would never have known about the rumble until it was over. I could have gone to the city with Johnny. "No use if-ing about it." I found out I was locked in. "My balls are on the line."

Eight o'clock arrived and nothing happened. An hour later there was still no sign of them. Gangs from Brownsville, the East Side, and other far-off places began to leave, believing it was a false alarm. By ten o'clock only the Fort Hamilton Boys remained to defend their turf. Finally around eleven Tony called the thing off.

Our mood changed from tension to buoyancy. Everyone left the corner to go somewhere. I squeezed into Lefty's packed car and we buzzed down to the Casa D'Ameche Café. Taking a couple of booths in the rear, we ordered pitchers of beer. As we sat around drinking we gave our versions of how we would have ruined them if they had come.

"Why doncha think they showed?" Cord asked.

"Ah, they're shit widout Dicky Boy," Blackie said. "They punked out, the creeps."

"Nobody wants ta fuck wid this neighborhood," Lefty said.

Guzzling beer in the dim café lulled me into a serene, secure feeling. What a relief that the thing fizzled. I really didn't care why they didn't show up. I was happy about it. I hated rumbles because they were crazy. Being good with your hands didn't mean anything in a rumble.

"They're on their way," Timmy whanged the door open. "I just saw them. They went by the poolroom, about ten carloads."

My impulse was, "Let's leave this place." The pale looks around me signaled the same reaction. But Tony wasn't budging. When I saw he wasn't running away I knew I had to stick. So did the other guys. Scared shitless, we moved slowly toward the door. Nothing was said. As the cars screeched into the curb and opening doors scraped the sidewalk, Tony bolted out ahead of us. He started yelling at them, "Get back in those fuckin' cars." Then he shot the guy nearest him. The train of cars closed their doors and pulled out. Tony ran after them shooting at the windows. They didn't fire back. Either they were scared or didn't have any guns. It turned out to be both, because they were back in an hour blasting the café with shotguns. Everyone dove to the floor as the pellets pierced the glass front. An innocent shoeshine boy was nicked in the back. They made two passes but never stopped to get out of the cars again. When it was all over we considered the outcome a big win for Fort Hamilton.

゠゠゠゠゠゠゠゠゠゠゠゠゠゠゠゠゠゠゠゠゠゠゠゠゠゠゠゠゠゠゠゠゠゠゠゠゠゠゠

28 Shoes—the provider of foot comfort, protector against weather, source of corns, incubator of fungi, memorializer of infancy, symbol of status, equipment for spying, elevator for short men, erotic stimulant to fetishists, gavel for dictators, traction for athletes, nest for scorpions, stabilizer for ballerinas, blockbuster to insects, and family shelter to a fabled old lady—have given me employment at three different times in my life.

As a kid in short pants I became a Sunday morning bootblack. I would hawk to passing churchgoers: "Wanna shine, mister? Only a dime. Ya gonna have ya foot up on the pew."

There was one regular customer, a guy in a natty suit who would lean against the building and clunk his needle-nose shoe down on my homemade shinebox. "Gimme one, kid," he'd say, and I'd go into my polishing routine. I don't know what this guy did for a living—I think he was a truck driver—but when I got down on my knees and started pampering his feet he metamorphosed into a bank president; his shoulders shot back and one hand dipped casually into a pocket while he perused the folded newspaper in the other, wagging his head knowingly as he read.

Dabbing on the orange liquid cleaner with my small brush, I spanked the leather skin with a large brush until it was as smooth as a barber-shaven face. Then I patted on the oxblood wax and swished with my rag. I repeated the waxing, adding a bit of spit, and resumed swishing. From time to time I would pause to assess the sheen. Experience told me when a shoe was at its maximum shine. When I finished, the pointy shoes were glinting Arabian daggers.

"How's 'at?" I'd say, looking up at him. Without a word or a glance he'd take a quarter from his pocket and dramatically flip it to the ground. Why he flipped it I never knew, but that's what he did every time. Maybe he wanted the neighborhood to know what a generous tipper he was, or maybe, in his momentary incarnation as a bank president, to him money was but a trifle.

When I was ten I moved into my second shoe job. I was the janitor for Sal's Shoe Repair Shop. I would go in once a week to clean the tar-blobbed, stained, gluey, gooey, grimy machines for sanding and stitching. I stewed all week in dread. That was a habit with me, worrying and procrastinating over chores that could have been done and out of the way in short time.

Now that I had left the bowling alley, I was again in the shoe business. This time as a machine operator in a shoe factory. My job called for me to set material in a press and punch it with statistics by stepping on a foot pedal. The owner's obnoxious twenty-year-old son managed my floor. He strutted around with his hands in his pockets looking over everyone's shoulder. A high-school dropout himself, he still thought it was the natural order that he should be the one managing the floor, as though it took a special talent to give simple orders. I boiled working under him. He was always taking me away from my machine to go on his personal errands. If production lulled he would send me for the golf clubs in his car so he could practice putts in the office. During the coffee break he would send me out for his pie a la mode. I even had to go get his theater tickets uptown and bring them to his apartment. I felt like a lackey handing him his tickets in front of a girl close to my age. For some reason it really grated me to be bossed by someone young. I often came home angry.

▲▼▲

One night after work at the shoe factory I went to the poolroom and there was a show going on outside. Richie was imitating all of the typical performers on the Ted Mack show. He even played Ted Mack. "Tell us, Shorty, how did you get started with your one-man band."

"Well, Mr. Mack," Richie answered himself with an Ozark accent, "I was sitting around the barn one day hankering ta find somethin' ta doo . . . . I picked up a musical saw, and then before ya know it I was playing spoons with my toes, and then I got around ta tootin' in a cider jug, too."

Richie's last imitation was the Pocatello, Iowa, Xavier High School Girls' Drum and Bugle Corps.

The older guys then requested him to put on his street-corner production of Shane. Timmy and I co-starred with him.

Richie leaned back in the dusk with his elbows braced on a car hood. He glared at Timmy, who was sitting on a bushel in front of Pop's. Timmy put his chin on his clasped hands and smirked. Everyone in the pool hall flocked out to watch. I bow-legged over to Richie. "I wouldn't pull on Wilson if I was you, Shane."

"Shut up, ya stinkin' old man," he snapped at me.

Bobby peeked down from the roof aiming a cuestick.

"I've heard a lot about you, Wilson," Richie stared at Timmy.

"What have you heard, Shane?" Timmy answered in a nasty, nasal tone.

"I've heard that you're a low-down, no good Yankee liar."

"Prove it, Shane."

"Okay, break it up," ordered a voice from the 66th Precinct squad car pulling up.

We picked up the props and hurried across the street to resume our act. The west corner of 69th Street was over the boundary line that separated the 64th and 66th precincts. Whoever complained would now have to call the 64th Precinct if he wanted to stop the show. Mappy lagged behind the rest of us trying to light a cigarette in the wind.

"I told ya ta move," snarled a wiry cop, getting out of the squad car.

Mappy looked over his shoulder with a sarcastic simper, but started for the other side.

"Why you little guinea bastard," the officer rushed at him with a kick, "get the fuck out of here."

Put down, kicked in front of everyone, but leery to hit the law, Mappy did the next most face-saving thing he could do. He stood his ground. This further incited the cop to more kicks. Most times his foot sank mutely into the flesh of Mappy's thighs, but you could hear other kicks crack on his shins. Mappy anchored himself grim-faced and refused to budge.

The rest of us watched from the other side of the street, tending to move back on an impulse to help, but afraid to break loose in case the cop panicked and pulled his gun. It remained a one-sided battering until the cop slurred Mappy's family. "I'll teach ya how to act," he ranted. "Your fuckin' family never did."

"Don't you talk about my family, ya bastard." Mappy's fingers gored into the policeman's chest and slammed him against the Fortridge window. The incident ticked off in seconds. As the other cop got out of the car to go to the aid of his partner, Mappy's older brother Jackie lunged at him. The policeman went for his gun, but before he could unholster it, Jackie hit him across the face and knocked him to the pavement. All of us mobbed onto the scene, grabbing hold of the second cop as he got up, but not knowing what to do with him. Mappy, sputtering curses, furious, overpowered the first cop and whipped him around by the shirt, draining his face, popping the badge and buttons, and finally ripping out a swath of blue. His partner, whom we had pinned to the floor, must have radioed the station before he got out of the car and he must have put in a 1013—Assist Patrolman Call—to which all cars in the vicinity must respond. Sirens were converging on the corner from every direction. Whirling red lights came into view. A slew of green squad cars darted to the corner with their grills to the curb. My heart leaped as nightsticks clanked against the opening doors. We broke to get away. Instead of running with the others, I turned my back on the police and casually walked into the Fortridge. I sat down at the counter between two truck drivers. Shots were fired outside, halting those who headed for the street. Thirteen were caught and lined up facing the Fortridge window with their arms and legs spread apart. The corner was teeming with cops. It looked like the whole 66th Precinct was out there. An emergency unit administered first-aid to the two policemen who had been roughed up. Their buddies were chafing to club the Mappito brothers, but the sirens had brought a big crowd of spectators.

A strapping, gruff, carrot-headed sergeant flipped a pad and went down the line. "Alright, gimme ya names."

"Joseph Mappito."

"Jack Mappito."

"Alfred Bagilla."

"James Marano."

"Carmine Tillclli."

"Danny Charmsalupo."

"Vincent Fazio."

"Anthony Lamonica."

"Ernest Amrosio."

"Vito Carpucci."

"Quido Pinolla."

"Timothy Kelly."

"C'mere, you." The sergeant guided Timmy over to the hardware store entrance. "Whadda you doin' wid these guinea bastards?"

"I don't even know them, Officer. I was waiting for the bus here."

"Awright, Kelly," the officer said in a friendly voice. "You stay here, and when things quiet down we'll let you go."

Minutes later Timmy's mother charged through the crowd, pushing and pulling everyone aside, and reached out for Timmy crying, "*Figlio mio, figlio mio.*"

"Is that yar mother?" The sergeant curled his lip at Timmy.

"Yeah."

"Why you guinea bastard," he snorted and backhanded Timmy in the face.

Rosie Kelly's liquid green eyes iced with fury. "Don't you touch my boy!" she screamed in high C, and buzzsawed into the sergeant, walloping him with some solid whacks before she was overcome by hysteria and fainted on the sidewalk. The sergeant dispatched another cop to get a glass of water while he kneeled down to revive her. Rosie awakened as fiery as before. When she saw the sergeant in front of her she threw the water in his face and flailed at him again. They finally restrained her with handcuffs, and Timmy was quickly shunted into the paddy wagon with the others and taken to the station house.

13 TOUGH GUYS
BATTER 2 COPS;
GUNS QUELL 'EM

Thirteen young toughs ganged up on a radio car team in the Borough Park section of Brooklyn last night, and for 10 hectic minutes the two cops were pounded, pummeled, punched, kicked and robbed of their nightsticks.

Only the appearance of two more policemen with drawn guns ended the fight.

All Are Booked

Hostilities over, five hoodlums were booked at the Borough Park police station on felonious assault charges and the other eight were charged with disorderly conduct.

The next day the *Daily News* reported the police version of the incident. Those whose families could raise the money were bailed out of jail. Mappy's image was different now. As Al said, "He kicked the shit out of a cop. That took a lot of balls." I was eager to find out what happened at the police station and took off for Mappy's house as soon as I arrived home from work. A block from his house I could hear his father's opera records. The Mappitos lived on the top floor of a four-story building. When I stepped inside the building, the resonant voice of Mario Del Monarco filled the hallway. For twenty years Mr. Mappito, a longshoreman, had given every extra cent to his mistress: music. A behemoth of a hi-fi console swallowed up half the living room. Columns of stacked records grew up to the ceiling. Mr. Mappito was in a sleeveless T-shirt at the kitchen table, listening to the music coming from the open door behind him. His triceps bulged at the slightest tensing of his arms. The sauce-stained tablecloth was cleared except for a half empty gallon of red wine. Mr. Mappito's face was flush from the warmth of the wine and the spicy spaghetti in his belly. He seemed entranced, reveling in his senses, as he listened to a soothing serenade with his eyes closed. From time to time he delicately pressed imaginary buttons on the stogie cigar in his mouth as if he were playing a flute. A romantic aria from *La Boheme* spun on next and Mr. Mappito, belting in his loudest voice, joined Del Monarco in a duet.

Mappy's family was obviously unshaken by the trouble with the police. Both of his parents came from the tough Mulberry section on the lower East Side. Mr. Mappito was the oldest and most respected brother in a family of ten boys. Some of Mappy's uncles who were only in their twenties had been involved in gun battles with the police. After one shooting his Uncle Frank came to hide at Mappy's apartment. The Mappitos were a close Sicilian family. If the rules of the law were broken by his sons, Mr. Mappito did not get upset. Only his rules were inviolable. Respect for the family was the highest order.

Growing up on the East Side in the same building with nine rugged uncles who all looked up to his father made Mappy more strong-willed and sure of himself than any of us. He was completely independent of Tony Bavimo. Being Sicilian might have also been a reason. Traditionally, Sicilians have favored extreme individualism. Personal vendettas plague Sicily because the individual feels he doesn't need the law.

Mrs. Mappito, with arms like steamrollers, was washing dishes at the sink. "Would ya like somethin' ta eat, Sarry?" she asked.

"What?" I tried to outshout the opera.

"Would ya like somethin' ta eat?"

"No, thanks, Jenny."

"C'mon, I'll call that bastard son of mine."

I followed Jenny through a short corridor narrowed by stacked seltzer cases. She knocked on the bathroom door. "Sarry's here." Then listened. "He'll be right out," she said.

"What?"

"He'll be right out."

While I was waiting for Mappy some of the other guys came over. We all went downstairs and sat on the baker's stoop, going over the details of the fight.

"No, that's not what happened," Al said. "He reached fa his gun as he was goin' down."

"Don't tell me. I was five feet away when Jackie corked him. He went fa the gun first," Richie insisted.

"What about fat Quido trying to run away," Timmy laughed.

The guttural grind of accelerating engines startled us. Whirring up 64th Street, a column of green police cars arrowed toward the bakery. Another column speedily approached the intersection from Eleventh Avenue. The whole 66th Precinct was attacking to get personal revenge for yesterday. No longer laughing, we jumped off the stoop like deer smelling hunters. The police-car columns interlocked around the corner. Cops sprang out grumbling curses and lashing with their nightsticks. Bobby tried to escape between the cars but was headed off and overtaken. The cops heaved him against the building, working over his gut with nightsticks until he puked. I hurdled a fence into a yard. Small nails punctured my hands going over. I saw the blood but couldn't feel anything. The jingling of handcuffs followed me over the fence. I scooted up a clothesline pole and swung onto a garage roof where I crouched, listening by the drainpipe. The cop who had come in after me was standing below breathing heavy. He flicked on his searchlight and looked around for awhile. When he went back out I raised my head to watch the orgy taking place. Society's guardians of law and order were splitting open skulls. I couldn't believe it. We were supposed to be the wild element with no respect for anything. But for the police to act the same way . . . what the hell is sane if even they resort to rumbles?

29 Lanky Norman Hilson skittered his hand over the wet strands of his flaxen hair, applying pressure where it got shorter and stalked up. His head bobbed and weaved trying to find a clean patch on the pool hall's rest room mirror. The law prohibited anyone under sixteen from being in a pool hall and Norman looked younger than his fifteen years, but Pop, nearing ninety, had long ago lost the ability to judge ages. After combing his hair Norman dried his hands thoroughly with a paper towel and sprinkled them with powder. Moisture acted as a glue on a poolplayer's hands, powder a lubricant, and the aim was a smooth stroke. Leering at Norman's actions from the other side of the hall, Tony flicked his fist at Blackie. "That kid's got some sweet ass."

"I can't believe you," Blackie shook his head. "Ya threw off how many girls last night? And now ya lookin' ta put it up this kid's ass."

"I go fa that light meat, it's sweet."

"That's jail bait. Get ya mind on the game."

"What am I goin' fa?" Tony's eyes returned to the table.

"We're up to the six ball."

"Check out this reverse English." He posed his stick.

"Seven of us were playing pillball on the table next to Tony. "Pick up a pill." I overturned a plastic milk bottle spilling M&M-size numbered objects on the table. Each player was given a pill bearing a number corresponding to a ball in the rack. The first player to sink his number took the cash pot.

Tony, deep in his game with Blackie, forgot about Norman, but when the game was over he sat down leering at him again. He joked to others around him about how he would love to see that kid's pants down. I laughed, not taking Tony seriously. Norman smiled feebly too, but his shooting grew unsteady. Meanwhile the audience swelled as more and more of the older guys drifted into the poolroom and sat down by Tony. Their laughter became a mental spotlight to Norman. Flustered, he miscued his next shot. Then the laughter receded into whispering. Suddenly four guys jumped up and muzzled Norman. Fright gagged him. Then he begged, "Don't, please don't." Disregarding his words, they yanked off his clothes and threw him face down on top of the pool table. He tried to squirm but they each tugged on a limb so that he was spread-eagle. Tony, half smiling and half serious, climbed up on the pool table and unzipped his pants. Then an agonized cry resounded through the hall.

Months before Tony had committed another perverse act in the poolroom. Olie, a forty-year-old, soupy-eyed wino, had straggled in to ask, "Can anybody spare a dime?"

"Whadda ya gimme fa it?" Tony asked, holding out a coin.

The desperate wino followed Tony down the stairs to the poolroom cellar. Cord peeped and relayed what was happening. The wino was on his knees a few steps below Tony on the stairs. Reaching up to Tony's fly, he uttered, "Now let's see, what do we have here?"

To the guys who had been in stir both incidents were nothing. They still considered Tony straight. In the street world only the male who took the submissive role was called a queer. The first reaction of the younger guys to the incident with Norman was disgust, but eventually we saw it as further proof of Tony's *spoostiness* (years later Norman bragged in prison about how he knew Tony). Only Tony would do such a wild, maniac act in broad daylight on a pool table. Anything extraordinary he did, even if repulsive, added to his charisma. Some guys were even talking about how virile it showed Tony to be, still lusting for any form of sex after a full night of lovemaking. It seemed Tony could get away with anything. The most unforgivable, despicable sexual act a man could commit according to poolroom mores was to have oral sex with a woman. Yet everyone knew Tony forced girls to let him do it to them. He never showed any guilt nor did anyone put him down for his lapses. Tony lived almost completely free of all rules.

When word got back to Norman's older brother about what happened, he wanted to get someone to maim Tony, but it was hard to find anyone who could. Tony only weighed 150 pounds but he could floor guys the size of piano movers. Once at the movies a mountainous man twice Tony's weight slapped him for being noisy. In the next instant the man was toppling to the ground from a left hook. There were a few guys from the old Fort Hamilton Boys who might have been a match for Tony: bruisers like Augie Chief, the ex-leader, who could ring the bell at Coney swinging a sledgehammer with one hand; and Ernie Mo, who buckled iron bars by running into them with his chest. But none of them took on Tony. The feeling was you couldn't beat him to settle anything. With his *spoosty* head, he would come back to fight you again and again. And if you kept beating him with your hands he would come back with a bat and then a gun. The only way to win against him was to kill him. But aside from the risks, Norman's brother wouldn't find anyone in the neighborhood to help smash Tony because everyone was Tony's friend.

The feast of St. Rosalie began the next week. The floodlit church grounds looked like a carnival dotted with game booths and gambling tents. People rambled around the barren dirt grounds spurring up clouds of dust, and tried their luck at the dice wheel, card wheel, and the rest. Foxy Timmy Kelly was a winner every time. He put his money down when the wheel stopped. Outside on the street, which the police had closed to traffic for three blocks, swarms of people strolled under the rainbows of colored lights arching across the buildings. Food stands hemming the way oozed a rhapsody of savory smells. Fresh yellow pumpkin flowers fragrantly fried in melted butter. On another grill, sausages sizzled in a rain forest of green peppers and shredded onions. Egg batter for *zeppoles*—Italian dumplings—fizzled and firecrackered in a basin of hot oil heated over a trash can with a sparking fire inside. Near a lemon-ice stand kids turned their paper cups inside out to lick up the sweet slush sticking to the bottom. At the seafood stand, where shells steamed over boiling water, a man sopped a half dozen clams with hot pepper sauce and then in rapid succession sucked the clam bodies down his gullet. Old-timers from the mountain villages around Naples ravished toasted lamb head, eating the eyes with the ecstasy of deliverance to heaven. "You don't know what's good. That's the best part," a mother reproved her son for sneering at the old men. Other stands were decked with colorful pinwheels, abstract-art lollipops, necklaces beaded with nuts, white-frothed anisette cookies, blood oranges, peaches steeped in wine, and Sicilian pizza as thick as custard pie. On top of a platform a band was playing the tarantella as old people including Grandma, were dancing in the street. Grandma took herself very seriously as she clicked her fingers over her head flamenco-style.

Tony forded the river of people to the church grounds. Twenty of us followed him in a knotty file. As he approached a new Plymouth being raffled off, a guy in a turtleneck stepped up to him. "Are you Bavimo?"

"Yeah."

The punch that followed spun Tony around. He groped to hold on as the guy threw a fast broadside at his head. One punch jolted him into the raffle table, stampeding the volunteer workers and causing an upheaval of dust and chairs.

"Cops," someone yelled.

The guy disappeared back in the crowd. Tony dove under the Plymouth and hid there until the police left. On parole, he didn't want to get caught in a fight. Word was out the next day that it was Whitey, the leader of the Rampers, who stepped out of the crowd. The Rampers were broadcasting all over Brooklyn how their leader romped on Bavimo.

Tony sulked and brooded for days. He couldn't eat. He couldn't sleep. All he thought about was finishing the fight. No one could talk to him. Cord, his best friend, tried to tell him to forget about it, and got slapped in the face for his advice. Tony wanted to go after Whitey, but the 66th Precinct was on the alert. Word had also gotten back to them about the skirmish. Extra cops were put on the beat outside of Whitey's hangouts. If Tony was seen on Fourteenth Avenue he was to be arrested. The cops didn't want a Ramper–Fort Hamilton war on their hands. The older guys decided Tony should challenge Whitey to a rematch fight in another neighborhood. Blackie was sent to Fourteenth Avenue with the message. Whitey agreed to the challenge right away. The exchange at the feast left him with contempt for Tony. He figured now he would have his chance to finish the beating, and once and for all establish himself as the toughest guy in Brooklyn. The rematch was booked for Mikey Mom's cellar in Bath Beach. That was neutral territory and outside the 66th Precinct's jurisdiction. Fort Hamilton was deserted the night of the fight. We took buses or drove to Bath Beach. Everyone was searched before he could enter the cellar. Only the neutrals could have guns. The long cellar's whitewashed walls were coated with dust. We lined up on one side and the Rampers watched from the other.

Whitey came down first. At the feast from where I had stood all I saw was his towhead. Now, up close, his appearance was awesome. Foremost was his heavy casing of skull. You could see it in the length of his head. Thick cables of neck tendon secured it to his body. He pulled his sweater and T-shirt off at the same time, uncovering a hairless torso padded with smooth and supple muscle. His wide shoulders tapered down to a knotted midsection. I guessed him to be a light-heavyweight. He acted cool and confident. It was exciting standing near him, like the time I reached out to touch Johnny Mize at Ebbets Field. Even though he was on the rival Giants it was still a thrill to be that close to a major leaguer. Whitey had a rep as one of the toughest gangleaders in Brooklyn.

Tony jaunted down the stairs a few minutes later. His face was imprinted with smouldering rage. As he passed Gary Blue, one of the neutrals, Gary remarked, "I got my money on Whitey."

"Ya better fuckin' keep it on 'im," Tony answered, glaring over at Whitey. "He's gonna need it fa the hospital."

Coming over to where we were lined up he tugged off his undershirt and handed it to Jackie Map. The huge ball in his bicep seemed to breathe as he righted the St. Christopher's medal on his neck. He walked over to confront Whitey and the neutrals in charge. Conditions were agreed upon right away: no wrestling, no clinching, no kicking. Mikey said this fight should show class. There were to be no rounds and no decision. It was bare fists to the finish. They squared off in the center of the cellar. My temples throbbed. I knew how much this fight meant to Tony. I was afraid that maybe the short fight at the feast was a herald. Maybe Whitey could have finished him off then if the cops had not come.

They gave the signal to start. Tony charged in to overcome Whitey's height and reach. The punches he got hit with coming in were so fast they were almost a blur. The bare knuckles smacked loudly on his skin, tearing open the flesh over an eye and reddening his whole face, but he bulled forward to close range. Leaping up with a savage left hook, he ripped Whitey off his feet and dropped him on his side.

Elation surged through me. Tony had Whitey down. He lay there shaking his head to clear the dizziness, and then slowly rose to his feet. His side was filthied and bruised from the concrete floor. He resumed his stance. "C'mon, Whitey, you can beat this guy," his friends encouraged. Tony raced in like a javelin thrower and in one motion crashed a right cross on Whitey's huge jaw that literally lifted him off the ground and drove him on top of a washing sink. He quickly sank to his knees and hunched his head, spitting out blood and teeth. He picked himself up in deliberate sequence. Trying to take advantage of his superior height, he pumped his jab as Tony charged in. Leaping over the jabs, Tony landed another solid right to Whitey's jaw that staggered him. He followed unrelentingly with more bone-shaking punches until Whitey's legs collapsed. This time he was sprawled out on his back. He rolled over on his stomach and lay there face down for a minute hoping to regain his strength. Struggling to his feet he plodded forward flatfooted, blooping impotent swings. His face was smeared with thick coagulated blood, his eyes were drunken, and a hunk of his lip was hanging like a raw flank steak. I was wishing he had stayed down for his own sake. It was no longer a match. He was only proving how much heart he had. He got crucified, pounded down ten more times, thirteen times all together. But he still came on. I never saw a guy with so much heart. Finally, one of the Rampers jumped between them to stop it. That night Pop saw one of the biggest blowouts ever to rock his pool halls. Now we were not only sure Tony was the toughest in Brooklyn; he was invincible.

30 No one would have found him lying face down buried under brush in a ditch, but rigor mortis raised his leg in an ice skater's arc. A passing motorist stopped when he spied a shoe in the air. Before he was identified the newspapers gave his age as mid-thirties, but Tony Bavimo was only twenty-one when he was killed. A .45-caliber pistol held behind him at point-blank range had torn away part of his head. The list of suspects was as endless as the number of people Tony had clashed with in his short life. The reaction of the police was "good riddance," but they still went through the motions of an investigation.

Upon first reading, Tony's death was unreal to me. I still expected to see him on the corner again as I had countless days before, but when I hurried to the poolroom that night he wasn't there. No one was. The police had rounded up everyone for questioning.

The next day he was laid out at Terregrosa's Funeral Parlor. The line of mourners overflowed into the street as gangs from all over the city came to pay their respects. As I entered the jammed vestibule I could hear the hand-stifled sobs of men and the hysterical screams and unrestrained crying of women. The mood was contagious. I started to cry before I could see the corpse. The column moved into the casket room, proceeding slowly down the center aisle between two sections of folding chairs filled with veiled women in black. Many were older women, friends and relations of Tony's mother, who was in her sixties. Directly below my shoulder I glimpsed a pair of gnarled hands splotched with age grasping rosary beads. Blackie, his eyes reddened, was stationed at an upright desk in the rear, taking contributions for the family. Other Fort Hamilton Boys leaned against the purple drapes on both sides of him. The satin-lined coffin was open in the front of the room near where Tony's immediate family was sitting. The rest of the space was packed with floral wreaths and bouquets in all shapes. The oversweet fragrance of refrigerated flowers crossed in the air with the scents from wax and musky perfumed handkerchiefs.

When I knelt at the casket I was shocked by the sight. Tony was wearing a navy blue suit and tie with a dandy's pair of patent leather shoes—clothes he never wore in life. There was a bald patch on his head because the gun had been held so close his hair caught on fire. Charcoal was smudged over the spot to give the appearance of hair. His powdered face was swollen to the size of a melon and noticeably stuffed with wax where the bullet had pushed out. He lay chilled stiff and yellow in a tame prayer pose that made me sickly sad. I felt faint. They should never have opened the casket. As I got up in a daze I noticed a detective hiding behind the flowers. Suspecting that the killer was among the mourners, he listened for incriminating remarks. The police thought the killer might whisper some vengeful word at the corpse.

I went over to Tony's mother and hugged her. She put her cheek on my shoulder. "Who coulda do sucha thing to my boy?"

"I don't know," I said crying.

"*O figlio mio,*" she screamed, and brought her hands up over her face.

I moved over to Tony's father and squeezed his hand in mine. "I'm very sorry, Mr. Bavimo."

"Thanka you," he said, his face drawn with bitter, obstinate grief.

Tony's older sister sat stricken, being fanned with a handkerchief by another woman. His younger sister, who was mentally retarded, stared ahead blankly. I kissed them both on the forehead and followed the file moving out.

Taking up a position in a back corner, I would cry for awhile and then stop, listening to the others cry. Richie caused a commotion at the coffin. "Please, get up. Please," he cried, embracing the body. Those behind him had to pull him away. I felt pained by the scene, but a part of me also resented Richie showing more sorrow than I did. Moments later I provoked someone else's jealousy by whispering across the room, "I'll get the guy, Tony."

"Never mind you," Cord grit his teeth. "I'll get the bastard."

The second day I returned to the funeral parlor in the morning to stay until it closed. Quite a few others took off from work to be there, too. My daze had thawed out. I was getting accustomed to the wake. With Tony the center of our attention, it was as though he was still with us. We sat downstairs in the lounge trading stories about him. Someone mentioned how impressed the mortician was with Tony's muscles when he embalmed him. That's how crazily we idolized him.

All of us were angry over the newspaper stories describing Tony as a "punk," "a moocher," "a bum." I complained, "How the hell could they say anything? They don't even know him. What do they do, go ask the police? As if their word is God."

Together Grassy and I wrote a letter, reworded by Timmy, and sent it to "Letters to the Editor." We were irked most by the label "punk," which to us meant a coward. "Tony wasn't afraid of anything," we wrote, "and his fights in the ring proved it. If he was a punk how could he have such a rep all over Brooklyn? And he was no moocher either. He worked at Bush Terminal as a welder for the last three years. Every kid in the neighborhood looked up to him. He was like a second father to us. We went to him if we needed money for a date or wanted to borrow a car. He was always ready to protect anyone in trouble. He taught us things about street life."

Ironically, one of the pointers he taught us was to never sit in the front seat of a car with strangers or anyone else you don't trust. The police believed he was shot in a car.

Tony had been able to go into any neighborhood bar and a dozen drinks would be put in front of him. So many men wanted to show their respect for him. In an immigrant section surrounded by hostile people, toughness was a respected trait. Psychiatrists would probably assert that Tony wasn't really masculine. They would resolve that he acted fierce only to compensate for feelings of inferiority caused by his small size. None of us were aware of any complexes. We didn't try to psychoanalyze him. To us only his concrete actions defined his personality.

One of the policemen at the funeral couldn't understand the weeping and accolades and dismissed him as a lunatic. Tony may have seemed insane to a middle-class person but in the eyes of the street culture he epitomized manhood.

The coffin went from the undertaker to Calvary Cemetery. The church refused to perform a requiem mass. A murdered person of notorious character was forbidden holy sanction. This rule was to punish the deceased, but the only ones who suffered were his family. There were four flower cars followed by a five-block funeral procession. The motorcade drove into the cemetery past the mausoleums, the trimmed lawns and walkways, into an area crowded with tombstones. We got out of the cars and walked to the gravesite. As the squeaky rope lowered Tony into the grave, we all tossed a flower on top of the coffin. The women screamed hysterically. Once more I vowed under my breath to get Tony's killer. Others near me muttered the same promise.

After the burial I started to feel the loss. Throughout the funeral my mind had been caught by events. And there was Tony's presence given life by the stories we related to each other. Now there was nothing. Only his memory. Richie asked me to go to a tattoo shop with him the next day. He requested a special tattoo from the man—a large cross with the words IN MEMORY OF MY GOOD FRIEND TONY. Tony meant more to Richie and me than to any of the other young guys. We were basically timid before meeting him. He implanted boldness in us. A part of him became a part of us. Without that part we would not have been able to raise ourselves later. For weeks Richie was morose. Finally, in a spontaneous act, he hitched a ride to California.

Tony's immigrant father, who had been so devoted to his son, tried to find the killer himself. "I getta 'im," he shook his fist and then sunk his teeth into his knuckles. He hounded the poolroom for months hoping to learn something. In those months his face became wizened and his eyes bloodshot from lack of sleep and the agony of his thoughts. He smoked incessantly. Not long after Tony died his father passed away. People said he died from "a broken heart." The real cause was that he gave up caring for himself.

My father's reaction was a promise to move the family, but I had heard him say the same thing often before. Tony's wasn't the only violent death in the neighborhood. So I was surprised when Dad borrowed on his pension and started hustling extra jobs, saving for a down payment on a small house in Flatbush.

Tony's death was a cataclysm for the Fort Hamilton Boys. The gang continued a spell longer and then began to come apart as if the glue was gone. The membership dwindled. Guys weren't coming around as much anymore. There was speculation that maybe that's what his killer or killers wanted to happen. Before Tony's death the Fort Hamilton Boys was at its peak. The gang was rampaging all over Brooklyn, wrecking dancehalls, honky-tonk bars, luncheonettes. Strong action produced strong reaction: Tony was murdered. He might have been killed by someone he hurt physically, but the gang was also injuring property interests. Local shop-keepers and businessmen were roused by the violent turbulence. Police were hounding Fort Hamilton and were less susceptible to bribes now because of pressure on the department. A special task force had been dispatched from headquarters to patrol the neighborhood. This concentration of police patrol on Fort Hamilton was threatening another kind of property interest: The shylocking, bookmaking, and other illegal enterprises felt hamstrung. The "Good People," being conservative businessmen in a sense, were against any tumult that fretted the public. Since the wars of Prohibition they had been operating in a relatively subdued and cautious style. Society allows them to carry on because of this unprovoking quiet. The "Good People" didn't want an incorruptible task force patroling one of their business districts. Whether they enforced their interest by ordering Tony's execution was never revealed to outsiders, but the murder was committed in their patent. The detective on the case was quoted by the *News* as saying, "it would be a very good guess that the murdered man was sitting in the front seat of an auto when he was slain, and that the killer, sitting in the back, had calmly held the gun an inch or two from the unsuspecting victim's head." An autopsy confirmed the estimated closeness of the gun. On the night of the killing Tony's parents saw him get into a car outside of his house. Certainly he would not have entered with Rampers or Avenue U Boys. Even if they pulled a gun to force him in it's unlikely he would have climbed in. Someone he knew well must have been sitting in the back. He never trusted a stranger behind him. The "Good People" were known to use a victim's close friend to make the hit or set it up. Mindful of this, the police arrested everyone in the poolroom the night the body was found. They were taken one at a time to the ditch where Tony was laying and asked, "Why'd ya do it?" by a detective as he pulled a blanket off the messy body. It was thought the killer might break down. Since the case went unsolved, we never found out who killed Tony.

Some of my friends saw me as the one who could succeed Tony and restore the gang if I won the Golden Gloves.

31 Training for a fight is a battle with yourself. I was never taught discipline but it came to me partly out of hate. I resented the teachers with their violin-playing sons and education who contemptuously frowned at "uncouth Italians." I was peeved wearing cardboard patches in my shoes, drudging in a bleach factory and the garment center and going to bullshit agencies. I rankled at being the lowest flunkey on the totem pole on every job, with the crud always coming down on my head. I was sick of going out for other people's pie and coffee. I hated the loan companies, the pawnbrokers, the thieving grocers, and all the other bastard mercenaries leeching all they could out of my family, and I despised the government that let them. I hated the snobs skirting "the wretched slums" in their chauffeured limousines. I hated the phony justice that said when a rich man's son punched someone it was a little misunderstanding, but when a streetcleaner's son like me did it, then it was a felonious assault. I hated the police goons who harassed us and the newspapers that always made them right. And I hated whoever it was who killed Tony on the sneak.

A typical training day for me began at six in the morning. Down in the cellar there was a homemade sandbag, a big postal sack loaded with sand and pebbles that Anthony had helped me heft to the rafters. Before leaving for work I mauled the bag for three rounds. When I first had put it up the bag was immovable and I sprained my wrists, but as the months passed my joints hardened and the bag began to yield. I showered and changed next, but I didn't shave. I wanted a heavy beard to protect against cuts in sparring. I would keep it stubbled on the night of my fight for the same reason—and to look mean. A mean look has a psychological effect on yourself as well as your opponent.

For breakfast I brewed a malt from six eggs, blackstrap molasses, Hoffman's protein powder, wheat germ, ice cream, cod liver oil, and honey. After I drank it my stomach felt like a seething lava pit. On my way to work I squeezed handsprings on the train. I didn't want to waste any time. I was now a loader at an export-import warehouse. I left the shoe factory for heavier work to help my boxing. I treated my job as part of training. Unloading seventy-pound boxes of Iraqi dates, I sprinted back and forth from trailer to platform. Fifty-pound bales of agar-agar I tossed with one arm onto the pushcart. Cumbersome two-hundred–pound gum arabic I lifted over my head at hour intervals. Before we finished unloading one trailer another one jackknifed into the platform. Work was continuous except for lunch and coffee breaks. In spring it was nice being outdoors, but in the winter we sloshed through freezing sleet. At five o'clock we punched out and went down to the warehouse dressing room to get out of our company uniform and boots. For me the change of clothes was only going to last until I got to the gym. On the subway I squeezed handsprings again.

The Trinity Club Gym was in the annex of a Protestant church in Brooklyn. Punctually awaiting me, my trainer, Johnny Mandello, had my things neatly arrayed outside my locker. As I wrapped gauze around my fists he instructed me on what punches to practice in sparring. The track coach at Fort Hamilton was right. Johnny did nurse along his fighters. A half year passed before he let me step into the gym ring with anyone. When I did start sparring it was with professionals. Johnny believed that if I boxed with amateurs I could only learn wrong habits. Some of the pros he put me in with were main-eventers—Carmela Costa, Angelo Defendis, Hardy "Bazooka" Smallwood. Sparring is the most important phase of training. It coordinates all the separate themes of practice, and callouses you to punches. My nose no longer pained or bled easily, and my eyes didn't blink anymore.

After sparring I sharpened my reflexes on the speedbag. I moved to the pulleys to strengthen my shoulders. During this exercise I put my body on automatic pilot while my mind daydreamed about Dutchy. She was going steady now, but I wasn't giving up on her. I thought that if I could show her that I was a winner, she would want to go with me again. I climbed back into the ring to shadowbox. I concentrated on footwork. I liked to carom off the rope, bobbing and weaving, and open up with combinations. Johnny watched my maneuvers closely, shouting pointers: "Keep your left up," "Tuck your chin in." My favorite training activity was jumping rope. Johnny said it prevented arm weariness. I was proud of being able to do fast one-handed whips, hand switches, and other fancy rope steps. I thought it gave me a dancing finesse that impressed girls.

I worked out longer than anyone else in the gym. Everyone was gone by the time I plodded down to the locker room. I did my calesthenics on the rubdown table. For neck strength I did the wrestler's bridge. For the abdominals I folded my body in half on the bench and kicked the floor over my head. I exercised for an hour. To make sure I burned off every bit of flab, I suffocated my pores with cold cream and wore a plastic raincoat under my sweatsuit. Sweating profusely in perpetual motion, I was like the tiger who ran until he melted into butter. I left a puddle of sweat.

I squeezed handsprings on the subway coming home. I arrived at the apartment at nine o'clock. Dehydrated, I chug-a-lugged a quart of milk. Ma cooked a special dinner for me. I wouldn't touch pasta, bread, cake, or any other starches. My diet in the evening was strictly lean meats, fresh vegetables, cheese, fruits, and plenty of milk. I drank a half gallon of milk for dinner. I spent my pay on the right foods for training. If one of my friends came by with a girl, I told him I wasn't interested. Christmas and New Year's were just training days to me. All my energy was channeled toward winning the Golden Gloves. After dinner I changed into my roadwork outfit—a sweat jacket with a Klan-shaped hood, two pairs of corduroy pants, and heavy combat boots. I tied barbell plates to the boots or held them to increase the drag. I figured the more resistance I gave my muscles in training, the more force they would have in the ring. Before going to run I would lay down on the couch to rest for awhile. As soon as I put my head down I was asleep. Only an alarm kept me from being out until morning. Sometimes even the alarm wasn't enough. My body was so drained I slept twenty thousand leagues beneath awakeness, almost in a coma. My brother Anthony had to shake me to get me up for roadwork.

By eleven o'clock I was hiking to "the dust bowl," a dirt field used by Norwegians for soccer. To get in I climbed over a high fence. The first lap around I felt my legs to see how hard they were getting from all the months of roadwork. I used to say, "I wanna make myself like steel." That way all those people who were dumping on me couldn't beat me. I wasn't just training for my ring opponents. I felt that life was combat and it was the whole world against me. If I beat my opponents in the ring I would be pushing my way through the others, too. I jogged around the field's quarter-mile perimeter thirty-two times. Roadwork was a monotonous treadmill but I drove myself. Wind chapped my lips. The last hundred yards I put on a fast burst. I was a slow runner before, but now I could outsprint my friends even in heavy boots. I finished my roadwork after midnight. The neighborhood was asleep. The lights were out in all the buildings and not a soul passed. It was serene to lay down in the middle of the dust bowl and look up at the stars. I felt a close communion with myself. The disciplined life purified me of all the guilt I felt for past failures. My mind was full of fantasies. Alone at midnight, I magnified Dutchy into a pure goddess. I envisioned myself sweating and bleeding in the ring, but winning for her. I was living in a world of reveries, but I knew what I was doing had a relation to reality. In January after almost two years of training, I was going to step into the arena. Thousands of people would be watching.

I climbed out of the field and started for home. My dry throat tasted of dirt, reminding me of the time "Natie the Jew" and I were forced to fight each other in the dust bowl. The older kids threw us at each other. Natie punched me in the face until I cried. I could never forget losing to him. None of the older kids would let me.

Trudging up to the apartment I felt I could drink an ocean. When I turned on the kitchen light a cockroach scurried from the sink. I guzzled from the faucet until my belly was bloated. Going to the closet I took down the new black satin robe with white trim that I had bought at Davega's. I was as excited by that robe as a girl is by her wedding gown. I put it on in front of the mirror, striking boxing poses. I imagined myself going up the ring steps with everyone seeing my name on the back.

The dressing rooms of Ridgewood Grove Arena were down a ramp under the bleachers. In the central room an official teething his cigar sat at a drawerless desk recording the weights of fighters as they stepped up on the scale. Trainers milled around the desk re-checking the matches. Off to the side in a small compartment, other fighters who already were wearing their regular gloves sat on benches spliced together in a square. The only Golden Gloves were the little prizes for the winners. I weighed in and had a pair of gloves laced on. I joined the other fighters sitting in the waiting compartment. Bare cinder blocks formed the walls. A low-watt bulb hanging from the ceiling emitted a dim light. It was like being in a bomb shelter as we sat there quietly looking at each other. We could feel as well as hear the reverberating noises of the crowd above. Although we couldn't see the fight, the crowd reactions gave us an account of what was happening. If there was a loud "ooh" we knew a hard punch missed. A loud howl meant a hard punch landed. A steady uproar meant someone was hurt on the ropes. And when they were up stamping their feet, a boxer was down.

Cool sweat trickling down my armpits was rerouted by the elastic band of my trunks and collected in a pool around my navel. My new leather shoes squeaked as I balled my toes in them nervously. I tried to relax but tensed inside as my eyes measured the physiques I might have to battle. The crowd started screaming and stamping wildly on the wooden floor above. Someone must have been knocked out. I worried most about that happening to me. It seemed a terrible humiliation to be sleeping on your back half naked with thousands looking on as your conqueror jubilantly jumped around your body.

Johnny rubbed the back of my neck the way you make a cat purr. He was trying to circulate the blood. The opening seconds of a fight are the most dangerous because the body is cold. I did neck exercises, rotating my head to warm up.

"Your boy is on now, Mandello. Take him up," a man with a throaty voice called in.

"Okay, he'll be right up," Johnny said, and then turned back to me for last-second instructions. "Remember, stick wid the left. Use ya jab, ya got a good jab."

"Awright, Johnny, I know." I pulled a ball of tinfoil out of my robe pocket and swallowed a glob of honey wrapped inside. Trainers recommended it as a transfusion of energy to replace what was drained by fear and worry in waiting.

Going up the ramp I passed a fighter hurrying down with his handlers. From the pained look on his face I could tell he was the loser in the previous match. Spectators reached out to pat the winner, who shuffled up the aisle with a grin. He was a black boy with well-defined muscles glossed by sweat. I brushed by him nodding at a bleacher section on its feet whistling. Over a hundred people from Fort Hamilton were in that section. I could see Dad sitting in the front row with Uncle Tony and Uncle Louie. Another burst of cheers sounded on the other side of the arena as my opponent made his way out of the dressing room. The only thing I knew about him was that his name was Sheldon Diamond and he weighed 160 pounds. At ringside Johnny smeared Vaseline over my face to reduce the risk of cuts. Hardy Smallwood climbed up on the other side of the ring apron with a towel. He was going to be my other corner man. Springing up and down, blond, crew cut, Diamond unhinged his arms to loosen up. I remained motionless, afraid of squandering energy. I glanced over and our eyes met. Seconds later we were staring at each other in the center of the ring as the referee gave us instructions. When I returned to the corner Hardy shoved a mouthpiece in my mouth. I genuflexed and made the sign of the cross for luck.

The gong rang. I whirled around and moved warily from my corner. Diamond rushed across the ring. I expected a slow feeling-out the first few moments, but he fooled me. His first punch was a right hand with all the force of his body behind it. It tore through my guard and knocked me to the canvass. I came to my senses when the referee's count over me was three. The crowd was agog, shaking the arena to its foundation. "Ya got 'im, finish 'im," his rooters shouted as I got up. The referee wiped my gloves and examined my eyes. He stepped aside and waved on Diamond from the neutral corner. I could see him spring toward me, but his figure was silently vague. I was in a mental twilight, somewhere between waking and sleeping. All my mind's lights were still out but the pilot light. My head took the full brunt of his hooks and I bounded off the ropes. Through reflex my gloves shot up to protect my face. For the remainder of the round Diamond trounced me from ringpost to ringpost. My head rocked and vibrated, absorbing his hardest punches, but my legs held up, girded by the hundreds of miles of roadwork.

At the bell I trodded back to my corner unwinded and untired but in a grog. My cornermen immediately went to work to get me out of it. They plopped me down on the stool, removed my mouthpiece, and made me sniff stinging smelling salts. Hardy stretched the elastic band of my trunks and poured a bottle of cold water down my crotch. One of Johnny's strong hands squeezed the back of my neck while the other sponged my face. When the gong rang for the second round, I got off the stool halfway restored to a clear head. As I moved out Johnny prompted me to use my left jab. Diamond rushed out headhunting again with roundhouses, but I was able to stave him off with jabs. I had the reach advantage, so my left prevented his husky-armed clouts from landing. My instincts were defensive. He was stalking me. I could see riled frustration in his eyes. Each second that I kept him away lessened his chance of knocking me out. Before the bell ended round two, I drew blood from his nose with a jab.

Round three was the last round. I moved out of my corner breathing easy and strong. I had finally shucked the dizziness from the first round. This time I went after him. I wasn't romantically inspired by Dutchy. The crowd's cheers were only a low din now because I was engrossed in my opponent. I was moved by venomous anger. I feinted a jab and harpooned a straight right into his gut. His legs melted and he was sitting on the canvass. The referee counted five over him before he towed himself up. Itching in the neutral corner, I raced over to him. I grazed his hair with a wild looping right. Before I could throw another punch he bogged my arms in a clinch. The referee quickly rived us apart. Diamond's eyes were glassy. I hammered a right to his jaw. He shot through the middle strand of the ropes stretched out on his face. The referee stopped the fight without a count. Diamond's handlers hurried over to revive him. My friends flooded the ring. Baldy, one of the older guys, carried me out on his shoulders.

"The kid was great, huh, Johnny?" he shouted, carrying me down the roaring aisles.

"Got up off the floor ta win, didn't he."

"He's got killer instinct. The crowd loves him. He can finish a guy when he's got him hurt."

"That's what ya need ta make a bundle, killer instinct. My boy comes ta fight."

The *Daily News* wrote up the fight the next morning.

Joey Sorrentino, a 17-year-old Brooklyn warehouse clerk, representing the Trinity Club, also shaped up as a definite title threat. Joey tangled with Sheldon Diamond, a student from LIU, in one of the best fights on the card. Diamond dropped Sorrentino with a crackling right early in the first round, but the Trinity boy came scrapping back and by the middle of the second round was in command.

Early in the third, he drove a rocketing right to Diamond's midsection. Diamond dropped to the deck, but he got up still fighting. A left and a right floored him for the second time and the referee stopped it at 1:50 of the round.

When the Golden Gloves tournament began there were sixty-four middleweights. By a process of elimination that number would be cut to two. As the number steadily diminished the following days, writeups in the papers said I had a good chance to take the Gloves. "Pump-ups," street public relations men, relayed to Dutchy how I was winning. They showed her the writeups. She wasn't impressed. I couldn't understand her. If she wasn't impressed by toughness, why was she going with her big-talk boyfriend? Then I realized that ring guts didn't mean anything to her. The kind of tough guy she wanted was one who could stand up to her.

The fighter I had to beat to win the Golden Gloves was Danny Russo. Months before the tournament opened he was touted as a strong favorite. His trainer was Pete Mello, a former boxing coach of the United States Olympic Team. For two years Mello had tutored Russo at the CYO Gym, perfecting his skills far beyond the subnovice class of the Golden Gloves. My bout with him was scheduled at Sunnyside Arena. In the dressing room that night, Carmine Natalie, one of the older guys, came back to talk to me. He said that Russo was a picture boxer who fights out of a set stance. The way to beat him was to not give him a chance to get set. "Get on top of him right away. Drive him into the ropes. Throw punches like a windmill."

My training the week before the fight was slack. I didn't have the inspiration of Dutchy's image anymore for roadwork. I knew all those puddles I sweated before didn't have any meaning. It was all futile. Even if I won the championship she wouldn't care. What she wanted I couldn't be. You can't go back into a poker game when you've already lost your pants. I was hung up on her and she knew it. There was no way to reverse things to start out again. The only incentive I had left was hate, which was stronger because it was now welded to bitterness.

I got angry at myself for letting soppy feelings stop me from doing my roadwork. Because of hate I wanted to get on top of Russo at the bell and smother him with punches. And I wanted to keep it up every round so, like Carmine said, he could never get set. But I didn't know if I had the wind to keep up a sustained barrage of punches for the entire fight. If I had done my roadwork I was sure I could.

Russo sat next to me on the bench before we were called up the ramp. He talked to me in a very calm, friendly voice. I didn't want to get to know him personally. As long as he was just Danny Russo, the name the newspapers were always acclaiming, I could hate him. If I got to know him as a nice guy it would rob me of the malice to tear into him. I moved away from him so as not to listen.

"Get ready, it's the last round out there," someone yelled to us.

"Well, see ya soon," Russo smiled good-naturedly, getting up to go out to the ring.

"Good luck," I said, out of habit and not knowing what I should say.

The arena erupted into cheers when he made his way up the aisle. Russo came from the rough East New York section of Brooklyn. I swallowed a glob of honey and followed him out.

At the opening bell I flew at him. He was out of his corner for a second before he richocheted back from a double barrel of punches I had thrown at him. He tried to throttle my arms in a clinch but I shoved him away. My hands were quicker than his, and beat him to every punch. I cornered him the whole round and never let up with punches. His knees buckled several times but he wouldn't go down. His face was bewildered and worried but there wasn't a hint of quitting.

Going back to my corner at the bell, I wondered why I couldn't knock him down. I had tremendous confidence in my punch. Johnny said that I was landing too high, my punches were hitting his forehead instead of his jaw, and I was throwing them too fast to get leverage.

The next round I charged him again but he was anticipating the move and pedaled out of range. He used the same manuever on me that I had used on Diamond. Whenever I made a foray he pistoned his long stiff jab in my face. I couldn't get in on him anymore. Disgusted with his unwillingness to slug it out, I stopped pursuing him and moved back a few steps. I waited for him to come into me. My feet were planted flatfooted and my right shoulder was cocked back for power. But he never came, playing a waiting game with me. I recharged him. His jab hashed my face but I broke through and riddled his head with short quick punches. I fired another flurry before the bell.

The third round I was worried about my wind. I was afraid I didn't have much left. I tried to coast through the round. By my scoring I was ahead. I had repeatedly staggered him in the first round, and in the second I had been the aggressor and got the edge in the exchanges. Russo abided by his jab for most of the last round but jolted my head with a good right.

The judges awarded the fight to Russo. The crowd booed the

decision but it was all over. The sports column in the *Daily News* described the bout the next day:

> *Danny Russo of the C.Y.O. and Joe Sorrentino from the Trinity Club battled toe-to-toe for three rounds last night in a real thriller. Russo was awarded the decision in a very close call.*

Russo went on to become the champion. My feelings fluctuated that night after we fought. At first I was in deep despair. Then I soared high, euphoric. The straightjacket life was over. No more thirty-two times around the dust bowl every night. No more sweat puddles on the bench. No more Spartan life. The next morning, I ran out to a bakery to buy a pumpkin pie. It was my favorite and I hadn't tasted one in a year. Grabbing hunks with both hands, I shoved them into my mouth and ate the whole pie. Then I cried. Not long after I joined the Marines.

▰▰▰

32 Parris Island, the Marine Recruit Training Depot for the eastern half of the United States, is a forlorn island entwined by marshy water in the swamplands of South Carolina. Along the northern horn, sentries are posted to check all persons who go on and off the island. To the east and west, treacherous tidal rivers form barriers two miles wide. The southern tip of the base juts into the Atlantic Ocean. The location for the most brutal military training in the world was not an accidental choice.

The train from New York deposited us at a saloon town on the mainland across from the northern shore. Here at noon we boarded a mud-mantled bus and chugged over the causeway to the island. Normally, new enlistees report to interim quarters in "Receiving" until enough men accumulate to form a training platoon. On our bus we had seventy-eight, a full complement, so we headed directly for the training area. Cruising through groves of moss-covered trees, the bus bounced and buffeted over the nubbly gravel road. I was sitting in a waffle iron in the back, over the engine and under the scorched roof. Beginning to retch, I ran for the window. After calming my insides, I took in a deep breath of the warm, steaming air. "We must be getting close," I thought. There was a network of tents on a hill up ahead. Along the side of the road a series of monuments faced us engraved with historical battles: Nassau 1776, Tripoli 1801, Seminole War 1836, Nicaragua 1912. . . .

Swinging near the parade field we were surrounded by a fossil world. Officers in blue and white dress uniforms with gold buttons and pleated shoulders strutted across the blacktop grasping their flashing scabbards. Drums and bugles readied for a ceremony. Platoons hoisting pennants linked up in a long procession and began marching with synchronized steps. Smartly stepping alongside, noncoms wearing the campaign hats of World War I grunted an ancient cadence: "La pa bey, ladee la pa bey," "un oo ee, ee oo ya lef." The band cabooSed onto the last column. Erectly waiting to review the phalanx, a brigadier in a motor chariot tapped his knuckles with a swagger stick.

Deboarding the bus in front of an ordnance shed, we were met by three drill instructors in campaign hats and starchy kale green fatigues.

"Hurry up, get outta there you lards of shit," one of them barked.

"Get in ranks, get in ranks, and stand at attention," another screamed.

Like lemmings, we all tried to squeeze through the door at the same time, cricking necks, colliding skulls, and mashing toes only to be welted across the face when we got outside. I jumped down and lingered for a second to stare at the D.I. the way you do at an exotic creature in a menagerie.

"Get a move on, turd." He barbed his fist in my ribs.

The last fumble out of the bus was a tubby recruit with quavering hips.

"Whatsa matter, boy, somethin' wrong with your legs?" the D.I. asked softly with concern.

"No, sir."

"Then you better move, fat boy, or this boonie here is gonna make your ass have a jet stream."

The boy, who was running as hard as he could before, grit his teeth and flailed his arms, accelerating with the upper half of his body. His face was as intense as a runner dashing the hundred in nine flat, but the friction of rubbing thighs stalled his blimpy legs.

As we stood stiff and silent in our several versions of attention, the three drill instructors walked down the columns inspecting us.

"Why is your chest moving, private?" one of them asked a blond-headed boy. "I told you to stand at attention."

"My chest isn't moving, sir."

"Are you calling me a liar, maggot?"

"No, sir."

"Ya sassin's buggin' me, boy. So you are movin'?"

"Yes, sir."

"I thought I told you to get at attention. You spastic shit, are you breaking my order now?"

"But it would make a liar out of you . . . "

"Ewe!! Do I look like a female sheep, dippy. You got fog on your eyes, boy. I got some medicine that'll clear them right up." He forced him to drink a whole bottle of Worcestershire sauce. The boy had to be carried to sick bay.

The smallest of the three D.I.s stopped at my spot and stared at my shoulders. I became more rigid and looked blankly ahead, ignoring him. His pygmy hand just fit around the swagger stick he held at his side. Putting his chin on my chest, he looked up at me with his lips pursed pugnaciously. "Ah like em big. Ah just wipe em out."

I thought, "You little imp, you wouldn't wipe out anybody if we stepped around the corner." Then it crossed my mind that maybe this guy was a karate expert.

The senior drill instructor welcomed us. "Before you boys got all fired up about coming down here to my corps, I was swinging in a hammock under a shady magnolia tree with ma Smoky Bear hat down over my eyes, sippin' my good Southern bourbon. Now I don't think kindly o' no Yankees who come down here and upset ma sweet time. Ah'm puttin' you yardbirds on notice. You have had the green weenie."

Feeling like products on an assembly belt, we were zipped through connected buildings to be fingerprinted, photographed, scalped, searched, stripped, hosed, and fitted in new, olive uniforms. Herded into ordnance for our M-1 rifles and field equipment, one of the recruits made the mistake of calling an M-1 a gun. The D.I. ordered him to hold the rifle in one hand and take his penis out with the other. In this stance he had to walk all over the base repeating: "This is my rifle, this is my gun. One is for shooting and one is for fun."

Shoved into a windowless van, we sat along a center bench on each other's laps like shish kebab. The van shuttled us to Dog Company where we moved into half-barrel–shaped tin huts, twenty-eight to a hut. Inside, bunk beds with foot lockers underneath bracketed the concrete floor. I was assigned the upper rack of the bunk, which was a boyhood dream come true. On the first night the drill instructors introduced us to a "field day." They splattered the hut walls and floor with mud and commanded us to clean the mess. Gunny Sergeant Michaels, the highest noncom in the battalion, inspected our effort five hours later. "We'll make men out of ya yet," he said, looking at our teenage faces. His words flashed back the recruiter sign: THE MARINE CORPS BUILDS MEN. I wondered how I would know when I was a man. The gunny sergeant was a man. I was sure of that. His worn khaki uniform was faded from countless washings. Not like my stiff, bright new pair. His uniform was also neat and pressed. He had a wallet in his back pocket and he wore a watch. I couldn't imagine him crying or being impulsive. Everything about him was well-ordered. That's what I would be like if I became a man.

The reveille bugle blew at 5 A.M. the next morning. I squinted out of a cranny at a nipping black night. "It must be taps," I thought, nestling again under the warm blankets. Seconds later the door crashed open, lights flicked on, and a human Roto-Rooter whizzed through. Recruits were wrenched from their bunks, bedding and all, and pulled in a pile on the floor.

"Ya got thirty seconds to be on the street, girls," the D.I. shouted, going out the back door.

"What did I do?" I thought as I picked myself up at 5 A.M. "What am I doin' here? John Wayne, you bastard."

▚▚▚

"Heels, heels, dig 'em," the D.I. shouted as we marched to chow. They watched our feet. Anyone out of step got knuckled in the head. Going into the chow hall, we had to perform a ritual with caps, slapping them against our hips in unison. After a curdy "shit-on-a-shingle" breakfast spiced with saltpeter, we double-timed back to the huts. Even our running steps had to be in unison, and our legs were kicked until they were. Given a minute for a head call, we all sat on the pots at the same time. There were two rows of toilets connected back to back so that my knees clinked against the knees on each side of me and my rear kissed the goose-pimply rear of the guy behind me.

"Ya made momsy angry, girls. Ya sat on the cocky seat too long," the D.I. scolded in baby talk. "Now I wanchas all to take ya clothes off and go in the itty bitty shower and do a hundred squat thrusts." Cramped together in the nude like sardines, we had to squat down and throw our legs back.

"Come out here, Jones. Ya not keeping up with the rest of the girls. Now get down and give me a thousand push-ups." The D.I. tugged him out by the ear. The boy's skinny arms collapsed after ten push-ups, provoking the D.I. to stomp his face in the mud the way you put out a cigarette.

"I don't wanna see nothing but assholes and elbows hit that door," the D.I. ordered us out of the shower. We raced out as if our lives depended on it, but not fast enough for him. "I don't know when you girls are gonna learn. So you wanna play fuck fuck, I'll play your game, girls. It's gonna be Cynthia on your bellies." The D.I. double-timed us to a hill called Cynthia, and ordered us to worm up and down on our bellies. Degrading abuse hacked away self-pride. I resisted the efforts to break me. I scored the highest in the platoon in athletic competition and I.Q. tests. At the chow hall I was swindling the Marines out of an extra meal by running out the back and coming around the front on the tail end of another platoon. According to military regulations it was mandatory to say "by your leave" when passing an officer. I wouldn't say it even for the company commander. When he tried to reprimand me I acted like a dunce. On Sunday mornings we were supposed to spit-polish our boots until they gleamed. The night before I would switch boots, putting mine under a farm boy's bunk. After he had my boots gleaming I would tell him about the mistake.

Close-order drill brought automatic responses to commands. "Left face, right face, about face, forward march, to the rear march, port arms, right shoulder arms. . . . " After three hundred hours of drill, reaction to orders became almost instantaneous. There was no interval of thought. In combat the orders change from "left face" to "take that machine gun bunker." Conditioning is at its maximum immediately after boot camp, and it declines after that. For this reason the best fighters—and the ones sent into combat right away —are the fresh recruits who have just finished their training. Also, the younger the person the more amenable he is to conditioning. Draft policies that prefer eighteen- to twenty-one–year–olds first are based in part on this fact.

The first class we attended was political indoctrination. For two hours a rabid corporal drawled into his collar microphone about communism. He introduced the subject by saying: "Communism was founded by a fanatic, Karl Marx." Concluding, he equated the Reds with a rattlesnake, "slippery, deadly, and out ta get ya."

A nondenominational meeting for religious inspiration was conducted next. The chaplain told us that if we had to go to war in the Middle East, which seemed imminent at the time, it was God's will that we should go. We shouldn't disobey God even if it's hard for us sometimes to understand His ways. I questioned—to myself—how the chaplain knew God's will. I also wondered how he was any different from the witch doctors in the movies dubbing spear tips in voodoo juice. I wasn't denying God, but I had doubts about anyone divining His will. It seemed more logical to me that God would disapprove of war. Jesus preached a gospel of brotherly love.

In our history class we were shown films of actual Marine battles. The camera zoomed in on Japs being charred by flamethrowers. Always forging forward, the Marines annihilated the enemy. The films edited out any sights of Marines being killed. Heroes such as General "Howling Mad" Smith, Chesty Puller, and John Basalone were eulogized.

Hollywood movies portraying war as romantic and manly were also run. *Battle Cry* with Tab Hunter was a big favorite. We learned the song "Honeybabe" and added verses on bivouac. Traditional parades were held with flags flying and the Marine Corps hymn in the background. An esprit de corps was developing. The average height of recruits was below average. Every one of the little guys was feeling important because he could call himself a Marine.

▆▆▆

"Depending on how you best feel comfortable with the weapon, you can come in straight to jab the Adam's apple, swipe to behead, swat to slice the jugular, axe to lop off an arm, or swing around the buttplate to crush the skull." The bayonet instructor crisply executed each maneuver, skewering a dummy. I thought I was a tough kid and gang fights were bad, but my insides were getting queasy at this butcher-shop talk on human beings.

After bayonet class the platoon jogged to the athletic field for physical training. The instructor stood on a raised platform.

"Do you know what FMF stands for?" he shouted.

"Fleet Marine Force," the platoon shouted back.

"No, Fighting Mother Fuckers, and that's what you are, and don't forget it. Awright, you Marine tigers, let's hear some growls."

"Graa raa, graa raa."

"Ah can't hear ya, girls."

"Graa raa, graa raa."

"Ah still can't hear ya."

"GRAA RAA, GRAA RAA."

"Now ya sound like Marines."

Jujitsu lessons were part of the physical training program. The instructor picked a volunteer to demonstrate. "When you're gonna be fighting another man and you want to kill him, you better get rid of the bad habits you learned about fighting. A bad habit is hitting a man above the belt. A good habit is going right for the groin. A bad habit is striking a man's jaw. A good habit is gouging out his eyeballs." He turned to the recruit. "Make believe you're Luke the Gook and you got a knife. Now come at me, boy, and try to stab me."

The recruit pumped his hand back, but before he could come down with it the instructor darted in like a mongoose and brought a karati chop to the groin. "You handled that knife all wrong, private. Don't slash or lunge when you're fighting with a knife. Jab like a boxer, and just as you hit a man, whip the blade up and across."

We played combative games, too. Teams scrimmaged on opposite sides of a tank-size ball. The object was to outpush the other side to move the ball over your goal line. The rougher the platoons played the more praise they received from the watching D.I.s.

During the first week I inwardly recoiled at the Marine Corps, especially at Parris Island. Every phase of life was regimented. The D.I.s said, "We will tell you when to eat, how much to eat, and how long to take to eat; we will tell you when to sleep, when to get up, and how long to take to dress; we will tell you when to shit, where to shit, and how long to take to shit." Everything was done en masse. There was no such thing as going for a walk by yourself. Either you marched indistinct in a platoon of seventy-eight men or in a battalion formation ten times that number. It was like living in an ant colony. The reason I joined the military was to escape the frustrating cycle of lousy jobs and my disappointment in losing the Golden Gloves. The military, especially the Marine Corps, was no outlet for frustration. I guess I expected something more glamorous and less mass-oriented, the Hollywood version I had learned. The movies were a part of the reason I chose the Marines. John Wayne must have impressed me in *Iwo Jima*, because I sat through it three times. From leathery Wayne I had the idea that the Marines were a tough, individualistic outfit. The newspapers depicted the Marines as the best fighting men in the world. Growing up in an environment where toughness was an ideal, I was inclined toward the toughest branch. But I didn't know that meant dissolving in a herd.

My attitude toward boot camp never detracted from my respect for Marines as men. There were noncommissioned officers at the base with campaign ribbons matting their shirt pockets. It took courage to earn those ribbons, more than it required to fight in the rumbles in Brooklyn. There was a big difference between a war with armies and a gang war. The latter only lasted a few minutes. In a year's time five to ten teenagers might be killed in New York from all the rumbles that year. In big wars millions are killed. I quarreled with myself the nights of the first week, trying to repress an impulse to rebel. My Fort Hamilton Boys' mentality and raw emotion made me want to run out the door and keep running. My family side was telling me to stick it out, that the right thing to do was to obey. I also had the red-blooded strong-man stuff from the movies working on me. This conflict continued through the next week, but never showed on the surface. I was named a squad leader. At the end of the second week there was another complication. The drill instructors were telling us that war in the Middle East seemed probable now. I couldn't sleep anymore. My mind churned with thoughts about going to war.

"Why should I go fight over there? They're our friends. Friends, my ass. They're strangers to me. Some old bastards say you're our friends, ya havin' trouble, don't worry about it I'll send a few thousand kids to bail you out. Well, you old bastards, you wanna help, go put your asses on the line, not mine. You've seen life, mine is just beginning. Besides, I never even picked youse. They call this a democracy. What they mean is a fogeyocracy. We ain't mature enough to vote. Only the old people know how to run the country so that it always gets into war.

"I could give a shit less about all the con words—hero, brave, coward. I'll make up my own con words. I'm not gonna fall for the shit that these things mean something. Whadda they mean? Just a bunch of people making up words that suit their interests.

"If they come over here and try to hurt my family, I'll fight. But who do I know in Lebanon? My life might not mean much to the gung-ho generals strutting around here with their big fat asses, but it's all I got. They look like they can't wait ta be unleashed so they can sit behind the lines and get in more chess action wid young bodies. War is the name of the game ta these guys. They twiddle their thumbs in nowhere without it. Because they got those stars they think they're better than me, but to me I'm worth more than any of them. A millionaire would give his fortune to be young again like me; he wouldn't give shit ta be an old general.

"The chaplain is saying we'll be the good guys in Lebanon. He doesn't even know a fuckin' thing about it and he's opening his mouth awready. No matter where we war God is ready ta back us, accordin' ta this flunkey.

"It's in the national interest to fight in Lebanon. We have to protect our oil there. What the hell should I worry about oil for? I ain't got none of that oil money. All I got is a dumpy t'ree-room apartment. I gotta go get blown apart because we might lose oil? What am I, some kinda jerk? Wid or widout the oil all I got is a dumpy t'ree-room apartment. The rich bastards are worrying about oil, but see if they care about the slums. They tear down the new office buildings, but the old ones where people live they let rot, and take the rent. We gotta be there, they say, but see if they had ta fight if they'd say it.

"They keep telling us about the communist menace. Menace ta who? Menace ta the fat cats in Long Island wid big estates. I should give my life so that they can keep hoggin' everything? Some people gotta be on top and some gotta be on bottom, I'll buy that. Ya gotta give 'em more fa runnin' things. But I don't buy the raw deal that the ones on bottom gotta starve for a bottle of milk while the ones on top are banking millions.

"Why should I believe these lecturers that the reds are rattle-snakes? Where do I know these lecturers from to trust them? I don' know them any better than I know the communists. I never met a communist, but I figure they're full of shit, too. I'll bet they tell their soldiers about the American menace. No matter how they tag themselves, they're just people like anybody else. I bet in Russia there are some on top living it up and most on the bottom getting crumbs so they can keep the machines going. Even if the communists are full of shit, why should I go fight them? Either way I'm getting the shaft.

"Maybe I won't get killed if I go. Maybe I'll just have part of my face blasted off so they'll take part of my ass and graft it where my face was. You can see goin' around fa the rest of ya life wid a hunk of ass flesh growing on ya face. The girls would make a fuss at first and then I'd be a freak. God gamme a nice lookin' face and He di'nt intend it ta have no ass growin' on it.

"And what happens if they put my young bod ta sleep? Don't sweat it. You get an honor burial. Remember '*a bon anima*' Nicky's funeral? They have six Marines there in dress blues. They shoot rifles in the air and a bugler plays taps. The flag is on the coffin first and then they take it off and give it to your mother. And then your warm eighteen-year-old life is sealed under dirt. Your mother probably gets a medal for you. Everybody says you're a hero. But what do you hear or see? Nuttin' that's goin' on in life matters. You're in that dark box wid your eyes closed forever.

"All the big speeches about the worthy cause is a lotta hocus-pocus ta me. Millions of kids my age have been handed that bullshit since the beginning of time. They all were goin' off fa the great cause. In the Roman movies ya see the leaders give 'em the same pep talk and they go marchin' off. I'm not gonna be caught in these imbeciles' madness. All the bugles blowin' and the drums, and the talk about sacred cause, that's all noise to me like the Pied Piper. The nitty-gritty is being on a patch of dirt wid artillery blastin' ya into chop meat. None of these people in high positions are looking out for me. They don't know I exist. To them I'm just one of a million specks dumped into a big river. And that big dumb river just keeps going the same way for thousands of years over a waterfall. No dumb river is gonna sweep me along in its current and push me over that fall.

"Get outta this Marine Corps. Don't go ta no Lebanon. They'll call it a disgrace if ya don't. Ta me 'disgrace' is noise out of someone's mouth. Life is life and everything else is talk. What people do is like raining and snowing. They're just movements. Running off the base is like a stone rolling. I'll say whether it's good or bad. I'm not gonna dance to other peoples' tunes.

"Plenty of these recruits are like frightened cows going in which ever direction they are yelled at ta go in. Like the ones I saw go into the slaughterhouse."

I had a fear of the severe authority of the Marines represented by the tough drill instructors and officers. But I also had the habit of doing what I wanted to do and not obeying authority. In a way the feelings inside me were the same as when I was told to do an errand by Ma and I went to play ball instead. Backing up my self-will was what I learned from Tony: "I don't give a fuck fa these drill instructors or anybody else."

"Where are those balls ya supposed ta have?" I told myself. "Just walk out that door and leave this place."

"If you do," another side warned, "it'll ruin any chance you have of making somethin' outta yourself. Wid a dishonorable discharge ya're through. Ya'll disgrace ya family."

33 Everyone in the hut was asleep when I slipped out. I didn't get far. A patrol on watch tackled me in the street. They called for the sergeant of the guard. He ordered me put in the guardhouse. It was late at night so no formal action could be taken until the next day. The guardhouse was only for temporary custody. It was a small single-story building made from thin plasterboard. The one room inside was bare except for a desk. The sergeant put me to work dusting the bulkheads. When I finished that chore he handed me a mop and bucket. "Give the deck a good swabbing," he said chewing a wad of gum. I stroked the floor a few times with the mop, and then threw it at him. "Swab the fuckin' thing yaself." I wanted to get out of the Marines and here they had me tamely mopping their floors. I punched the wall in anger. The plasterboard was so brittle my fist went through. I decided to walk through the wall. Aghast at first, the sergeant sounded the alarm. The patrol on duty collared me again. A court-martial was convened in the morning. It was a summary proceeding with one stern officer presiding. When he read the report that I had walked through a wall he looked astounded. After lambasting me for my actions, he sentenced me to two weeks in the brig. Two M.P.s came to take me away.

The brig was a fortlike mound of granite blocks painted yellow. An armored door outside opened to a corridor leading to a wall of bars. Behind the bars an open compound sloped back about a hundred feet to two tiers of cells. The M.P.s took me to the warden's office and then left when the brig guards entered. The warden, who had the eyes of a barn burner, sat at his desk puffing on a pipe as he calmly told me how much he missed the stench of death in the trenches and how he despised playing jailer to a bunch of malingering scum. The government spent $20,000 to train him as an artillery officer. That money was going to waste unless there was war, and he would feel cheated, too, unless there was one soon. He didn't sign on for twenty years to sit at a desk.

Reveille was at 0400 the next morning. We were shocked awake by the grating clatter of garbage cans hurled against our cells. The next sound was the cannon voice of the burly bulldog-mouthed sergeant in charge of the compound. "Muster in a column of two's for perfume." Bending over, we dropped our skivvies so he could spray our behinds with delousing powder. After dressing we marched to the chow hall for breakfast. The march took an hour because of "air raid drills." Every puddle we came to we had to fall into at the command "prisoners down." On the chow hall steps we were given the command "to the rear, harch," and marched back to the brig. After ten trips back and forth we finally were allowed inside to eat. The posture for eating was attention. Our shoulders had to be rigidly upright and we couldn't talk. A prison chaser with a shotgun stood behind us enforcing the rule. If anyone moved he got jarred in the back with a rifle butt.

Returning to the brig compound, we remained in formation until everyone was frisked for utensils. Then ten minutes were granted for a head call. There was a single tile bowl projecting from the side wall. It jutted out above the ground with no enclosing partitions. The first time I saw it I took it for a drinking fountain. We lined up in front of this one toilet bowl like patrons at the box office of an Academy Award movie. Around sixty prisoners faced me in a single file as I sat on the pot. Within seconds they were yelling, "Hurry up. What's takin' ya so long?" For three days I was constipated, unable to go in front of an audience. Another inmate told me he had the same trouble but found that if he drank loads of coffee it acted as a laxative. I drank a full pot the next morning and almost couldn't hold off the cramps during the march back to the brig. No one yelled at me this time. As soon as I got on the bowl it was like opening the hatch of a cement mixer.

Work commenced at 0600. The turnkey passed out scrub

brushes to the prisoners. Hot water was then hosed into the compound until it was flooded up to our knees. We duck-walked back and forth through the water scrubbing the concrete floor. My knees ached from the continuous squatting. Hours seemed to go by, but when I looked up at the enormous clock on the wall only minutes had passed. Anyone who stalled to rest was kicked in the ribs. When our legs began to shake we secured for a new detail. The hot water was drained out of the compound and a junk peddler's wagon rolled in, heaped with rusted cheese graters, plumbing pipes, strips of fender, and other metal scraps. We were each given a scrap and a piece of steel wool. We polished the scrap long enough to revive our legs and then secured to scrub the floor again.

This alternating sequence of scrubbing and polishing went on through the day. No talking was allowed during work. Permission had to be requested to step over painted lines. The slightest infraction brought a punch to the solar plexus. The main purpose of the brig was to punish. It wounded prisoners to the breaking point but never allowed them to break. The big clock was intentionally put in front of us so that we had to watch the minute hand move slowly, like a glacier, to each dot. The maximum period of detention at the Parris Island brig was a few months, which was as long as most recruits could stand such intensive nerve jagging. Serious offenders sentenced to long terms were committed to the federal penetentiary. They were considered dangerous to personnel or property and were confined to protect the military establishment and society. The short-term inmates of the brig were not there for serious violations. They were regarded as rebels who needed a lesson in misery to be squared away. The object was to terrorize the recruit, to implant such a dread for the brig that he would do the things he rebelled against rather than go back.

Even the brig had its pauses of normal life. Sergeant MacIntosh, who was on turnkey duty three nights a week, relaxed the unreal treatment and talked to us as a friend. He was the Pat O'Brien type: a soft-hearted, down-to-earth, gutsy Irishman. Once he called me outside the compound to give me advice about the Marine Corps. He said if I made a bad record it would be O.C.S. (over choppy seas) with the Grunts (infantry). They would probably make me a B.A.R. man—an automatic weapons man who's given thirty-seven seconds to live in combat. Talking about the Middle

East, he said, "I hope to God we don't have to go to war. Anyone who says he ain't afraid is wacky. Listen, ya only got one mark against you. Square yaself away and ya can still get that good mamasun duty in Japan." I respected Sergeant MacIntosh and promised him I would straighten out.

When I was released in two weeks I was transferred to another platoon. The platoon was in its first day of training so I had to repeat the initial processing again. That meant another visit to the plyer-happy dentists who already pulled three of my molars; to the health center for immunization shots (each recruit got seventeen needles by the end of training); and to ordnance and hygienics for issuance of a rifle, bayonet, cartridge belt, field equipment, and Listerine. All Marines in boot camp had to gargle with Listerine before going to bed.

I competed again in the five physical fitness events: pull-ups, push-ups, sit-ups, squat-thrusts, and the 220 dash. I did thirty pull-ups and scored the highest combined score in the platoon. My new drill instructors appointed me a squad leader again. One of the boys in my squad was from a farm in Tennessee. At chow we traded stories about our home towns. I told him how in summer when it was hot we showered under a fire hydrant in the street. He said in the country they cooled off by floating down the river in a tire tube. My hangout in the city was the poolroom. He said he spent a lot of his time dragging Main and in the barn. He used to plow sheep in the barn.

The first week after the brig I applied myself to training, determined not to go back. But toward the end of the second week the feelings that bothered me before were surfacing again. As the memory of the brig receded, the rebel impulses in me grew stronger, but I was still able to contain them, never showing any sign of discontent. Occupied with tasks during the day, it was mainly at night that I would look inside myself. "Who am I?" I wondered. One Joe tries to run away. Another Joe is a squad leader. One voice inside of me tells me to break out of this fuckin' Marine Corps. Another feeling urges me to become a good Marine.

The third week things were still within bounds until the morning they served powdered eggs in the chow hall. The eggs were scrambled, so looking at them I couldn't tell they were powdered. When I tried to eat them I had trouble swallowing. My throat heaved them back up. No matter how hard I tried I couldn't get them down. They made me nauseous the way liver did. The rule was that you had to finish everything on your plate. I stuffed the eggs in a cereal box hoping to get by the mess officer. At the rear of the chow hall trash cans were filled with hot water. Recruits lined up in front of them to bus their trays. The mess officer standing at the head of the line inspected each tray as it passed him. Knowing all the gimmicks, he snooped in my cereal box and saw the eggs. He dumped them back in the dish.

"You better go back and finish your chow, private."

"Listen, I tried ta but I couldn't. I didn't know they were powdered. They make me sick."

"You took them. You better eat them."

"But I told ya they make me sick."

"If you don't take these eggs back and finish them yourself, I'm gonna shove them down your throat."

"Well, I'm not gonna eat the fuckin' things."

Wresting my head with one hand, he took a gob of eggs and tried to force it in my mouth. I dropped the tray and drove him into the barrels. They fell making a loud noise and swashing water all over. He tried judo on me. I knocked him down between tables. The buzzing of recruits clamored all the way to the other side of the chow hall. My drill instructors came running over. I zigzagged past them to make it out the door. It would be another month in the brig if they caught me. I headed for the swamps. I was through with the Marine Corps. I wanted out. Rifle Range Baker was the last flat area before the everglades. There were no fences around the training area. The drill instructors said they weren't needed. The boondocks, as they called the swamps, were a maze of growth, quicksand, and water moccasins. I didn't know how I was going to get off the island. I couldn't think. Reason vanished as mist. I had cut the string back at the chow hall when I punched the mess officer. Emotion took over. It told me to run. There was no weighing the obstacles or consequences. I was just impulse on the move. I waded across a silty creek. I didn't know if it was Ribbon Creek where seven recruits drowned in a forced night march. Croaking frogs were camouflaged in the moss and sumac. Deeper in the swamps I came upon moist sand pits and stepped on a bed of black shells that made a clapping sound.

Tired from running, I sat down to rest hidden by a thicket of reeds. My first thoughts were about the M.P. patrols that must have been sent after me. I wondered if they had hounds and how close they were getting. Then I started to think about the future. What was going to happen to me? I felt that I had blown everything. If they threw me out of the Corps with a dishonorable discharge that would exclude me from any civil service job. I shuddered seeing myself loading almonds at the warehouse the rest of my life. I would be a stick-up man before that. But being a gunman just wasn't my nature. I couldn't see myself killing people for money. The only thing that seemed left was to become a professional fighter. That was the last driftwood to grab onto.

But what if they wouldn't discharge me? I wanted to get out and didn't care what happened later. It seemed wrong that just because I signed a piece of paper they could keep me where I didn't want to be. I didn't own my own life anymore. They were going to lock me up in that bedlam brig again because I wouldn't let some guy shove eggs down my throat. To escape the nightmare of the present I pictured the future. I thought about where I would be in five years. I knew this would be all over by then. I would be somewhere else, probably in Pop's. "In five years it'll all be in the past, forgotten about. But now I'm stuck here in the middle of breakin' a rule, wid the whole base after me."

I sat in the thicket and kept scratching my upper arm. It was itchy at first but then it felt like a bite. I crooked my arm around and saw a tick. I tried to scrape it off but it was buried in my flesh. The little parasite was blown up like a pea from sucking my blood. Relieved that it wasn't a water moccasin, I still worried it might give me a disease. I took off my belt to use the corner as a blade. I tried stabbing the tick with the point, but it wouldn't come out. The thing burrowed its claws into a fold of skin. I got up and ran on in the swamps. From the change in temperature I could tell that a couple of hours had passed. Early morning in South Carolina was chilly, but by noon the sun was sweltering. On base we had to wear caps and we had salt tablets to protect against heatstroke. Roving, with no sense of direction, I came to a road. I followed its course hoping it led off the base. The road forked a few hundred yards from where I picked it up. I stayed on the side that looped into a woodland area scattered with picnic tables. I thought it was strange to find picnic grounds on Parris Island. The families living on the base probably used it. No one was around except a pair of squirrels pacing on top of a food stand. Hungry, I thought about breaking into it, but then remembered the Uniform Code of Military Justice. The penalties under the U.C.M.J. were primitively severe. Breaking into the stand would be classified defacing government property, and removing food would be stealing government property. In the brig we were required to learn the U.C.M.J. By the language of the code such acts could carry twenty to thirty years. I didn't know whether they really inflicted such grave penalties, but the possibility deterred me. The military had a way of magnifying a small wrong into a solemn offense against the United States of America.

An M.P. truck pulled up to the picnic grounds and a squad jumped off. They spread out to screen the area. If I tried to run they would have known I was the man they were after. Thinking quickly, I picked up a pole with a sticker on the end. Then while the M.P.s were approaching I went around sticking leaves and emptying them in the litter basket. It was like in the supermarket. I acted as though I was going about my normal business. The M.P.s walked by, continuing their search. The deception didn't last long. They were back five minutes later to get me. Put in the back of the truck at gunpoint, I was taken to the provost marshal's station. It was a two-story wooden building with offices on the bottom and barracks on top. The M.P.s burned the tick off my arm. A cocky Nazi-type lance corporal remained with me as the others went upstairs. The frilly M.P. uniform must have gone to his head. He had on a tidy green suit with white spats, a white cartridge belt totting a big .45 pistol, a red armband, a silky white scarf, braided shoulder emblems, and a white cap with a shiny brass insignia.

"Where are you from?" he asked.

"Brooklyn."

"Brooklyn what, maggot?"

"Brooklyn, sir."

"Oh, a bad ass from New York and a Wop, too. Do you know what the sound of shit makes when it hits the wall? Wop!" he taunted.

I wanted to punch his face.

"I don't like bad-ass Wops. Ya know that? You're not going to be a bad-ass in my Corps. Understand that?" He jabbed his finger in my chest.

I lunged at his head and rattled it against the wall. He paled, and yelled for his buddies. The whole garrison came swarming down the stairs. I raked the faces of the ones in front, knocking them down. More swept around. Finally, they overwhelmed me. I was forced to the floor and handcuffed. They carried me out to a truck and put me in the back, face down. An M.P. with a nightstick straddled my head. If I moved he butted my skull. The truck stopped after a short ride. When we got out I saw the brig. They dragged me up to solitary. Shoving me in they banged shut the solid door. I yelled out curses, but no one heard me. The walls and floor were padded with wrestling mats.

There was nothing else in the cell except darkness. I sat on the floor for hours. Then the heavy lock turned and the door opened a bit. Light rayed in accompanied by the sound of scrubbing. A guard put a tray of food down. I was rationed to sandwiches. He closed the door so I couldn't see what was in the bread. It tasted like apple butter and cream cheese. Later the guard came back for the tray and tossed in a bedpan. I sensed when it was night outside, but I really didn't know. It was night all the time in solitary. My moods ranged wildly. I felt sorry for myself. I cried. Other times I felt comfort in being alone. It was peaceful in the silent dark. I sang songs. "Blueberry Hill" was my favorite. Before enlisting I loved to listen to Fats Domino sing it. Nostalgic images skipped in my mind. I longed to go for a walk in my neighborhood. I craved spicy Italian foods. I was starved for a baked *calzone*, a puffy crust filled with ricotta cheese and prosciutto ham. I missed girls, too, but not for their bodies. Saltpeter took away that urge. I missed the pleasurable pang of having a crush on a girl and the exhilaration of coming home after the first date with her. I remembered the girls I had gone steady with and thought about the nice times we'd had.

As days passed, which I counted by meals, I started to feel afraid. I worried about being left in the dark cell and forgotten about. It was unreasonable, but being alone has strange effects. At times I felt the way I did once when my brother put a pillow over my head. It was a panicky feeling of suffocating.

34 The M.P.s came for me again on the eighth day. I must have looked weird to them with thick black hair on top and a fuzzy red beard below my sideburns (a souvenir of the Vikings who had raided Italy). Instead of reporting to Battalion Head-

quarters for a court-martial, the M.P.s headed in a different direction. The jeep pulled into the driveway of a white hospital building on stumpy stilts. They ordered me upstairs to P.O.U. (Psychiatric Observation Unit). We entered a wing with bunk beds on each side. Patients moped around the ward. All were dressed in the same blue robes and slippers. One with mobile eyeballs followed our path to the desk. A Navy corpsman with a clipboard was sitting there, flanked by two orderlies guarding the swinging doors. The corpsman talked to the M.P.s out of my hearing. Before leaving they warned me that if I pulled any more stunts I would be back in solitary. The corpsman remarked that the whole base knew about me. I was actually glad to be in the nuthouse, seeing it as a way off the island. I thought of things I could do to make them believe I was crazy. There was a bottle of ink on the desk. If I poured it on my hair that would be a good starter. Talking to the corpsman I blinked my eyelashes like Morse code. He was evaluating me on a chart. By society's view, going out beyond a margin of conformity signifies a person is crazy. To me society was mad in its practice of human butchery, and sanity lay outside its margin.

I played Ping-Pong the rest of the afternoon. At night I couldn't sleep. An orderly with a bedpan and flashlight made rounds waking up chronic bedwetters. In the morning two psychiatrists examined me. Both were Naval officers. The first man questioned me in a clinical but friendly manner. During our conversation I mentioned my grandmother in some connection. "Oh!" His eyebrows raised as though he was onto something. He pursued the subject. "Your grandmother is very important to you, isn't she?" At the same time that he perceived the key to a mental mystery, I had a flash of the ripcord out of the Marines. If he thought I had some kind of grandmother complex, I wasn't going to quash it. I talked the rest of the hour about my grandmother. I gibbered silly things like how I liked to watch her boil lobsters. He took down everything I mentioned in detailed notes.

The second psychiatrist was hostile to me, and acted more military than doctor. He predicted that I would end up in the electric chair. I talked to him straight. I told him I hated the military. He tried to taunt me. "You can't take it. The training is too much for your fragile body." I laughed inside. I beat everyone in the platoon in physical competition. Boot camp was a burlesque next to boxing. "What I can't stand," I told him, "is the ant-hill life." I also couldn't accept a war with Arabs over oil, but I never expressed that feeling. Instinct warned against it. My chance of being discharged would be better if the issue was solely my inability to adjust to military life. If they had any inkling that feelings against war were involved it would have been a different poker game. The second psychiatrist had me remitted to the brig. I didn't stay long. Within a few days I was summoned to a hearing before a board of officers.

After deliberating for an hour they recommended my release on grounds of unfitness. Higher-ups soon finalized it. On the day I was to leave Parris Island, my uniform was taken away and I was given a pink suit to go home in. They ordered me to parade around the base in it so all the recruits could see the disgrace in being banished from the Corps.

Ashamed to face my family in the pink suit, I wanted to buy a uniform when I arrived in New York. There was a string of army and navy surplus stores on 42nd Street. The owner of the first one I tried, eyeing the pink suit, asked for my military I.D. When I told him I didn't have one he looked at me as if I was a contaminated grub and walked away. Several other patriotic storekeepers spurned me after him. Finally, I found a place on Eighth Avenue that didn't ask any questions. The only full Marine uniform they had in stock was at least a size too small, but I bought it anyway. Taking it down to the men's room of the Automat, I changed clothes in a toilet stall. On the subway going home, I was treated with extra courtesy by workers because of the uniform. "G'head, gyrene, sit down," a man got up to give me his seat. "My boy was in the Corps, too." Their kindness added to the guilt I felt wearing the uniform. I got off at the Fort Hamilton Station. As I walked up my block I thought about the scenes in the Marine movies where the boy's family has welcome-home signs in the window and his mother and father happily embrace him at the door. It was a quiet scene when Ma let me in. Dad was sitting at the table eating. Both of them looked hurt, which hurt me. I expected Dad to holler at me, but he just sat there. Ma's first words were about the chaplain's letter. She tried to console herself by his statement, "Not everyone can be a Marine! God might have another design for him." But I could tell she was disappointed.

The rest of my relatives thought there was something wrong with me in the head. All my uncles served honorably in World War II. They wanted to know why I couldn't stick it out and get an

Honorable Discharge. Grandma's feelings must have been strong because she insisted that I visit a psychiatrist, and psychiatry was unheard of to immigrants.

At Pop's I got an entirely different reception. Being bounced from the military was normal for the Fort Hamilton Boys. Practically everyone in the gang lasted only a few months and then was thrown out with Bad Conduct, Section 8, General, or Dishonorable discharges. One of the few who completed his tour of duty, whom the army considered sane, was the guy who went amuck crowning people with bowling balls at the time of the Avenue U trouble. Ralphie Shades held the record for the shortest hitch: one week. To get his Bad Discharge he got up in the middle of the night and pretended to sleepwalk into the officer's tent with a bayonet. Richie received an Undesirable in a month by dancing naked on the roof of the barracks. Of course, others like Tony never made it past the induction center. When he went for his physical Tony mussed his hair to "trick" the doctors into thinking he wasn't all there. The examining psychiatrist asked him if he would be able to get along without women for a long period.

"Oh, yeah," he answered. "I seen a lotta sweet lookin' lieutenants I wouldn't mind canning."

A few days after Cord was drafted he was committed to the Valley Forge Mental Hospital. Considered dangerous because he assaulted an officer, he was placed in a padded cell. On the wall inside there was a shoe-polish scrawl, "Doodles was here." Not to be outdone by anyone from Pop's, he proudly scrawled his name in bigger letters, "Cord was here."

The best story involved Baldy and a guy from the East Side during the early occupation of Germany. Tracked down as deserters, they barricaded themselves in a farmhouse. The captain of the troops seiging the farmhouse called to the two men through a loudspeaker, "Give yourselves up. You don't have a chance. The place is surrounded by water. There's no way out."

"That's what you think," Baldy cried back. "We're building a boat."

After they were apprehended they were flown back to the States under ice cubes and committed to Valley Forge, where they were kept in ice cubes. It was part of shock therapy, which included the administering of insulin and electric currents. The purpose of the treatment was to bring the patients for a short while into a state of mental clarity and greater contact with reality so that the therapist could communicate with them. The problem the medical people overlooked was that Baldy and the East Sider had their own reality.

Timmy Kelly was the only friend who was sorry that I did not last in the Marines. We talked about it going for a walk one night. I told him I saw certain things to be the main goods in life and others as window dressing. Eating spaghetti and drinking wine, conversing with your friends, having a family—to me these were the essentials of life. To die for a word like valor was stupid. I viewed the Marines as not just a corps out there now but part of a billion men fighting over something labeled time. To me it was all one cauldron—the cavemen smiting each other with clubs, the Roman legions coming over the hill with pikes, the troops charging into tanks. Neither uniforms, weapons, nor time divided anything for me. Stripped of all the artificial word dividers, history was just a continuous rash of killings. I didn't express myself in educated words but I could separate action from language.

Timmy agreed with some of my beliefs and challenged others. As a law student he respected the Bill of Rights. "If we didn't have it, some bureaucrat would be telling us what to do, what to say, what to see, what not to do, and the rest of it. Like you say boot camp was an ant colony, that's the way society would be. When it comes to protecting those rights I'd go to war myself. People don't live by bread alone."

What he said made sense to me, yet I still considered war madness. Nothing was ever resolved by war because it was an unending process and nations disappeared. Statesmen merely temporized with millions of lives.

I also couldn't see how Lebanon threatened the Bill of Rights.

35 I climbed up the rickety stairs to Stillman's Gym. A homely man with lumpy ears looked at my card and let me enter. Spectators who wanted to get in paid fifty cents admission. Inside, they could watch the action in two rings where sniffing pugs in headgear stood toe to toe, banging each other. Frequently, more attention was paid to the shady characters in flamboyant overcoats and felt hats who formed caucuses around the floor. Sometimes a legendary fight figure would be recognized. "That's

Whitey Bimstein, the trainer," someone would point out. "He sucked blood outta Graziano's eye in the Billy Arnold fight. They woulda stopped it if it wasn't fa that."

Gino, my new manager, intercepted me at the locker room door and told me to bring out my sparring gear. The smelly locker room was sown with dirty jockstraps and stale socks. I hastily changed into my sweatsuit and escaped from the dank quarters. Hurricane Jackson shadowboxed out to the gym floor ahead of me practicing his famous double uppercut.

I reported to trainer Johnny Zulo, who was getting me ready for my first pro fight. Johnny trained champions and contenders as well as apprentices like me. According to Gino, I'd have a couple of A.A.U. bouts. "Just ta tune you up," he said. "But after that, forget the amachoors, ya gonna be makin' money."

As it turned out, I couldn't get an A.A.U. match so I entered the Golden Gloves again in the open class. I weighed in at 178 now, so I was moved up to the light-heavyweight division. My first opponent was a lissome Negro from the Salem Crescent A.C. In the opening seconds my opponent's punches stung, but as the round moved on adrenaline had the effect of Novocain. Not every punch was painless; the impact of a fist driven into my solar plexus choked off my breath, an uppercut forced my lower teeth through my inner lips, and a bolo made me dizzy. There was a sluggishness in my right shoulder, but I won the fight with a knockout in the first round.

Word got around that I was a hard puncher, and a large following turned out for all my fights. Fight fans enjoy the spectacle of one boxer brutalizing another. Glancing out at the crowd when I had my opponent hurt, I saw faces inscribed with sadistic pleasure screaming at me: "put 'im away, put 'im away, kill him," reminiscent of the gladiator battles. The patricians at ringside disguise their gratifications behind stolid faces and tuxedos. Aroused women look up at us with carnal eyes. Members of down minorities thirsting for glory rally with ardor behind their kinsman. To the fighter the contest is often a bruising duel, but there are nights the destructive instinct takes over. With your blood heated by the hot lights and excitement gorging your veins, adrenaline flooding, nerve centers pulsating, and the roaring multitude, you feel a lust of power destroying another man.

Advancing to the quarter finals in the Golden Gloves I withdrew from the tournament. Gino judged I was ready to go pro. The pro limit for light-heavies is 175, but I felt weak at that weight. I stood only 5'10" but my heavy bone structure made my best weight 185. Gino was pleased: "That's where all the gravy is."

As I began to spar with heavyweights my body was in for new punishment. When a man weighing 250 pounds smashes his fist into your face, everything in your head vibrates, sometimes causing painful headaches that last for days. Ordinarily when sparring I would hold back. I liked to spar lightly, feeling that this was only a rehearsal so why go all out. But with heavies I found that tempers flare. When some Gargantua started bombing me it ended up in a grudge battle with both of us trying to knock each other out. Once I knocked out a 230-pound sparring partner with fourteen-ounce gloves. Gino jumped up and down with elation where the guy was draped over the ropes.

With my height and reach, in every case shorter than my heavy-weight opponent, the only way I could land punches was to get in close. This meant that I often rushed into punches that had the impact of a head-on collision. My headaches grew worse and purple-black puffs sprouted around my eyes. Back in my P.A.L. days I proudly wore a black eye as a badge of bravery. Now I worried about being disfigured. All around the gym there were warning wrecks in the pulp-nosed, porridge-brained ex-pugs. Whatever fame they once knew had been attained at the price of having their mental vitals gelded.

I went to see a doctor about my headaches. His prognosis was probably the same for every boxer he examined: "You'll end up with your hands just pieces of bone, your elbows full of cartilage buildup, your shoulders in pain from bursitis, and your brain impaired . . . . " Before leaving his office I asked him to take a look at my right shoulder where a vein popped out like a grapevine. It first appeared when I was doing the strenuous warehouse work. The doctor said he had never seen anything like it before and told me to get over to Bellevue's Skin and Cancer Clinic. At the clinic I was seated beneath a flying-saucer lamp as a team of medical men circled around me, poking at the vein and remarking "extraordinary." Finally came the diagnosis: "hypervascular development," nothing to be worried about but the vein would cause a tightening of the arm muscles at times. I was relieved. I also knew why my punches were becoming sluggish.

Although I fought a couple of "tune-ups," my professional career as a boxer never got off the ground. A few months after my visit to the doctor, I quit the ring. A lot of things went into my decision: the hypervascular development, the headaches from sparring, the prospect of being disfigured. But probably the strongest cause was the fear of becoming a mental eunuch.

▬▬▬▬▬▬▬▬▬▬▬▬▬▬▬▬▬▬▬▬▬▬▬▬▬▬▬▬▬▬

36 I got a night job as a porter at New York's Central Produce Market. Fruits and vegetables were spread over ten acres of cement. The merchants' beat-up buildings with their sagging canopies snuggled against each other for blocks. Cobblestone streets arched for drainage weaved down to the pier. Floodlights stared out the night. The market bordered on the spice belt, a stretch of warehouses storing herbs from all over the world. Delectable scents of ginger, sage, nutmeg, curry, and cloves mingled in the air. Cross-country diesels with refrigerated trailers smoked down the streets. Horse-drawn wagons clippity-clopped behind them. In midsummer the market was a sweltering greenhouse.

I worked for Carbone Brothers, a wholesale house trading in lettuce, carrots, grapes, peaches, and succulent cranshaw melons priced as much as five dollars apiece. I had never seen a cranshaw before. At that time only the delicacy stores in the townhouse neighborhoods carried them. There were forty-six porters on the payroll, and all except me were black. The foreman put me on the carrot detail. Bouncing back and forth from farm vans to the sidewalk, I stowed thousands of carrots on a corrugated steel platform. To keep the carrots fresh, ice was packed on top of the dirt-fraught crates. Mud slushed down upon my clothes every time I lifted a crate, and my chest was soon caked with dirt. I never wore gloves, so I nicked my hands on the abrasive ice grains.

Midway through the night the porters were told, "Grab yaselves a bite and get back." After a quick meal we returned to load the retail trucks. They were parked blocks from the house. To get there I stepped into a harness and hauled the carrots in a two-wheel cart. Fifteen crates were loaded into the cart, weighing over eleven hundred pounds. I pulled the cart over slippery cobblestones and sometimes hit bumps that shifted the weight to the rear and flipped me up in the air. My path was marked by horse plops.

I felt like an animal. The market was a spectator event for sophisticates. After a night at the theater and some posh club they came down to cruise around. Once I heard a woman squeal, "Isn't it marvelous." Nearby a porter urinated against the wheel of a truck. A man in a tux rolled down the front window of his limousine and called to me, "Hey, young man. Can we buy some of your carrots?" I gave him a bunch and watched them eat. "A raw carrot, how scrumptious," the woman said, biting into one.

"What's the big deal about a raw carrot?" I thought.

The sidewalk in front of our building was rancid with rotten fruit. But the foulest thing around was the melon salesman. He was a fish-eyed gargoyle with a malignant tumor for a heart. The filth out of his mouth was a cesspool. I couldn't believe the abuse taken by buyers dependent on him. The owner, who was a very nice man, viewed him as too pathetic to fire.

Most nights the porters stayed on for overtime; a common workday was from 3 P.M. to 5 A.M. When I punched out I felt like a turtle crawling from his shell. My lower back ached from the continuous stooping under weight. Time lost its separateness. Once I was on the subway it was a fifty-minute ride home. Sleeping eight hours, I had an hour to get back to work. Five days dissolved into one hazy grind. On Friday nights, however, everyone came alive at the market. Ernie Lem would always sing, "It's Friday, it's Friday."

"Hey, Ernie," I called over to him. "I'm glad, too, but what's the singing for?"

"Joey," he smiled, "if you could be black one weekend you wouldn't wanna be white no more."

The girls I dated on weekends were from the market offices. There was one woman, a bookkeeper, who was the brood mare of the market. Her apartment was like Grand Central when her husband was out. The day I was over her husband called to find out what groceries to bring home for dinner. Stroking my body, she recited a recipe to him for a casserole. She rolled on top of me giving him the last ingredient, "And a can of cream of chicken, dear." Click! After two hours I wobbled out of bed and groped for my clothes. She jumped up angrily. "Damn it, what about me now?"

The weekend was a brief pause from the same scene of crates and carrots. On Sunday the market reopened and my senses lapsed back into limbo. I would trudge up the dressing room stairs to change into my coveralls. The walls were shingled with Negro pin-ups from *Jet* magazine. Sometimes Charlie Joe and Streamline sat on the bench looking at them.

"They sho sumpin," Charlie Joe said.

"They sheet. They all too skinny," Streamline said.

"Donchoo wish you had em heah? Whadda you think, Joeih?"

"I think they're great."

I always stuck up for Charlie Joe. We worked side by side every night on the carrot detail. Tall, lithe, and without a wrinkle, wearing his cap he looked forty, but when he took it off a blizzard of white hair showed his sixty years. Chewing on a cigar, he walked out the door on fungo legs with a slow bounce to stack mud-dripping carrots again, something he had been methodically doing forty years of his life. He disliked the job but wasn't resentful like me or self-pitying like the melon man. It was honest work, and for Charlie Joe that was the main thing. Because of seniority, it was his prerogative to make deliveries with the company truck, which would have been a break from the tedium of carrots, but he always let me or one of the other young men take his place. In all the little advantages he put the young porters ahead of himself. Though gentle in his ways, he took no guff from the salesmen.

Streamline was a more defiant man. Once he choked the foreman for raising his voice at him. He drew a sharp line: the company owned his effort but not a smidgen more. Not even the boss could trespass on his integrity. At first I disliked him. He seemed offish and arrogant. Most porters used the handtrucks and carts randomly, not Streamline. Everything he used, even his broom, had his name on it and no one else could touch it. As I got to know him I found he was really a kind man. Having his own tools was his way. Because I was only nineteen, both Streamline and Charlie Joe had a protective attitude toward me. That changed after my fight with Jakey the Market Gambler.

Jakey roved around the market with a box of dice offering three-to-one odds to the player who bet the dice would come out nine or over. I started playing for fifty cents. I lost the first roll so I doubled my bet. This went on until my pay was gone. Brooding for days, I convinced myself the game was rigged. The next pay night I waylaid Jakey, picking him up feet first and shaking all the money out of his pockets. I took back my pay. Charlie Joe told the other porters, "Ya gotta give Joeih credit fo' not lettin' Jakey get away wit' it."

I made a lot of black friends at the market. My closest one was Hardy "Bazooka" Smallwood, who earlier had been like my stablemate at the gym. According to some scuttlebutt, blacks were yellow inside. There was a saying, "fights like a shine," which meant a black gets aggressive only if his opponent is hurt or afraid. But Hardy, who lost an eye in one bout, never took a backward step in his life. I tried not to get too tight with him because he was black, but he was such a warm, genuine friend I thought of him only as a person. In the Golden Gloves he was my cornerman, and many in the crowd considered it an outrage.

In parts of New York bigotry was imbedded in a bedrock of ignorance. Most of the working class were hyperconscious of race, creed, and nationality, and it was in the open in so many ways. New York's beaches were segregated. Italians bathed on Bay 15, Jews went to Brighton, blacks to the lower bays, "Americans" to Jones Beach, etc. At the polls a candidate's last name was perhaps his most important qualification. Parents of a girl asked out wanted to know "what is he?" Every group prized their blood as superior. Each pointed to the greats of their own kind, ignoring the lowly ones. Differences in culture should be preserved, but this was carried to where it became a crutch for an individual's own worth.

The worst hate was reserved for the blacks. "If they ever try to move on this block," Lefty once said, "we'll burn down their houses, their fuckin' babies, and everythin'." At Coney Island once, an elderly Negro crossed the invisible line separating black bathers from whites. He ventured over to watch the dancing under the boardwalk. Within seconds he was circled by whites five deep. The frightened man tried to say he was sorry, but before he finished, jagged beer bottles were knifing into his bare flesh. He was left for dead on the sand, his skin punctured with gushing rips. Someone called for an ambulance, which arrived shortly with the police. No one was questioned or arrested, not because the police approved but because they knew the whole beach community acted. Later that day the blacks retaliated. Five of them with glinting barber razors came onto a white bay and sliced bellies open.

I used to hate blacks. From boyhood on I was taught why. Uncle Joe complained about "the coons gettin' on the job." The man next door talked about "those *melanzanas* living in shit up in Harlem wid fodder screwin' daughter and brodder whoring sister." His wife mocked, "Those ugly things, they ain't God's children." Uncle

Ernie rasped, "Those jungle bunnies, all they know how ta do is go on welfare." The grocer talked about "nigger food—they eat shit like pigs knuckles and chitterlings." On the jobs I worked there were the Rastus jokes. In the bars you heard, "Ya can't take ya wife to a ballgame anymore wid them animals there." In the poolroom they were "those fuckin' boogies rooming in a purple Cadillac."

At the market I came to respect blacks but I never accepted the market. I wasn't going to spend the rest of my life in this sweat-pool. I tried to get out, but my past failures were like a dense layer of ice overhead. Nothing better was open to a dropout with a bad discharge and a police record. The only way to move was down.

I got in on a burglary. It wasn't as if I said, "Well, now I'll become a burglar." I was approached by Al the Gopher, who worked in a nearby warehouse. He said it would be a cinch to knock off his place. The miserable way things were going for me, I was interested. I didn't care what happened anymore. We planned the heist in an hour. Two others were involved, Al's cousin and a guy with a stolen station wagon. I had qualms that night, but the next day I went through with it. Al let me in the back door of his warehouse, and I sneaked down the cellar to hide until closing time. It was a clammy, dark place with burlap sacks of bean pow-der piled as high as levees. Bags were gutted where marauding rats had gnawed into them. I sat in the dark beleaguered by scratching sounds, almost more afraid of the rats than of being caught. They grew huge at these food-laden waterfront warehouses. Hand trucks clanked above me for hours. Then the floors were silent. When I went upstairs it was eight-thirty by the office clock. The key was hanging on the file cabinet, where Al said it would be. At nine o'clock I opened the door for them. As they hurried in I realized a blunder in our plan. How were we going to close the door when we left? The manager locked the front door from the outside and took the key home with him. I couldn't take home the key to the back door. They would notice it missing the next day and suspect an inside job. Al couldn't bring it in the office in the morning ei-ther. That would look suspicious because he never went in there, and he might be seen trying to put it back. We decided to leave the door open and go ahead with it anyway. Al's cousin stood look-out as we loaded a thousand pounds of raisins in the station wagon. Nobody passed. All went smoothly leaving, too, but then Al blun-dered driving the wrong way on a one-way street. A lurking police car noticed and tore after us.

"Oh, Christ, fa raisins," I thought.

"Make a left," his cousin yelled.

Flooring it, Al swerved the car into a side street.

"Left again," I hollered. Before turning we could see the police make the first left.

"Right, quick, right."

We were going at breakneck speed but they were still barreling down. Now the siren was on. My heart dropped. "Turn again," I hollered. The back wheels snaked as the station wagon skidded into another side street.

"Right now." The only way to lose them was to keep turning in the short warehouse streets. We all ducked our heads expecting shots to start zinging through the rear window. Finally we pulled ahead that little bit more so that they couldn't tell which side street we went into and they guessed wrong. We sped back on the bridge to Brooklyn. The tunnel was always webbed with cops. At Al's place we unloaded the stuff in his garage. It was weeks before we found a fence, and it was a haggle to get fifty bucks from him. Al's share was twenty dollars. The rest of us got ten each. If the cops had caught us we would have faced a charge of grand larceny. That carried five to ten years. I realized how stupid it was to steal. Even if our haul was thousands of dollars instead of only ten it still would have been stupid. Ten young years are too precious to risk losing for the flashier car and clothes the money would be blown on.

I felt disgusted with myself. Everyone in my family was honest and hard working. I could steal at fifteen for fun, but now I was going on twenty and stealing was no way to make a living. I refused to go on any more burglaries with Al.

The next score he planned he bungled again. He and his cousin broke into a supermarket. Unable to crack the safe, they carted it out on a truck. Even away from the store they could not jimmy the safe open. It ended up scuttled in the East River with the money still inside. Al's second nickname was *malafagouda* (one who botches everything). A few years later this characteristic killed him. He strangled himself trying to perform an Asian rope trick.

Still miserable working at the market, I tried on weekends to find a new job. Nothing materialized. There were short-order cook and busboy jobs available but they were no better than being a market porter and they paid less. One day the thought occurred to me to go see Father Russo. He was a young priest I met at the confraternity dances. I knew he was influential with business people. He wrote a letter in my behalf to the Caristo Construction Company. I anticipated construction work would be a toilsome grind, but it was only thirty-five hours and paid $140 a week.

▚▚

37 Bricklayers on scaffolds were filling in the third floor of a new parochial school under construction. A row of gyrating cement mixers rattled in the street. One parked at the entrance released a fusillade of fluid rock down a metal chute. A Cyclone fence outside quarantined an area infested with crushed beer cans. Electricians, plumbers, and pipefitters trafficked in and out of the building's open archway. Husky laborers powdered with cement dust clambered aboard a construction elevator lugging buckets. Another struggled trying to steady a broncking wheelbarrow. I stepped into the supervisor's shack.

"I'm supposed ta report here." I handed my letter to the supervisor.

He glanced at it and then looked me over. "Young blood, huh? Go see Davey Brown. He'll put ya ta work with the cement crew."

"Where's that?"

"In the back."

I went inside the half-completed building. The bare walls were slotted for doors and windows. Uncovered wires and pipes crossed the ceiling; the floor was soggy dirt. A man in a robot mask was tempering metal with a flaming blue acetelyne torch.

"Gangway!" A laborer toting a beam approached me.

"Do you know where Davey Brown is?" I asked.

"Yeah, there's Captain Marvel over there." He pointed to a massively muscular guy wearing dungaree shorts and combat boots sprightly running up planks with a buggy full of cement.

Davey "Brown" Tannaro was a legend in the construction industry. I had heard of his feats of strength before, but I never believed them. I thought they were exaggerated like most things you hear. But after working with him a few days I became a believer. Standing 5'10", his clothes had to be specially tailored for him because he measured forty-nine inches around the chest and slanted down to twenty-nine at the waist. The girth of his arms was large but not overblown like Mr. Universe. He was strong in all ways, but phe-nomenally so in his wrists and shoulders. During lunch hour the la-borers competed to see who could lift more bricks by wrist action. (A bottom brick was held vertically palm down, like a skillet, while other bricks were stacked across the far end.) The average was two bricks. Five was exceptional. Davey could do thirteen. I always prided myself on being strong. In junior high I won the pull-up championship. In the Marines I had the highest strength score in my platoon. And when I worked at the import-export warehouse I could lift a 225-pound bale over my head. Yet Davey put me down like a baby in the arm wrestle. He beat me in one second. They brought a weightlifter around once to challenge him and he made short shrift of him, too.

Davey's shoulder power was even more extraordinary. The first time he ever threw a javelin he became champion of the 7th Army. Though inexperienced, he also trounced one of the best handball players in the army: General Gavin. It was the dot speed of Davey's serve from shoulder power that did it. After their match General Gavin and Davey became regular partners and they were unbeatable. For a year they played together and Gavin's chauffeur picked up Davey for every match. But the general would never stoop to converse with his partner. Davey was only a private.

Davey's comic-strip feat was his football throw on the fly 110 yards. He could stand behind one goal line and heave a spiral over the other. Only eyewitnesses could believe it. But Davey down-played it, pointing out that if there was a "Football Throw" Olym-pic event others would eclipse 110 yards. Still, he might have been an All-American or decathlon champion had he gone to college. In-stead he became the most prized worker in construction. Davey could have gone to college. His Regents scores in math, science, and biology were over ninety. He left school because it was what everyone else in his family and the neighborhood had done.

In the beginning he was happy as a laborer. He thrived on physical activity, and a cement laborer was one of the most strenu-ous jobs around. Many new men don't last a day. You shovel ce-ment all day while a foreman verbally flogs you, "*Yoma, yoma.*" The nickname "Brown" was attached because Davey loved the sun. While most laborers tried to duck into the shade, he turned toward the rays like a plant. No matter what time of year it was, his face was bronzed. In the winter he basked under ultraviolet. In the fall he compensated for the weak rays with intensifiers on his roof. He had one tinfoil reflector the size and shape of a coffin. He used to lay inside this sunbox for hours. Neighbors chuckled at the spectacle, and he realized he was going overboard. Married to a beautiful girl, Davey was a striking Sicilian with blond hair and electric blue eyes. When he was at McKinley Junior High School the girls' vote elected him student body president.

I was nineteen and he was twenty-eight but we still hit if off right away as friends because of our mutual craze for physical fitness. Every workday we ate lunch together at a health food store. He ordered organic soya beans shredded over organic cottage cheese mixed with uncooked, organic egg yolks. That was a little too healthy for me. Broiled beef patties were my usual selection. Fruit addicts, our dessert was always pounds of fresh grapes, nectarines, cherries, and bananas. We would take them back to the construction site and then sit in a nice sunny spot against the building for a symposium. Davey had read the classical epics of mythology and told me the stories of Ulysses, Achilles, and Beowulf, who had been his heroes and inspiration for strength since boyhood. Since he was twelve he had been lifting, pushing, squeezing, tensing, and resisting all kinds of weights. He did not want to become a "tape-measure athlete," as he described bodybuilders. His obsession was strength. Tigers fascinated him because they could perform magnificent feats of strength with such ease and grace.

Davey's reading was not confined to mythology. In the trunk of his car he had a small collection of paperbacks. His books included the Bible, a popularized version of Freud, one on flamenco music, several on health, and a primer to Greek philosophy. It surprised me because I never read books and didn't know any other laborers who did. I was sapped when I got home from work and in no mood to read. I had no inclination, either. I read two books in four years: *The Amboy Dukes* by Irving Shulman and *I, The Jury* by Mickey Spillane.

Davey treasured his philosophy book. When I looked at the long words at the top of the pages—NICOMACHEAN ETHICS, PLOTINUS-ENNEADS, EPICUREANISM,—I thought, "Oh, this is really hard stuff," and threw it back in the trunk. Davey said the chapter titles did injustice to the contents. A lot of the reading was down to our level. He explained some of the ideas in simple language. His understanding might not have been as deep as a college professor's, but he seemed to grasp the basics. "Stoicism," he said, "teaches the principle of mind over matter. It's almost like Freud's psychosomatic idea. Your brain controls your body. If you get walloped on the back you don't have to show pain; you can ignore it. Your mind can also say whether it's good or bad. A wallop on the back is neutral until you make a judgment. I'll give you another example. If you get shot down by a girl you don't have to show hurt feelings and you don't have to say it's bad. Like you might say it's a good thing she dumped me cause now I can meet other girls. The point is that getting shot down isn't inherently bad. Nothing is. Some stoics believe that not only attitudes but feelings are also in the mind. By will power you can shut off the pain impulses from your nerves."

The idea of controlling pain appealed to me very much.

Plato enthralled Davey. His method of dialogue made him very readable. The important idea Davey got out of Plato was that we can never find the truth. "There are a number of reasons for it. Our senses are imperfect. For example, an X ray can see things our eye can't. A dog can hear a dog whistle but we can't. Even with extensions like a microscope our vision is limited. Realms exist that even the microscope can't see. Another reason we can't know truth is because our feelings twist everything we see. You know the song 'Smoke Gets in Your Eyes.' When you care for a girl she can do no wrong. That's one example. Everything we experience is distorted by emotion."

Davey liked to philosophize. He often asked the question: "Why are people miserable?" Imitating Plato, his answers were usually framed in an analogy, and, naturally, in terms of a physical task. He said the average guy can only lift a hundred-pound stone, but everyone says he has to lift a two-hundred pounder to be worthy of respect. "You know, like they say a good person is not supposed to have sex, curse, drink, smoke, lie, lose his temper, and the rest. Then there's the things he's supposed to do like make a lot of money, own a new car, buy a house. It's like giving him a two-hundred pound stone to carry that he can't shoulder. And so he feels self-contempt or doesn't respect himself. I think it's stupid to say the guy has to carry it. Tell him he should try. The better he does, fine. But don't say he's nothing unless he measures up to two hundred."

A related idea of his was that a man is given many different stones to lift in life—a physical, spiritual, sexual, moral, social, financial, parental stone. He felt that mány people unfairly underrate themselves because they're bad in one event. "A man is the sum of his stones, and shouldn't put himself down because he's weak in one category."

Dormancy was his favorite theory. "So much of our potential is just sleeping there. If we make the effort we could do much better. A guy might think a hundred pounds is his maximum, but if he wakes up that dormant side he'd probably get up to a hundred-fifty. That applies to everything—making money, making girls, shooting pool.... While you and me are sleeping some guy is staying up all night thinking of ways to make money. He might not have as much potential as us, but what counts is that he's using all of his and we're not. That's why he's gonna be the one who makes important money."

Davey regretted the course of his life. At eighteen all that mattered to him was physical fitness and pocket money for dates. But now he wanted to provide his family with a nice home. He thought it would be exciting to travel around the world. His interest in health grew to a fascination with medicine. But it was too late to get out. He was nearing thirty and had a family to support. Externally he was always in good spirits, but he was really unhappy. The crags in his forehead and a receding hairline were making him realize the folly of having placed so much emphasis on the physical. Once he said, "Why do we think we're gonna stay young forever?"

After three months the job closed down because the contractor and union deadlocked on the new contract. For the time being I was out of work again.

▗▖▖▖

38 The Fort Hamilton section of Boro Park from 60th to 69th streets was not a squalid ghetto, but primarily a populous working-class neighborhood of multiple brick buildings from two- to four-stories high. Dad had moved the family there to get away from the violence of South Brooklyn. It turned out that while Fort Hamilton was not as run down, it was equally as violent. Killings were rampant. Frankie Yale was machine-gunned down in the street. Charlie Sige was machine-gunned in half in Dick's Candy Store. Butch Mecla was found shot in the street. Eighteen-year-old Freddy Adiro was garrotted, shot, and run over. Nick, the luncheonette owner, was stabbed to death. Jimmy B., the bookie, was found shot in his car. Ruddy Lupa was shot behind the Fortway Theater. Ralphie Shades bashed a Negro to death with a full gallon of wine. Jimmy Talma was shoved into a printing press.

After Tony Bavimo was killed, Dad started borrowing and saving to move the family away from Fort Hamilton. He bought a white-shingled, one-family house in East Flatbush. To help meet the mortgage he remodeled the second floor and converted it into a separate unit for a tenant. With four small railroad rooms and kitchenette downstairs and one tiny closet, it was a net loss in living space over the old apartment. The house was free of cockroaches but hosted hordes of whopping water bugs. Dad wasn't interested in finding more comfort. His main concern was to get the kids away from the gangs, racketeers, pool halls, and other bad influences of Fort Hamilton. Our new block was bounded by a playground, a library, and a series of shingled one- and two-family dwellings. I felt isolated in the new neighborhood. The only guys my age on the block were Jewish students from Brooklyn College who studied most of the time. Fort Hamilton was an hour away, but I drove there every night.

Since Tony's death the Fort Hamilton Boys had steadily declined. No one was interested or brave enough to risk moving the gang again. The days of thrills and license were over. The focus changed to gaining money. Cord was sentenced to thirty years in Sing Sing for armed robbery. Twinny was sentenced to twenty years in Auburn for armed robbery. Lefty was in Greenhaven for grand theft. Jackie Map was in Leavenworth for hijacking. Big Ed was on the lam in Cuba. Ralphie Shades got the electric chair for shooting a gas station attendant.

Johnny Shira was also having bad luck as a con man. His chance of a lifetime aborted. He had struck a friendship with a wealthy elderly woman he had charmed for weeks with flowers and cordials. He even brought her salt *amalagadania* for her stomach trouble. She was on the verge of buying "real estate" from him, but fell asleep in bed one night with a cigarette. In the morning all that was left of her was ashes. "Can you imagine something like that happening?" he moaned. "It's Him up there. I'm telling ya, I can't get a break. If I went into the hat business He'd stop making heads tomorrow."

Most of the guys settled down in married life. Bobby married one of the most beautiful girls in Brooklyn and soon became a devoted father. Mappy got married, too, and in time had four daughters, but he always retained his youthful spirit. Years later he was imitating Peter Fonda varooming around on a big Harley wearing sun glasses and a motorcycle jacket. On the West Coast Richie was rising fast as an actor. It turned out he really wasn't German after all. He was Jewish. His father's friendship with Milton Berle and Henny Youngman seemed more logical in retrospect. All those years his mother had kept secret the fact that he was Jewish to protect him. Natie Weinstein, the grocer's boy, ended up in an insane asylum.

Davey Brown remained a cement laborer for a long time. I never worked with him again after the job closed down. The dispute went unsettled longer than expected. Through Father Russo I got another construction job hoisting steel. I rarely got to see Davey anymore because he lived with his family on the other side of Brooklyn. One morning I read his name on the front page of the *Daily News*. He and two other laborers tried to hold up a construction payroll. He must have felt at a dead-end after running with a wheelbarrow for fifteen years.

My brothers all quit school. Nicky was doing house painting, Ernie boilerwork, Anthony became the top cop in his precinct and eventually was promoted to detective. It didn't surprise anyone. Ever since I could remember Ma was always saying, "Anthony is such a good boy." And he was kind of a model son. If she sent him to the store he would come right back with the groceries. If she sent me, I would follow my impulses to play ball and let the errand wait. As a newspaper carrier Anthony won a turkey for soliciting twenty new starts on his route. I never won anything and got fired for dumping papers down the sewer. Being a musician, Dad wanted his sons to play an instrument too. He bought Anthony a clarinet and me a trumpet from a pawn shop. Anthony blossomed into such a fine musician he was asked to perform solo in the school assembly. On holidays all the relatives sat around listening to him play "Come Back to Sorrento." Dad's side, the Sorrentinos, regarded the song as a personal tribute to them. The only song I could play was "My Darling Clementine." Dad's friend Freddy said I could become a good horn man because I had an excellent embouchure, but I was always sneaking out of practice. Once I put on a Harry James record and climbed out the window. Ma thought,

"Gee, he's getting good," until she went into the room.

Anthony was much neater than I. Even as an infant he outclassed me. He spoke his first words in half the time it took me. I was silent until sixteen months old. Ma was worried that maybe something was wrong with me.

When Tony Bavimo was alive, Anthony was impressed with his toughness, the way most young guys must have felt about Jessie James, but he didn't care to copy him. He chose to go into civil service like Dad.

Timmy Kelly was applying himself full gun at St. John's law school and ranked in the top one percent of the school. His grades qualified him to be a regular judge on moot court. Over the years we had become best friends. I could talk to him with deeper understanding than anyone else. I didn't have his vocabulary or formal concepts, but I could express myself beyond one dimension on some subjects. The law appeared exciting the way he talked about it. I was interested in knowing the legal rules for everything. The crux of my interest was to know my rights when arrested. I always felt helplessly insecure in the hands of the police.

Although Timmy was engaged to be married and a serious law student, he never lost his boyhood devil. His mother, who was so attached to him, was responsible in a way. She let him get away with anything as a boy. He could urinate on Santa Claus' lap in Macy's, which he did, and she wouldn't punish him for it.

As a young man his pranks were different. Once he and his fiancée were out with another couple. They were at the Bourbon Street Restaurant sitting at a table near the door. When an out-of-town party came in, Timmy got up with a napkin over his arm. "This way please." He had them follow him to the outdoor patio. An hour later they came back in incensed, realizing they were the only ones sitting out there. The patio was solely for show.

Gang life was dying everywhere. In 1945, according to *The New York Times,* there were five hundred gangs in New York City. Ten years later the number halved. In the 1960s only a handful of gangs remained. It's easier to understand why gangs disappeared if you know why they were born.

The first street gangs emerged on the lower East Side where minorities hostile to each other lived on separate blocks. An individual could not walk safely around the corner. Youths banded together to protect themselves. During World War II blacks migrated to the city in large numbers because of higher wages. With this influx of blacks into white neighborhoods the number of gangs grew to its highest. Racial hatred and fear continued to be the main reasons for gangs, but other factors became involved when gang life fulfilled other needs. In a poor, overcrowded tenement section where the street was the only place to go, gang life was an escape from frustration. It provided a separate culture where the underprivileged could vie for distinction apart from society. Sons of families moving away from depressed areas established gangs in new areas without racial antagonism. Gang life offered thrills and a sense of belonging. Territorial conflicts became common between members of the same minority group. The Avenue U and Fort Hamilton battles were territorial. Both sections were predominantly Italian. The home had an important bearing. The violent emotional nature of uneducated parents made violence more acceptable to their children. Apathy, neglect, and ignorance by parents contributed, as did the financial struggle, the burden of a large family, and language barrier. In some of the better Jewish neighborhoods no gangs appeared. These well-organized communities provided playgrounds, parks, good police practices, and social centers for their youth. In Chinese sections, even where poverty existed, there were never gangs. Strong parental control arising out of the ingrained tradition of ancestral worship held Chinese teenagers in check.

When the gangs disappeared in New York the newspapers claimed better youth programs and social workers were responsible. Their account was a misemphasis. The post-war prosperity was more important. It brought a building boom; factory inventories were low and shipping multiplied, opening up good-paying positions to dropouts. Families could afford television. Kids stayed home instead of going to the pool hall. Cars brought mobility. You could leave the block. The three pool halls in our neighborhood were starving for customers and eventually closed. Pop's was renovated into a cycle shop. The pool tables came out and tricycles and baby carriages went in. The general appearance of the neighborhood improved, too. Buildings were painted, factories replaced billboard lots, bricks supplanted store windows. Inside, apartments were redecorated with imitation Spanish or French furniture.

Economic opportunity still was not the biggest factor. Harlem was as bad off as before, yet street gangs waned there, too. Its two worst precincts—which had seventeen gangs in the early 1950s—

reported only two in 1960. A dope plague hit New York in the late 1950s and laid the gangs to waste. Bodies emaciated. Minds died. The next generation was blowing its mind on heroin in junior high. They weren't interested in rumbles. Junk was the new escape.

39 Charlie's Candy Store was the only hangout left after Pop's closed. When Tony was alive as many as sixty guys congregated outside. Now only a dozen of us came around. We were the odds and ends after jail and marriage claimed everyone else. Our ages ranged from eighteen to thirty-nine. None of us knew one another well because we had belonged to separate clicks. My close friends were gone except Timmy, and he only came around once in a while. I got along well with the guys in the leftover crew, but didn't feel a close bond with them. We didn't do much together and there seemed so few things we knew how to do. Mainly we played pinochle on the newsstand or talked about the way the neighborhood used to be. No girls were left for us to date. The fifty Lancerettes had all vanished to become housewives and mothers. If it was warm out we rolled bocci balls at the court up the block. It was as though our youth was as long past as the seventy-year-old men in the bocci league.

The police still badgered us now and then. One of the reasons was because the notorious Quido Pinolla was hanging out with us. Every cop in the two local precincts knew and despised him. Just looking at him you could tell why. He stood 5'5," a fortyish twenty-five years old, weighed 300 pounds, and had a huge, almost water-in-the-head size face with festering skin and deeply recessed slitty eyes that gave him the expression of a Japanese suma wrestler. A convicted rapist he hounded teenage girls. "Virgin red, that's the most beauteeful color in the rainbow," he loved to say. In moments of lust he went amuck, once ripping a door off its hinges to get at a fifteen-year-old girl who was in bed with her boyfriend. The police broke bats over his head when they caught him. Paradoxically, some of the girls who went with Quido willingly were the prettiest around and from the best homes on Shore Road.

A few of the guys transacted illegal business on the corner playing big operator. One night a stranger walked up motioning for Mikey Lanto to see him on the side. "Excuse me a minute. I got some business to attend," Mikey said, flaking off with a solemn eye intended to let everyone know he had a crucial deal waiting. Leaving our huddle, he crossed the street with the stranger for a hallway conference. They talked for hours, gesturing and nodding like heads of state. The "big" negotiations involved the price of a single carton of untaxed cigarettes. Mikey was a truck driver for a ring running them up from the South. Previously he could never last as a driver—he overslept too many mornings. Now he punched in punctually every day for the same pay. The untaxed cigarettes he hauled changed everything. He felt entrusted with a daring mission. More illegal opportunities would have ended the unemployment on our street corner.

Weekends were as dull as weekdays. Friday nights we drifted to Rudy's Tavern. In the window display a stuffed snake was coiled around a stuffed armadillo. The dust-ridden drapes could have been inside-out vacuum cleaner bags. The door pushed open to a long barroom dimly lit by a bubbling beer prop. Drinkers in short sleeves rested their elbows on the bar watching the fight on TV. The only woman who came in was a graying widow who screamed a banshee wail when she got crocked. We stood around debating the outcome of the fight. If we got tired of talking there was table shuffleboard. Philly Marko, a loud would-be tough guy hanging out with us, had a stock remark if a drunk got surly. "Get the pipes, we got a little plumbing ta do." Before coming around Marko was the leader of the Twelfth Avenue Cardinals. Once he went around the corner to fight the leader of the Apaches, another wimpy gang. Twenty minutes later both returned unsoiled and unmarked but with their hair disheveled. "It was a draw," they said. "We kept staggering one anudder wid bombs but neither of us would go down." Leo Vittorio slapped them both in the face.

At Rudy's we each ordered a round of drinks. By the end of the night we spent only as much as we would have if we had bought our own, but it made us feel big to order a round. I drank only orange juice. My system was still tied to the habits of training. I couldn't let myself lush it up, and I hated the kerosene taste of alcohol. As the others got buoyed, my mood sank. They acted dreamy and silly and talked in a groove I wasn't in. It bored me as a spectator. After drinking until late someone would say, "Let's go get a bite." I knew exactly what would be next. "Let's go ta the

Chink's." At the Chinese restaurant we all studied the menu and then ordered the same "Number 4" dinner. Lenny Pimples entertained us by showing us how far he would befoul his food and still eat it To cap off the stale evening we played pinochle.

On Saturday nights we put on our spiffy clothes to go dancing at Roseland. The place was as spacious as an armory inside. Mirrors adorned the walls and revolving harlequin globes glittered above the dance floor. Everyone came stag. The girls, shimmying in low-cut dresses, enticed at a distance, but up close most were the blind-date types, the ones who would be described as "a lotta fun" by their girl friends. Age averaged in the mid-twenties. The girls were husband-hunting. We were up to get a lay. Most nights we struck out and came home to play pinochle. From time to time to refresh our memory of a female body we went to burlesque in Union City.

I seldom had trouble with girls before, but at Roseland I was feeble. I didn't drink or smoke, but my biggest drawback with husband-shopping girls was my boyish face. I was twenty but looked sixteen. The scruffiness from boxing had disappeared. My eyebrow covered the only grisly scar. I thought the girls were avoiding me because my face was too chubby. Studying my face in the mirror, I noticed that my cheeks were puffy. The more I examined them the more convinced I was that they were my problem. So I coated my face with Vaseline and did roadwork to burn the fat off. Nothing changed at Roseland.

The movie *Love Is a Many-Splendored Thing* depressed me. I felt I was missing a beautiful experience not having a girl. I loved picnics but had no one to take. When Mappy and Bobby passed with their wives I would duck into a hallway rather than face them. I felt inferior being the only one from the old click who hadn't found a girl.

On Sundays I had dinner at Timmy Kelly's. It was always the most enjoyable time of the week. After dinner we listened to his albums by the Platters and sat around talking. We often talked about school but only because he was still a student. I had left school four years ago and said I was never going back. Both of us assumed that was final. He related the cases he was judging in moot court and I plunged into the issues with him. We talked about movies. I understood most films only on their surface. *The Old Man and the Sea* was simply the story of a fisherman to me, but Timmy saw the symbolic struggle between the man and the ocean. It was the human spirit against nature. I viewed scenes in a more concrete, common-sense way. His brain filtered facts through abstractions learned in college.

Timmy recited poems, too. We made vows to be true to our tinkered version of Kipling's "The Thousandth Man."

> One man in a thousand, Solomon says
> Will stick more close than a brother.
> Nine hundred and ninety-nine depend
> On what the world sees in you,
> But the Thousandth Man will stand your friend
> With the whole world against you.
> Nine hundred and ninety-nine of them call
> for your looks, or glory, or money in their dealings.
> But the Thousandth Man is worth them all
> Because he's interested only in your feelings.
> Nine hundred and ninety-nine can't bide
> The shame or mocking or laughter,
> But the Thousandth Man will stand by your side
> To the gallows'-foot—and after!

Later Timmy went out with his fiancée and I went to the corner to play pinochle.

40 My car was in the mechanic's shop so I had to take a bus to Fort Hamilton. I waited at the stop for ten minutes, then began walking to pick it up further down. When the bus did come I was too far from the nearest stop to catch it. It was a nice night so I kept walking. At the corner of Bedford and Church, about a mile from my house, I noticed what looked like a high school a short way up the block. I wondered if it had an outdoor track. To keep in shape I was still doing roadwork, but the only open space near me was the cemetery. It was a bad place to run because dog walkers got in the way. Crossing the street I snooped around the school grounds, but I couldn't find an athletic field. On my way back to Church Avenue, the bus route, I glimpsed a sign-post:

REGISTER NOW—FREE
ERASMUS HALL EVENING HIGH SCHOOL
SPRING TERM BEGINS FEB. 14, 1957

Lights were on in the building behind it. I moved closer.

248

"Maybe I should go in an' enroll," I thought. But then I asked, "Fa what? I tried four times before. It would be the same thing if I tried a fifth time. I'd never finish. Besides, I'm twen'y years old. Even if I did finish I'd graduate at twen'y-four. Where could I start out at that age. The subjects are too hard anyways. I ain't never been able ta pass algebra and foreign language. Ya'd have ta take those fa an academic diploma."

But I wasn't a tough guy anymore. I knew real tough guys were buried young. The new crop blasting around on motorcycles didn't impress me.

I had the awareness of Davey's example that no matter how endowed with talent a person is, if he didn't use his potential he could spend his life doing brute labor.

I saw how varied and deep life was through Timmy's eyes because of education. I sampled the beauty of poetry through him. And I never forgot the stirring tidbits of philosophy offered by Davey.

The hate that drove me to train so hard for boxing was gone, but the discipline acquired remained a part of me. It only needed a new goal and motive to set it in motion.

Tucked away in my memory were the words of immigrant Nick Marotta that "education is the best hope we have of bettering ourselves," and I never forgot what Mr. DeMeo said, "You can become anything you want to be." The only time I had ever applied myself was in Miss Lawsen's class and I did well. Maybe if I applied myself to algebra I could handle it, too.

About to back off in doubt, I pictured the guys standing in front of Charlie's, some bald and nearing forty. I thought of them playing pinochle, trying for a sense of power from a hundred aces.

I went into the office to enroll. When the guys on the corner heard about it, one of them laughed. "What's he wastin' his time fa? A leopard can never change his spots."

Commencement at Harvard has something of the grandeur of a British coronation. For more than three centuries this annual rite signifying a new beginning has been a Crimson tradition.

On this sunny day, June 15, 1967, seventeen thousand guests made their way to the folding chairs set outdoors on the grass facing the speaker's platform erected between the marble columns of the college chapel. Across the way on the steps of the library, people sat shoulder to shoulder in rows up to the doors, as in a gallery.

Ma and Dad passed through the ivy gate onto the campus taking in the preparations for the pomp and ceremony to follow, walking across a landscape that had felt the young steps of Emerson, Thoreau, James, Santayana, John Adams, John Quincy Adams, Theodore and Franklin Roosevelt, the Kennedys.

I was told later that Grandma and Aunt Rose were too excited to sit down. They examined an old hand pump off the path. It had been the source of water for the campus near the time of its founding in 1637. Moving on, they peered in the doorways of dormitories with high brick chimneys. Then they stopped at an arts building cloaked with ivy. The classroom inside once sat Eugene O'Neill, T. S. Eliot, Robert Frost, and more recently Updike, Mailer, and Bernstein. They returned to their seats when the orchestra began playing. At the same time a cab from the airport brought an affluent Wall Street businessman and his wife, Mr. and Mrs. Timmy Kelly.

By a quirk of fate Richie Berder was also in town. He was here for the East Coast premiere of his first starring role. He was cast as Sonny Barger, the leader of the Hell's Angels, but Richie was actually portraying Tony Bavimo. To get a feeling for the Hell's Angels, Richie had lived as one for two weeks. His opinion of them—given to a national magazine—was that his old friends would have gone through them like paper bags.

At the Law School we gathered outside the law library. This day marked the end of our formal study of law. We passed in a knot to the college campus. I saw it as the climax of a long odyssey, which had started with night school and had taken me through two institutions of higher learning and another stint in the Marines. I had reenlisted to vindicate my record, to prove that I could endure boot camp and serve honorably if I put my will to it. I was concerned that people wouldn't respect me if they believed I couldn't stick with the Marines. I had never doubted that I could. To me it had been a matter of being master of my own destiny. The first time I chose not to serve; the second time I did.

Scholarships helped me to pay for my college and law school educations, and I was grateful for them. They contributed to a belief I acquired that though there is a lot wrong with this country, there are a lot of people committed to its ideals and working to change things.

Scholarships did not pay for everything. I worked summers and part-time during the school year. I had been a cab driver for Yellow Cab in Los Angeles, a claims adjustor for Allstate, a singing waiter at Tates Nightclub, a counselor at Deveraux, a trampoline instructor in Santa Barbara.

The Law School class entered the college gate. Some of the graduates turned around—sentimentally or relieved—and waved goodbye to the old buildings. I had chosen Harvard Law School because it had a great reputation, almost a mystique. Leaving, I knew why. It wasn't the number of books in the library or its financial assets. It was the teachers and the quality of those who had studied there that made the school's reputation, students such as Adlai Stevenson, Robert Taft, Dean Acheson, and the ones who became legal monuments—Holmes, Brandeis, Frankfurter, Hand, Wigmore, Storey, Pound.

My youngest sister Sally was standing on her chair as I passed my family coming down the aisle in the procession. Ma and Dad had tears in their eyes. Even Grandma had her handkerchief up to her eyes. Sitting down in the front row, I rubbed my knuckles nervously. As the moment approached for the valedictory address, I reached down under my gown and pulled out a glob of honey wrapped in tinfoil. The Grand Marshall lifted his staff and thumped it down, twice, announcing: "Calculus and Spirit" by Joseph Nicholas Sorrentino.

I walked up to the microphone and began to speak.

In this epoch of history man has enthroned science. Science charts the course of the universe. It logs the voyages of light beams from distant stars. It predicts the arrival of comets and the moon's eclipse. It launches satellites into space, plots their path, foretells their fall. And now the instruments of science are turned on the destinies of men, in attempts to measure an individual's promise for achievement in the future.

Psychologists at Berkeley report a series of tests to predict success or failure in a given career. Sociologists have constructed a test to predict success or failure in marriage. Criminologists talk of tests to predict delinquency. Life magazine recently pictured a new assembly of tests to help predict what traits in an infant will lead to his later personality. One shows a set of blinking lights flashed before a child while a television camera monitors his every reaction.

The direction of these thrusts is in view. The potential of an individual's life is being subjected to searching measurement.

Admittedly such knowledge will give guidance in career planning, prevent tragic marriages and delinquency, uplift the gifted but underprivileged child, but will it not also rob many of the young of their dreams? I believe that the most scientific and penetrating techniques of measurement will never measure the human spirit, but that this spirit will remain the individual's inscrutable last refuge of defiance, where he will always have the freedom to achieve his dreams despite grim verdicts and stark limitations.

On this day I am a graduate of a great university, but it has been a long journey to this honor, and not what social scientists would have predicted eleven years ago.

When I was in my first year I failed out of Fort Hamilton High school in Brooklyn. Not long after I enrolled in Bay Ridge High school at night. I failed there also. I tried a third time at Bay Ridge, but could not last the term. Then I attended Washington Irving at night, and again could not finish.

During this period I was also out in the business world, and achieved a record of distinction for failing which even surpassed my scholastic career. I started in a bleach factory at fourteen. On the first day, trying to impress my employer, I attempted to carry ten gallons of bleach to a truck we were loading. We lost all ten. At sixteen I worked in a sweater factory where I had the embarrassing experience of being awakened from a nap by the president of the company. After that incident I became a longshoreman. My next opportunity came through a furniture company's ad in The New York Times which read: "Want ambitious young man who seeks responsibility." After a month of aligning the wheels on teacarts I got tired of responsibility. Then I became associated with a Wall Street firm—in its messenger department. A shoe factory followed. Here I was so low in the company that even the office girls wanted me to address them by their last names. Discontent, I moved on to a printing plant, warehouse, a Rockefeller Center mailroom, the Erie Railroad, the Washington market, a cement crew. I even had an exposure to glamour, becoming an office boy at 20th Century-Fox. One of my duties was to send complimentary tickets for premiere performances to New York's dignitaries. I now would like to apologize to former Mayor Wagner, whose ticket I gave to my grandmother, and to the other celebrities whose tickets went to the poor.

This was also a period of wildness. I was one of the leaders of a street gang in a tough neighborhood. At eighteen came the first of two enlistments in the Marines. The first time I could not endure the severe authority and rebelled: fighting with recruits, rioting in the mess hall, trying to run away through the swamps of Parris Island. Within a short time I was released with a bad discharge.

Having done well before in the Golden Gloves, when I returned from the Marines I resumed boxing, preparing for a professional career, but after a time gave it up.

At twenty years old, realizing that my only chance for a better life was through education, I went back to high school at night a fifth time. I finished three years at Erasmus while working days hoisting steel. My grades were good enough to be admitted to the University of California despite inferior college boards. At the University I was elected a student-body president and graduated magna cum laude. After graduation I reenlisted in the Marines. This time I became a recruit platoon leader, highest scorer in athletic competition, and changed my bad discharge to an honorable one. And now after three years at its law school, I have the honor of being a valedictory speaker at Harvard University.

Do not look for mainly tragedy, or trauma to explain this change; it was mainly resolution from within.

I come here today not just to tell my story, but to emphasize that in America we can make such things possible.

In giving opportunity to the individual, our tradition has been generous, and from this liberality we have prospered and become a pattern to others. Let us go forward now and complete the task which remains in this land. A nation which denies opportunity to a part of its people diminishes its own strength in part, and a democracy which cannot carry out its own ideals cannot compete to be the ideal of others.

As for testing and the individual, low estimates will not dim the flame of high aspiration. For in the heart of every young person there is spiritual promise.

▪▪

AFTERWORD

Joe's speech was only seven minutes long, but as the Boston Globe *reported, "It was delivered with spirit as big as a ball park," and became an international sensation.* Time *magazine called it "the year's most moving graduation address."*

The United States Congress memorialized the speech in its Record. The Christian Science Monitor *devoted an editorial to it. But most importantly, it was a source of inspiration to dropouts all over the world.*

In the four years since graduating from Harvard Law School, Joe has attended Oxford; he has become an attorney and has served with the U.S. Job Corps and the U.S. Department of Justice; he has presented classes at U.C.L.A.; and he has written this book.

Ed Germain